THE NEW MPS of '01 - AND RETREADS

Andrew Roth and Byron Criddle

PARLIAMENTARY PROFILES

©2001 Parliamentary Profile Services Ltd

All rights reserved. No part of this publication may be reproduced, stored in a retrieval system, or transmitted, in any form or by any means, electronic, mechanical, photocopying, recording or otherwise, without the prior permission of the authorised representative of Parliamentary Profile Services Ltd.

Address: 34 Somali Road, London NW2 3RL
Telephone: 020 7222 5884 or 020 7435 6673
Fax: 020 7222 5889
Website: www.rothprofiles.demon.co.uk
Email: roth@rothprofiles.demon.co.uk

Computing Services by Padded Cell Software Ltd, London (www.paddedcell.com)

ISBN 0 900582 39 1

Printed and bound in Great Britain

Our thanks go out to those new MPs of 2001 who collaborated with our sometimes importunate requests for information and were kind enough to read and correct our draft profiles. We even give thanks to the new MP whose information strained our letter hole. Also to the few who warned us off libellous quotes from Private Eye. What we deplore is the increase in those who decline to give their parents' names and jobs.

A HUNDRED NEW 'FRESHERS' AND 'REFRESHERS'

Andrew Roth

One of the most curious things about the eccentric press coverage of the general election of June 2001 was its preoccupation with two contestants for safe seats, Shaun Woodward and Boris Johnson. More space was devoted to these two than to all the other 98 MPs who came into the new Parliament as new MPs or retreads. It was a symptom of hate and love. The press were united in hating Woodward, as a 'traitor' or opportunistic 'climber', and in loving 'Johnson' as an entertaining comic writer.

The loathing was shown by stunts aimed at Woodward, including hiring phoney butlers to parade St Helens South bearing silver salvers. Concentration on the high living of this ex-Tory married to a Sainsbury heiress wife meant pressmen took their eyes off two realities. One was that the Downing Street efforts to find Woodward a safe seat was not because he was needed as a Labour Minister. The intention was to send up a signal to wavering moderate Tories in a Rightward-moving, divided party: "If you come over, we will take care of you!"

The press and other observers also missed seeing that Woodward belongs to a new category of retreads which I call an 'instant retread' and Byron Criddle terms a 'seamless retread'. Usually retreads are defeated MPs who return to Parliament after an interval either for their own seats or safer ones. The 'instant' or 'seamless' retreads, all floor-crossers, concede that they cannot win their old seats after changing parties and seek their new party's help to find a safe seat. The pattern was set in 1979 by Reg Prentice who, having crossed the floor from the safe Labour seat of Newham North East, was shoehorned into the safe Tory seat of Daventry. Alan Howarth did the reverse crossover in 1997, being emulated by Woodward in 2001. Because Woodward was this special type of 'instant' or 'seamless' retread, there were 100 new MPs and retreads in 2001, not 99 as widely claimed.

In the case of 'Johnson' the press corps that descended on him - virtually ignoring another Tory journalist, Paul Goodman, fighting a similar seat next door - managed to disconnect their critical faculties. They did not discover that the very surname of this amusing charmer is not really 'Johnson' at all. Like Tony Blair, whose paternal grandfather was not called Blair and John Major, whose paternal grandfather was not called Major, Boris's grandfather was not called 'Johnson' but something more exotic. His great grandfather was a Turk called Ali Kemal, the Interior Minister to the last Sultan there, being killed as a result. His son, Osman Ali, found asylum in the UK, then changed his name to Johnson.

It is easier to become an MP sporting a British-seeming name, as shown by Gisela Gschaider Stuart, the MP for Birmingham-Edgbaston. When in 1994 she contested a Euro-seat using her maiden name of Gschaider, she narrowly lost. When in May 1997 she used her married name of Stuart, she became the first Labour MP to capture Edgbaston, Birmingham's most middle-class seat.

New MPs of '01

Knowing many voters' Europhobia, it was surprising how few newspapers twigged the increasing cosmopolitanism of would-be legislators. Not being in the candidate's interest to disclose this 'guilty secret', many decline to disclose their parents' names. It was not until they were safely elected that some of the 'mixed breeds' confessed, usually in their Maiden speeches. Tatton's George Osborne, whose father is the 17th baronet, disclosed that he has a Hungarian mother. The mother of Mark Francois, the MP for Rayleigh in chauvinist Essex, is Italian, with the evocative maiden name of Carloni. Mark Field's mother is German. Sion Simon belatedly confessed to a Corsican grandfather. The new Scottish Nationalist MP for Moray, bearing the authentic Scottish name of Angus Robertson, confessed in his Maiden that his mother was "Continental", a euphemism for German. This should have been easily discoverable by any journalist querying how come he had broadcast in German on Austrian radio.

As a Hungarian-American immigrant from New York, I have no desire to 'expose' other cosmopolitans, simply to point out how inadequate political coverage has become. Because the June 2001 election was long foreseen as a 'standstill' election, it was clear beforehand that only about 30 seats risked changing their party loyalties. By failing to take even this narrow sector seriously, papers accepted the opinion polls' prediction of 27 seats or so for the LibDems, instead of the 52 they won. After studying individual seats I bet on 54 or 55. Conservative newspapers even failed to anticipate the 'Essex effect' which gave the Tories two of their eight gains. 'Tory Boy' Andrew Rosindell chalked up the biggest pro-Tory swing to retake Romford. Next door another Thatcherite and Monday Club member, Angela Watkinson, retook Upminster. This 'Essex effect' meant two of the three Labour MPs in the Havering area were knocked out, leaving only John Cryer of Hornchurch.

Although preoccupied by Downing Street's 'parachuting' favourites into safe seats, the national press ignored the question of why able people gave up influential posts close to the centre of power to become backbenchers. David Miliband, formerly Tony Blair's manifesto-writer, said in his Maiden speech that he wanted his new constituents in South Shields to cash in on Blairite promises. Jon Cruddas, a former liaison officer with the unions, soon showed he was closer to rebel unions than to the Blairites by publicly disavowing his alleged support of Downing Street against Ken Livingstone over public-private partnership on the Underground.

Most significant of all, the national press ignored the concerted arrival as MPs of major union fixers: Tom Watson and Mark Tami of the AEEU, Anne Picking of UNISON, Kevan Jones of the GMB, Dai Havard of MSF. They show all the signs of being highly motivated and ready to flex their unions' muscles when needed. Although likely to be loyal on Afghanistan, they promised resistance to public-private partnerships, as made clear at the October 2001 annual Labour conference. ***

Richard (Michael) BACON   Conservative   NORFOLK SOUTH '01-

Majority: 6,893 (12.3%) over LibDem 5-way;
Description: A shrunken version of a previously swollen rural seat, first deprived of the overspill industrial town of Thetford, and later of two Norwich suburbs; it was held by Labour's Christopher Mayhew '45-50, but Labour's base in the Agricultural Workers' Union has shriveled with mechanisation; Diss and Wymondham are its leading towns;
Position: Associate Chairman, Hammersmith Conservative Association '95-;
Outlook: Strongly Eurosceptic financial consultant who wants to "retain control of tax and spending in the UK"; is hostile to PR and devolution; a Rightwing party activist ("auctioneer for Lady Thatcher and Lord Tebbit"); Rightwing libertarian Richard Shepherd is the Tory he most admires; in the social field he is more flexible than most Rightwingers: he is interested in getting the disabled into jobs and willing to see marital partnerships officially registered;
History: He joined the Conservative Party at 16, '78, becoming YC Chairman; he won the Conservative National Union award for increasing party membership Oct '94 he became Associate Chairman of the Hammersmith Conservative Association '95; selected for hopeless Vauxhall; he campaigned against devolution ("the break-up of the UK") and "handing over any further power to Europe" Apr '97; in the election he came 3rd behind the LibDem with 5,942 votes (15.2% or 13.2% lower than the 2nd place Conservative candidate in '92) May '97; he was a semi-finalist for selection for Leominster Feb '99; he organised an Action Day to highlight the threat to Harefield Hospital Feb '00; he was selected as successor to John MacGregor as the Tory candidate for safe Norfolk South Apr '00; he called for the abolition of the European Parliament and the European Commission May '01; he was elected for Norfolk South on a slightly smaller majority than his predecessor June '01; he asked Ministers how many disbled people were in receipt of the Disability Working Allowance and Disabled Person's Tax Credit July '01; he backed Iain Duncan Smith in early ballots for Leader July '01; he was one of 14 new Tory MPs who together wrote to the DAILY TELEGRAPH endorsing Iain Duncan Smith as a Leader who "can unite the party on Europe" Aug '01; he backed an effort to have marital partnerships registered Oct '01; in his Maiden speech he complained that "Norwich is now the only major city in the UK without a direct motorway link" and deplored the shrinkage of agricultural employment Oct '01;
Born: 3 December 1962, Solihull
Family: He does not disclose his parents' names or occupations;
Education: King's School, Worcester; London School of Economics (B Sc in Economics, lst class Honours); Goethe Institute, Berlin;
Occupation: Financial Consultant: Founder and Managing Director of English Word Factory (consultancy specialising in corporate and financial communications) '99-; ex: Associate Partner, Brunswick Group (financial communications consultancy) '96-99; Deputy Director, Management Consultancies Association '94-96; Financial Journalist, mainly for Euromoney Publications in London and Berlin '90-94; Executive, with Barclays de Zoete Wedd '86-89;
Traits: Dark, parted hair; Anglican; is fluent in German;
Address: House of Commons, Westminster, London SW1A 0AA; 86 Gloucester Street, London SW1V;

Richard (Michael) BACON   New MPs of '01

Telephone: 0207 219 3000 (H of C); London home: 0207 932 0605; office: 0207 932 0605; Fax: 0207 932 0511; rmbacon@hotmail.com;

Vera BAIRD QC   Labour   REDCAR '01-

Majority: 13,443 (35.2%) over Conservative 4-way;
Description: A Teeside industrial seat with high structural unemployment; its western boundary is the River Tees, with a narrow channel leading to Teesmouth, the UK's second busiest port; its economy is dominated by ICI at Wilton and Corus steel plants near South Bank; curiously, it is named after its North Sea holiday resort; in '95 its heavy commitment to Labour was unaltered by adding two balancing wards south of Redcar;
Position: On Human Rights Select Committee '01-; Vice Chairman: Society of Labour Lawyers, Fawcett Society;
Outlook: Leftwing feminist barrister inheriting Mo's abandoned seat; has appeared for the defence for the miners at Orgreave, trade unionists at Wapping and in the P&O seamen's dispute, Greenham Common, Hawk plane saboteurs; an opponent of tuition fees and Lord Irvine's legal aid reforms but a friend of Cherie Blair; conscious of being "born into an unskilled working class, northern family and I have achieved a successful career in a hard profession";
History: She joined the Labour Party '72; she joined the TGWU '82; she was selected as Labour candidate for Berwick '82; in the election, she came 3rd after Alan Beith and Julian Brazier, with 14.3% of the vote June '83; was runner-up to Ashok Kumar in selection for Langbaurgh by-election Oct '91; was consulted by Home Office on formulating rape law sections of Youth Justice Act '99; defeating Left-leaning Maureen Hall, with the backing of the GMB, was selected at 49 for Redcar, in succession to Dr 'Mo' Mowlam Dec '00; she retained the seat on a pro-Tory swing of 4.5% with a reduced majority of 13,443, over 8,000 below that of her very widely popular predecessor June '01; in her Maiden speech she welcomed the Export Control Bill limiting the exports of arms; she recalled that it was Teesport's customs officers who had detained the components of the Iraqi 'supergun'; she raised the blows to local employment of the closure of Cammell Laird and the cutbacks in the Corus Teesside steelworks July '01; she urged the extension to Redcar of referral orders for first-time offenders under the Youth Justice and Criminal Evidence Act 1999 July '01; urged an early debate on a Court of Appeal judgment that private trusts to which public tasks were assigned were not subject to the Human Rights Act, thus curbing "relevance to ordinary people" July '01; having served on its standing committee - where she spoke about the supply of Hawk jets to Indonesia - she argued against the absence of "sustainable development" in the targets of the Export Control Bill Nov '01;
Born: 13 February 1952, Oldham
Family: Daughter, Jack Thomas, maintenance painter, and Alice (Marsland), factory worker; m 1st '72 David John Taylor-Gooby; dvd '78; m 2nd '78 Robin Brian Baird, dcd '79; two stepsons, Julian Robert, Martin Alexander;
Education: Yew Tree County Primary, Chadderton Grammar School, near Oldham;

2   Copyright (C)Parliamentary Profile Services Ltd

Newcastle Polytechnic (LLB with Honours); Open University (BA); Guildhall University (MA, in progress);
Occupation: QC '00-; Barrister '75-; Deputy Head of Michael Mansfield's chambers with 46 barristers, including Barbara Roche's husband Patrick: "the most successful Leftwing chambers"; "I have established a grants budget from our joint earnings; so far we have supported a domestic violence research unit and financed an annual UK scholarship for a young South African lawyer"; Author: Rape in Court (1998), Defending Battered Women Who Kill (in progresss); ex: Visiting Law Fellow, St Hilda's College, Oxford '99;
Traits: Short reddish hair; "dynamic and fearless" (self-description); uncertain about dates: in her CV for selection for Redcar, she said she was the runner-up for selection for Langbaurgh in 1992, when Ashok Kumar, unexpected victor in the 1991 by-election, contested (and lost) the seat; she presumably meant runner-up in the 1991 selection;
Address: House of Commons, Westminster, London SW1A 0AA; 14 Tooks Court, Cursitor Street, London EC1A 1LB; Unit 3, South Bank Business Centre, Normanby Road, TS6 0RU;
Telephone: 0207 219 3000 (H of C); 0208 341 9165 (home); 0207 405 8828 (chambers); vera.labour@virgin.net;

Gregory (Leonard George) BARKER   Conservative   BEXHILL & BATTLE '01-

Majority: 10,503 (23.5%) over LibDem 4-way;
Description: An affluent East Sussex coastal seat containing the site of the Battle of Hastings; it was re-created in '83 out of much of the old Rye constituency, minus Rye itself and some of its rural hinterland; a quiet area for farming and retired commuters, with one of the highest proportions of middle-class pensioners; Tory since 1874, in '97 it was the Conservatives' 18th safest seat; this Tory oasis was disturbed by the ouster of its veteran MP, Charles Wardle, over his acceptance of a £120,000 directorship from Mohamed al-Fayed, highlighted by the DAILY TELEGRAPH editor, Charles Moore, whose mother lived locally; the successor's qualifications were challenged; this turmoil was intensified by the parachuting in of a vote-splitting UKIP candidate, Nigel Farage MEP, backed by Mr Wardle;
Position: On Environmental Audit Select Committee '01-; ex: Policy Advisor to David Willetts '00-01;
Outlook: Hyperactive young associate of David Willetts, who has won a supersafe seat on his second try; he has been supportive of Tony Blair's anti-terrorist actions but critical of Charles Kennedy's anti-blank-cheque postures; tends to be dogmatic about Tory economic issues but pragmatic about social affairs; he spent two years in Russia working for the Siberian Oil Company; although most of the pre-election noise was made by his detractors, they scarcely dented his majority; in the Countryside Alliance;
History: He joined the Conservative Party at 16, '82; he became Chairman of the Shoreham Young Conservatives '83; he became President of the Royal Holloway College Conservative Association, trebling its membership '86; he became campaign assistant to David Willetts Apr '92; he was selected as Tory candidate for Eccles, describing himself as Managing Director of International Pacific Securities '96; in the election he lost 12.4% of the Conservative vote,

Gregory (Leonard George) BARKER

which he later claimed to "beat the national swing" which was one of 10% May '97; he was in Moscow as a Director of the Siberian Oil Company when the city was convulsed by the "terrorist bombing of residential apartment blocks" '99; he became a Political Adviser to David Willetts and adviser to Lord Freeman on candidates May '00; he was selected for Bexhill & Battle after Charles Wardle stood down over his £120,000 directorship with Mohamed al-Fayed July '00; Charles Wardle backed rebels in Bexhill and Battle who vowed to field an 'Independent Conservative' candidate against him after they failed to secure a no-confidence vote against him, claiming he had exaggerated his business credentials; he claimed his CV had been cleared by an inquiry presided over by the party chairman, Lord Hodgson; the 'Independent Conservative' candidate failed to materialise Mar '01; the UKIP MEP, Nigel Farage, entered the lists against him, backed by Charles Wardle May '01; he retained the Tories' third safest seat by a majority of 10,503, only 600 votes below that garnered in '97 by Charles Wardle; the UKIP candidate won roughly the same vote previously secured by the Referendum and UKIP parties June '01; in his Maiden speech he described the Government's plan to reject the Bexhill bypass around Hastings, next door to his constituency, as "a kick in the teeth for the whole town"; "it was not just a measure to ease traffic congestion but was desperately needed to provide land for housing - housing to attract people into the town - but also for local families unable to get on to the property ladder"; it would have opened up land for a business park to provide much-needed, better-paid jobs; it would have provided land to build a new university"; he declared early for Michael Portillo in the Tory Leadership contest July '01; in the second recall of Parliament he supported the recruitment of President Putin as a "staunch ally in the global war against terror" Oct '01; he enthused about President Bush Oct '01; in the Westminster Hall debate on early education, he deplored the disappearance of private day care places but was sympathetic about pre-school education, his first child, George, having benefited from an international kindergarten in Moscow Oct '01; he joined lengthily in the Tory attack on the Blair Government for not sacking spin doctor Jo Moore Oct '01; his constituents were "appalled" by rail journey times to Ashford and London Oct '01; he pressed for a debate on emergency planning against a terrorist biochemical attack Nov 1; he contrasted the "staunch, if thinking" Tory support for the war against terrorism to Labour's "ragbag of rebels and dissenters" Nov '01; he complained about Labour's imposition of bureaucratic demands and burdens on teachers Nov '01; he was named to the Environmental Audit Select Committee, replacing Tim Loughton Nov '01;
Born: 8 March 1966, Shoreham
Family: Son, of Bernard Barker, company director, and Jill (Sawyer)l m '92 Celeste (Harrison); 2s: George '95, Henry '01; 1d Cordelia '00;
Education: Steyning Grammar; Lancing College, Sussex; Royal Holloway College, London University (BA Hons in Economic History, Modern History and Politics); London Business School;
Occupation: Deputy Chairman and Shareholder, of SimplyGames.com.ltd (online retailer of computer games) '99-00; Director and Shareholder, of Daric Plc (recruitment advertising agency) '98-01, when it was sold for £42m to TMP Worldwide; ex: Head of Investor Relations, of Siberian Oil Company ("I spent two fascinating years working...in Russia at the front line of efforts to reinvigorate the post-Soviet economy") '98-00, Associate Partner, of Brunswick Group Ltd (financial PR firm) '97-98; Director, representing an investment bank, of International Pacific Securities Plc '90-97, Small Companies Analyst, at Gerrard Vivian Gray '88-90, Policy Researcher, for Centre for Policy Studies '87-88;
Traits: Long face; contacts; curly dark hair; "fizzes enthusiasm on the stump" (Michael Brown, INDEPENDENT); was in the Territorial unit of the Honourable Artillery Company '89-94;

New MPs of '01   *Gregory (Leonard George) BARKER*

Address: House of Common, Westminster, London SW1A 0AA;
Telephone: 0207 219 3000 (H of C);

John (Charles) BARON   **Conservative**   **BILLERICAY '01-**

Majority: 5,013 (11%) over Labour 4-way;
Description: A recreation of the pre-'83 Basildon minus Basildon New Town; in the '95 changes it retained Billericay itself and Wickford plus Pitsea from Basildon New Town; it has four townships at each corner: Billericay, Wickford, Laindon and Pitsea; after Thurrock it has probably the second most Rightwing Conservative constituency association;
Position: Treasurer, Streatham Conservative Association '95-96;
Outlook: A Rightwing Eurosceptic Rothschild director and fund manager and former Army officer who secured a pro-Tory swing in Billericay after having lost Basildon in '97 after its abandonment by David Amess; prides himself on having been able to limit the '97 anti-Tory swing in Essex; wants more spending on police and defence; a sharp opponent of the burden of regulation and taxation on small businesses, particularly by the EU;
History: He became a life member of the Cambridge University Conservative Association '78; he then joined the Streatham Conservative Association; he was selected as candidate for Basildon, abandoned by its veteran Tory MP, David Amess Feb '96; as a candidate he raised substantial funds and increased membership '96-97; he lost Basildon to Labour's Angela Smith on a 14.7% anti-Tory swing, which he later acclaimed as "one of the lowest swings against [the Conservatives] in South Essex" May '97; he was selected for Billericay on the retirement of Teresa Gorman Dec '99; he retained the seat on pro-Tory swing of 4.27% with a majority of 5,013, almost four times Teresa Gorman's previous majority June '01; asked about Billericay's shortage of school places July '01; he was one of the first 15 to declare for David Davis in the Tory Leadership contest July '01; he was far from noncontroversial in his Maiden speech, deploring the alleged £26b increase in Labour taxes on business and pledging the Tories to cut regulations, abolish IR35, cut fuel tax, abolish the Climate Change Levy and end over-centralisation by government; he also urged a moratorium on the building of new incinerators July '01; at the second Parliamentary recall on terrorism he complained that Northern Ireland terrorists had not been disarmed and that the Army and police were under-funded and under-manned for their anti-terrorist roles Oct '01; he opposed the Bill ratifying the Nice Agreement, fearing it led to further political and economic integration which would stifle wealth creation Oct '01; said, "regulations and red tape have hit small businesses hard" Nov '01;
Born: 21 June 1959, Redhill, Surrey
Family: Son, of Raymond Arther Elmet Baron, and Kathleen Ruby (Whittlestone); m '91 Thalia Anne May (Laird), architect; 2d Poppy '94, Leone '98;
Education: Two grammar schools; Queen's College, Taunton; Jesus College, Cambridge University (MA Cantab in History and Economics; AMSI); RMA Sandhurst:
Occupation: Director and Fund Manager, for Rothschild Asset Management '98-; ex:

Copyright (C)Parliamentary Profile Services Ltd

John (Charles) BARON New MPs of '01

Director and Fund Manager, for Henderson Private Investors Ltd '87-98; Captain, in Royal Regiment of Fusiliers (after Sandhurst served in Northern Ireeland, Cyprus and Germany) '83-87;
Traits: Rounded face; specs; thin, greying, parted hair; forthright;
Address: House of Commons, Westminster, London SW1A 0AA; The Mallards, 125 Bramble Tye, near Bridge, Basildon, Essex SS15 5GRl 34 The Hastings, Wickford, Essex SS11 7EQ;
Telephone: 0207 219 8374 (H of C); 0207 978 1738 (home); 0207 634 2934 and Fax (work); 01268 520765;

John (Andrew) BARRETT   Liberal Democrat   EDINBURGH WEST '01-

Majority: 7,589 (19.2%) over Labour 5-way;
Description: Formerly the country's tightest Conservative-Liberal marginal, until Lord James Douglas-Hamilton failed in '97 to perform his usual Houdini-like escape from defeat; mostly the most affluent parts of the city with its best schools; in '95 it was extended into SNP-leaning Queensferry and Labour-leaning Muirhouse; Conservatives were pushed into 3rd place in '01;
Position: Edinburgh City Councillor '95-; Convenor of Lothian LibDems; Vice President of the Scottish Liberal Club;
Outlook: A cautious, low-profile Edinburgh City Councillor and company director, chosen from the Scottish LibDems' 'B list' as the successor to Donald Gorrie, who has withdrawn to the Scottish Parliament; he has shown an interest in the environment and in films (on the boards of the Edinburgh International Film Festival '95- and the Edinburgh and Lothians Screen Industries Office and Edinburgh Filmhouse);
History: He was elected to Edinburgh City Council '95; was election agent to Donald Gorrie May '97; contested Linlithgow in Holyrood elections '99; was selected as the LibDem candidate to succeed Donald Gorrie '00; was elected by a majority of 7,589, marginally more than his predecessor over Labour, with the Conservative pushed into 3rd place June '01; in the second recall of Parliament on terrorism he urged caution in moving against bin Laden Oct '01; he worried about improving security measures at the planned but delayed Prestwick air traffic control centre Oct '01; he led a motion hailing Energy Efficiency Week Oct '01; he complained that "Grampian Foods in my constituency has laid off employees in the airline food industry" as a result of the 11 Sepember terrorist attack and asked the British Government to emulate Washington in helping the airlines Nov '01; he led motions attacking new nuclear power stations and welcoming a lifting of the ban against exports of Scottish lamb Nov '01;
Born: 11 February 1954;
Family: He does not disclose his parents' names and jobs; m '75 Carol (Pearson); 1d;
Education: Forrester High School, Edinburgh; Telford College;; Napier Polytechnic;
Occupation: Edinburgh City Councillor '95-; Company Director, '90-;
Traits: Heart-shaped face with long nose; interested in films (on Board of Edinburgh International Film Festival), music;
Address: House of Commons, Westminster, London SW1A 0AA; West Edinburgh Liberral

New MPs of '01　　　　　　　　　　　　　　　　　　　*John (Andrew) BARRETT*

Democrats, 11 Drum Brae Avenue, Edinburgh EH12 8TE;
Telephone: 0207 219 3000 (H of C); 0131339 0339/476 7101 Fax;

Henry (Campbell) BELLINGHAM　　　　**Conservative**　　　　**NORTH WEST NORFOLK '01-, '83-97**

Majority: 3,485 (6.8%) over Labour 4-way;
Description: A largely agricultural seat which embraces Sandringham; it also has at RAF Marham, the largest Tornado base in the country; it has some light industry, especially in the port of Kings Lynn; it has been Labour-held as Kings Lynn by Derek Page (later Lord Whaddon) '64-70 and recently by Dr George Turner '97-01;
Position: On Northern Ireland Select Committee '01-; ex: PPS, to Malcolm Rifkind '90-97; Chairman, Conservative Council on Eastern Europe '89-94; on Select Committee on Environment '87-90; Vice Chairman 87-90, Secretary '83-87, Conservative MPs' Smaller Businesses Committee; Secretary and Vice Chairman, Conservative MPs' Northern Ireland Committee '83-90;
Outlook: The matured retread version of a locally-rooted traditional landowner-barrister-director and constituency defender, one of the 14-man rump of Tory Old Etonians in '01; well-connected, he was on cheek-kissing terms with late Princess Diana; a would-be exporter of monarchism to Libya, Romania and ex-Yugoslavia; a superloyalist formerly capable of feeding Tory PMs stooge questions handed out by the Whips ("Do they teach this sort of crawling at Eton? Is there some esoteric Etonian house or society called 'Bumsuckers'?" - Simon Hoggart, GUARDIAN); formerly "unofficial chairman of 'Young Fogeys for Major'" (Matthew Parris, TIMES); a Rightish enthusiast for small businesses, particularly in the constituency; pro-Serbian in Bosnia; opposed to ERM and German domination; a mildly-battered Lloyd's 'name'; scion of local landowning gentry who expunged the defection to the SDP of their Tory MP Christopher Brocklebank-Fowler, initially with self-effacing minimal impact; as a 12-bore type, became a firearms rebel in '88 over the "knee-jerk reaction" to the Hungerford massacre;
History: At Cambridge he was a Pitt Club blood and a bit of a 'Hooray Henry' rather than politically active; later joined Young Conservatives; after the defection to the SDP of Christopher Brocklebank-Fowler, was selected for North West Norfolk Aug '81; founded West Norfolk Small Business Bureau '82; conducted his campaign on the doorstep instead of in the TV studios, but was also supported by Mrs Thatcher in brief visit May '83; won seat, defeating Christopher Brocklebank-Fowler June '83; favoured postal votes for holiday-makers July '83; voted for restoration of death penalty for all categories July '83; urged code on stubble-burning Sep '83; in his Maiden emphasised the importance of small firms to local and national prosperity Nov '83; urged consultation by local authorities before business rates were set Jan '84; co-sponsored clause in Trade Union Bill for contracting in to political levy Apr '84; his over-enthusiastic agent tried to sell his constituents raffle tickets to cover costs of surgery Apr '84; accused Labour MP Tony Banks of dressing like a "football hooligan" May '84; sponsored a motion barring student unions from using their funds to charter buses for CND demonstrations June '84; his agent was fined and given 12 months' conditional discharge for

false declaration of election expenses Sep '84; sponsored motion opposing forcing existing shopworkers to work on Sundays May '85; demanded an urgent statement on failure of Bristow's bid for Westland June '85; loyally accepted phased-in poll tax although he would have preferred local income tax Feb '86; said he favoured reasonable closure of small schools in his constituency Feb '86; backed finding time for Unborn Children (Protection) Bill Feb '86; expressed considerable disquiet over bombing of Libya from East Anglia USAF bases Apr '86; elicited admission from John Stanley that shooting down of British helicopter by British troops and killing of two of his constituents should have resulted in a formal inquiry June '86; complained that local seasonal workers could no longer get benefit when laid off June '86; attacked Denis Healey for bias in refusing to meet Buthelezi July '86; participated in plot with 30 other Tory backbenchers to back Opposition effort which succeeded in raising MPs' secretarial expenses from £13,000 to over £20,000, annoying Mrs Thatcher July '86; accused Netherlands Government of bribery in poaching Lotus car company from next-door constituency Aug '86; complained to Home Secretary of leniency of six-year term for Norfolk rapist Nov '86; criticised Norfolk Broads Bill for incorporating too large an area Dec '86; complained that a rare, thumbnail-sized moth was holding up a £7m bypass for Dersingham Dec '86; in superloyal speech urged better local infrastructure and backing for West Norfolk Enterprise Agency Trust Dec '86; trebled his majority over Christopher Brocklebank-Fowler June '87; said of Townsend Thoresen ferries: "the management is obviously rotten to the core" July '87; signed motion congratulating Mrs Thatcher for resisting pressure for sanctions against South Africa Oct '87; as a responsible shotgun owner he objected to unnecessary Firearms (Amendment) Bill as an over-reaction to Hungerford massacre, while accepting need to ban some fully-automatic rifles Jan '88; with Opposition support, removed a clause forcing collectors of antique weapons to surrender their guns or obtain special certificates Feb '88; backed televising of Commons Feb '88; co-sponsored a call for a review of the Birmingham pub bombers' appeal judgment Feb '88; complained that Norfolk "a prudent, low-spending authority" was being treated unfairly in its Rate Support Grant settlement Feb '88; tried to amend Firearms (Amendment) Bill to exclude Kalashnikovs from ban Mar '88; backed restoration of corporal punishment Apr '88; backed anti-abortion motion Apr '88; accepting Nicholas Ridley's concessions, ceased backing Michael Mates' proposals to band poll tax Apr '88; met Rauf Denktash, President of Turkish North Cyprus while there Apr '88; as a member of the British Field Sports Society, voted against guillotine, warning that the Firearms (Amendment) Bill would annihilate "the sport of practical shooting" May '88; as Secretary of the Tory MPs' Northern Ireland Committee, welcomed non-sectarian Workers Party of Ireland May '88; was "appalled" by US Democratic candidate Michael Dukakis's promise to support "affirmative action" to favour Roman Catholics in Northern Ireland June '88; presented a petition signed by 17,000 against possible dumping by NIREX of nuclear waste in the Wash area July '88; visited Paraguay and Brazil, half funded by the respective governments Aug '88; visited South Africa as guest of its government Oct '88; said the escape from Ireland of Father Patrick Ryan had "got the whole extradition process off to an appalling start"; "the last few months have seen nothing but us giving and the Southern Irish Government taking" Nov '88; said "it is appalling to stop [the disabled] taking part in target shooting, stalking or other forms of rifle shooting" under the over-zealous post-Hungerford Firearms (Amendment) Bill; accused Douglas Hogg of having failed to win "the confidence and support of the shooting community" Nov '88; welcomed the separation of the National Rivers Authority from the about-to-be privatised Anglia Water because of the need for sea defences in his low-lying constituency; "water would lap up the front door at Sandringham" Dec '88; after a visit to South Africa, backed English cricketers being allowed to visit, to lend their coaching expertise to aspiring black young cricket enthusiasts Jan '89; was responsible for Pamela Bordes becoming a Parliamentary researcher by passing on an unused researcher's pass to his friend, Dover MP David Shaw for her use; claimed her "credentials were checked thoroughly"; "if she has taken us for a ride, it's a very clever ride; and if so she has pulled the wool over not only my eyes and David's, but a lot of prominent people who gave her references" Mar '89; as its first Chairman, launched Conservative Council on Eastern Europe Mar '89; congratulated Construction Industry Training Board in his constituency Apr '89; co-sponsored motion welcoming visit of South African President F W de Klerk's visit to UK June '89; backed motion welcoming removal of Apartheid in South African coalmining June '89; attacked Labour for pointing out East Anglia was fourth worst for water pollution; insisted privatisation would inject private capital; "I'm the first person to accept that there's a long way to go, but a tremendous effort is being made to clean things up" June '89; was one of six barrister-MPs to welcome Lord Mackay's reforms of the legal profession June '89; welcomed plan to end stubble burning Nov '89; protested trial of Slovak human rights activist Nov '89; voted against War Crimes Bill to prosecute as war criminals, aged immigrants from Baltic states Dec '89; backed restoration of monarchy in Romania: "what is needed is a figurehead to unite a nation torn apart by bloodshed" Dec '89; pressed for lower ceiling for rate increases for firms with rateable values below £10,400, saying "small businesses...are going to be hit very hard"; to Labour laughter, said the small businesses in his constituency supported the new Uniform Business Rate in principle but wanted a longer transitional period Jan '90; chaired meeting in Prague of Conservative Council on Eastern Europe Jan '90; "as the owner of land in Norfolk with rights of way going through it", co-sponsored Edward Leigh's Rights of Way Bill; complained that youngsters riding scramble motorcycles in the countryside and others using four-wheel-drive vehicles were badly damaging tracks Feb '90; again opposed War Crimes Bill Mar '90; said he supported Consumer Guarantees Bill of Martyn Jones, who was "a good friend of mine", but it had finance-raising implications which should not be in a Private Members Bill Mar '90; supported Horses Bill to improve safety for young riders because "I owe my life to the fact that I was wearing a crash hat when I had a number of bad falls" as an amateur steeplechase jockey Apr '90; as Parliamentary Adviser to the National Association of Waste Disposal Contractors, urged an amendment that waste disposal authorities should give priority to those national companies which were already approved of by other authorities Apr '90; invited press to meet Prince Idris, the great nephew of deposed King Idris "to discuss the growing democracy movement" in Libya Apr '90; invited press to meet ex-King of Romania, whom he acclaimed as "such an honourable man" Apr '90; said administrators in education's ivory towers should lose their jobs before "people at the sharp end" Apr '90; was one of 12 Tory MPs who rebelled in favour of dog registration May '90; urged withdrawal of economic aid from Romania after maltreatment of demonstrators in Bucharest June '90; expressed doubts about Agriculture Minister Gummer's agreement to export beef only from farms which had experienced no BSE: "any farmer who has an infected animal is going to hide the thing as quickly as possible" June '90; observed Bulgarian elections for Inter-Parliamentary Union June '90; abstained on dog registration Oct '90; admitted the Thatcher era was over: "my own ideal scenario would be for her to consider standing down in April or May and then we can have a proper leadership contest" Nov '90; was named PPS to Malcolm Rifkind, then Transport Secretary Dec '90; as a PPS came off Environment Select Committee Jan '91; attacked Saddam Hussein's oil spillage campaign as "eco-terrorism" Jan '91; inveighed against the CAP as aiding France Jan '91; put down amendment to Natural Heritage (Scotland) Bill to reintroduce the boar and wolf to the Highlands; the boar would add zest to a day's shooting and the wolf would be useful for the culling of hind deer; "the real reason, he tells friends, is that they would 'frighten off those bloody walkers who so plague the Highlands, wearing their ghastly plastic anoraks'" ('Black Dog', MAIL ON SUNDAY) Feb '91;

enthused about the Tories placing a £2,700 advertisement for T-shirts showing John Major and Norman Lamont in VIZ, the adult comic, claiming it was "a product of the Thatcherite enterprise culture, which has found a niche in the market" Mar '91; urged improved status for teachers June '91; found "grossly distasteful" the full frontal nude photograph of the Duke of York in the SUN June '91; urged cutting the aid for Seychelles because of its "numerous abuses of human rights" June '91; suggested restoration of monarchy in ex-Yugoslavia under "Crown Prince Alexander" July '91; enthused about the Norfolk fire authorities' smoke detector campaign July '91; expressed concern about the local "washed shellfish" industry July '91; asked questions about Yugoslavia, especially the supply of tanks to Croatian Muslims, publicised by lobbyists Ian Greer Associates Jan '92; highlighted problems of Norfolk's village schools whose costs were double but were "the focal point of village life" Feb '92; congratulated water companies on spending £28m on improving water quality, warning that renationalising them would cost £8b Feb '92; retained seat with majority up from 10,825 to 11,564, despite a swing of 7.26% to Labour Apr '92; listed as a loser on the Lloyd's insurance market, said there was "a crisis of confidence" in the leadership of Lloyd's; "although I am not involved in the LMX spiral syndicates, and my loss this year will be well below the average, I feel very sorry for those who have been caught up in this" May '92; enthused about the sewage policies of Anglian Water May '92; urged help for King's Lynn fishermen, with the value of their brown shrimps catch down to a fifth because of the flooding of the Dutch market by Danish high seas fishermen switching to inshore fishing June '92; welcomed Nicholas Soames as the first "Minister of Food who knows quite a lot about food" but worried that he might "change his usual breakfast menu from cold grouse and claret to Alpen and apple juice" June '92; chaired the press conference of Dr Radovan Karadzic, President of the Bosnian Serbs July '92; welcomed UK's departure from ERM: "we went into the rottweiler's kennel and we did not get just scratched and nipped - we had a limb bitten off and we came out of the kennel severely mauled; I hope to goodness that we will not go back into that kennel for a long time to come" Nov '92; welcomed 1% cut in interest rates and encouragement for builders and smallish businesses in Autumn Statement Nov '92; defended Prince of Wales against accusation that, by extolling virtues of French rural life, he was encouraging Paris to torpedo GATT negotiations on behalf of restive French farmers: "the Prince certainly would not intervene in the GATT negotiations; national governments must find ways of ensuring that the rural communities can adjust; my view is that he is absolutely right" Dec '92; backed statutory levy for training for the construction industry, not least because the Construction Industry Training Board was in his constituency Feb '93; declined the EVENING STANDARD suggestion that he might stand as a "stalking horse" against John Major, since his ancestor had murdered PM Spencer Perceval in 1812, said "I am not planning to shoot the present Prime Minister; my loyalty to John Major is absolute" June '93; welcomed the Deregulation Bill, complaining that during the boom times of the latter '80s "we forgot about small firms and tended to give too much leeway to pressure groups that wanted more regulation"; he wanted local small businesses helped through organisations like the West Norfolk Enterprise Agency Feb '94; voted to reduce the age of homosexual consent to 18, Feb '94; urged more safety barriers on roads in Scotland, where he preferred to holiday, rather than "in some grotty, overpriced, lager-lout-infested Continental resort" Mar '94; urged an investigation of the SUNDAY TIMES' for entrapment of two MPs who had accepted £1,000 for planting a question; he had been approached by "a Mr Calvert"; "the only suspicion that the newspaper could have had of me derives from the fact that, like most of the other Tory Members who were contacted, I am a member of Lloyd's"; July '94; he lost North West Norfolk on a swing of 10.2% to Labour's Dr George Turner by a majority of 1,339 (2.3%) May '97; he was re-selected for NW Norfolk Mar '99; despite rumours of an unofficial Lab-LibDem pact

against him, he regained the seat by a majority of 3,485, on a pro-Tory swing of 4.57% June '01; he made a vigorous defence of fox-hunting people June '01; in his "semi-retread" Maiden speech, he paid unusual tributes to his Labour predecessor but claimed Labour neglected rural communities like his June '01; he declined to disclose which Tory he backed in the Leadership contest June-July '01; he complained about "a waiting list to go on waiting lists" for hospitals in his area July '01; he urged that Ministers make their statesments to the Commons instead of on radio July '01; he was named to the Northern Ireland Select Committee July '01; in the second Parliamentary recall he urged speedier extradition of terrorists and solution of the Israel-Palestinian Arab crisis Oct '01; welcoming the impact on crime of the CCTV in King's Lynn, he urged CCTV be installed too in Hunstanton, to which crime was being displaced Oct '01; he was accused by Margaret Beckett of "a very silly remark" when he claimed "the Minister with dedicated responsiblity for agriculture is in the House of Lords"; she insisted she was responsible for agriculture and attended the EU's Agriculture Council Oct '01; he expressed concern about the location of wind farms on the coast of his constituency Oct '01; fearing that Norfolk's coastal waters "might one day be opened up to other European Union countries", and that coastal wind farms might hinder fishing, he backed the Marine Life Conservation Bill Oct '01; he deplored Zimbabwe's descent into "virtual anarchy" Nov '01;
Born: 29 March 1955, Cheltenham
Family: His ancestor, John Bellingham, was hanged for assassinating Prime Minister Spencer Perceval in 1812; son, late Henry Bellingham, local land agent, and June (Cloudley-Smith); m '93 Emma (Whiteley), a descendant of Lord North; "as a descendant of a murderer of a Prime Minister marrying the descendant of a Prime Minister, you could say I was marrying above my station";
Education: Wellesley House; Eton; Magdalene College, Cambridge (BA); Council for Legal Education; Middle Temple;
Occupation: Barrister, practicing in Norwich and London; Chairman, Global Tourism Solutions Ltd '01-; Director: Glencara Estate Company '97-, First Mercantile Plc '00-, Viking Internet Plc '00-, Lansdown Advisory Ltd (assisting oversead firms with advice on inward investment) '01-; Owner, of farmland and woodland in Norfolk; Founder and Patron, of West Norfolk Enterprise Agency; ex: Lloyd's Underwriter (in '94 was underwriting through RF Kershaw; 17 syndicates listed) '79-95; Director, Lothian Plc '90-98; Parliamentary Adviser, to National Association of Waste Disposal Contractors '90-97;
Traits: Greying parted hair; triangular face with long nose; "Slim, with wispy hair and a tenor drawl", "is one of life's mods" (Matthew Parris, TIMES); hardworking; has "disquieting energy" (DAILY TELEGRAPH); former amateur steeplechase jockey ("during an undistinguished career...I had the chance to ride in about 50 races"); with three 12-bores enjoys rough shooting and clay pigeon shooting; a crack shot (captained House of Commons team that beat the Lords - who "shoot five times a week" - in '89); also a fisherman; a friend of late Princess Diana since childhood; clubman (White's and Pratts); friend of Martin Howe; unpolitically other-worldly (he asked Michael Brown for whom he had voted in the '01 Leadership contest, not realising Brown had been defeated along with him in '97 and had made a new career as a political correspondent on the INDEPENDENT); has had a black labrador called 'Maggie';
Address: House of Commons, Westminster, London SW1A 0AA;
Telephone: 0207 219 3000 (H of C);

Kevin (Denis) BRENNAN **Labour** **CARDIFF WEST '01-**

Majority: 11,321 (33.2%) over Tory 5-way;
Description: A very mixed seat formerly the base of Speaker George Thomas '45-83, later Viscount Tonypandy; it includes Llandaff Cathedral, the gentrified Latin Quarter of Pontcanna and now embraces villagey suburbs like St Fagans with its Folk Museum; it also has Ninian Park, "the home of the sleeping giants of British football, Cardiff City; sadly, they have been sleeping since 1927...when they won the FA Cup" (KB); its problem area is the massive, poverty-stricken Ely housing estate, which has seen riots;
Position: Cardiff City Councillor '91-; on Labour's Welsh National Executive '95-; ex: Chairman, Cardiff West CLP '98-00;
Outlook: A quick-witted new partisan; Rhodri Morgan's former adviser and local party chairman inheriting his boss's abandoned seat; he "designed the Welsh AMS system" (RED PEPPER); a pro-PR campaigning Leftwing Welsh-Irishman; one of the beneficiaries of devolution, with its consequent shift of senior Welsh and Scottish politicians to the Welsh National Assembly and the Scottish Parliament;
History: His first political affiliation at 16 was to the Young Communist League '75; he joined the Labour Party Oct '79; he became President of the Oxford Union '82; he campaigned for PR for the Welsh Assembly elections '95, '96; he led the 'Yes for Wales' pro-devolution referendum campaign in Cardiff '97; he organised both of Rhodri Morgan's leaership campaigns '97, '98; he was selected to succeed Rhodri Morgan as the Parliamentary candidate for Cardiff West July '00; he retained the seat on a 2.79% pro-Tory swing with a majority of 11,321, 4,000 down on Rhodri Morgan's '97 majority June '01; he made a brilliant Maiden on the first day of the Queen's Speech debate, in which he agreed that William Hague was "probably the best received" of the English proconsuls sent by the Tories to Wales June '01; claimed that "this Labour Government have done more for pensioners in the past four years than the hon Member for Uxbridge (Mr Randall) and his party would have done if they had been in power for a further 18 years" June '01; attacked MPs, especially Boris Johnson, who brought mobile phones into the Chamber July '01; he urged a more widespread use of anti-social-behaviour orders July '01; he urged Commons Leader Robin Cook to legislate for all-women short-lists, "allowing the Conservative Party to have an all-women short-list instead of an all-loser short-list" July '01; he urged consideration of the alternative Tenon proposals to improve pension provision for those of modest means Oct '01; he insisted that devolution had helped Wales dispose of foot-and-mouth carcases despite "the topographical nature of Wales" Oct '01; he asked Margaret Beckett whether it was safe to feed British lamb to children Oct '01; challenging the Tory charge about "burying" the "bad news" story of the Railtrack takeover, he insisted that "doing something to sort out the mess of the Tory privatisation of Railtrack is a good news story" Oct '01; he urged a change in the Code of Conduct for Special Advisers in which they were permitted "devilling" on behalf of Ministers Oct '01; welcoming a once-in-a-generation reform in the Adoption and Children Bill because of "pain and sadness" in the existing system, he urged strongly the need for parental consent in adoptions Oct '01; he led a motion warning against the "nuisance caused by reckless and dangerous misuse of fireworks" Nov '01;

Kevin (Denis) BRENNAN

Born: 16 October 1959, Cwmbran
Family: From a family of "Irish tenant farmers and Welsh miners" (KB); son, Michael Brennan, steelworker "from the green fields of west Cork", and Beryl (Evans), Nantyglo-born dinner lady; m '88 Amy Wack, poetry editor born in Pensacola, Florida; 1d Siobhan '94;
Education: St David's RC Primary, Pontnewydd, Cwnbran; St Alban's RC Comprehensive, Pontypool; Pembroke College, Oxford University (BA, President of Union '82, in the term after William Hague); University College, Cardiff (PGCE); University of Glamorgan (MSc);
Occupation: Ex: Researcher '95-99, Special Adviser '00-01 to Rhodri Morgan, MP then First Minister of National Assembly for Wales; Teacher '85-94; Author: 'Voting the Vision' (with Huw Edwards and Mary Southcott 1996); 'The Money Myth' (with Rhodri Morgan 1997);
Traits: Dark, slight, short; articulate; Catholic by education;
Address: House of Commons, Westminster, London SW1A 0AA; 5 Church Road, Canton, Cardiff CF5 1NY;
Telephone: 0207 219 3156 (H of C); 02920 223207/230472 Fax (office); kbrennan@net.ntl.com;

Mrs Annette BROOKE   Liberal Democrat   **DORSET MID & NORTH POOLE '01-**

Majority: 384 (.9%) over Conservative 4-way;
Description: A '95-new, affluent, fairly compact semi-suburban and rural seat curling around the north and west of Poole, made up of parts of former Poole, Bournemouth West, Dorset North and Dorset South; it was once the home of T E Lawrence; its strong LibDem presence in local government finally broke through; in its first election in '97, Conservative Christopher Fraser won it by 671 votes; this made it No 3 on the LibDem target list;
Position: Former Mayor of Poole '97-98, Sheriff '96-97, Leader of ruling LibDem Group on Poole Borough Council '00-01; Chairman of its Education Committee '96-00, and Planning Committee '91-96; on Standing Committee of Association of Liberal Democrat Councillors '96-98;
Outlook: An initially-faltering skin-of-the-teeth LibDem victor, one of three new LibDem women MPs in '01; a veteran economics lecturer and high-profile local LibDem Leader who nudged Tory Chris Fraser off this seat's political stage; proud of her achievements in local education and said to be passionate about improving opportunities for children and for adults with special needs;
History: She joined the Liberals '81; she was elected to Poole Borough Council Feb '86; she was elected Chairman of Planning May '91; she became Deputy Leader of the ruling LibDem Group May '95; she was elected Chairman of Education May '96; dubbing it "my home seat, which is very winnable", she was selected to contest the Dorset Mid and Poole North seat Jan '99; she won the seat, ousting Chris Fraser on a 1.11% anti-Tory swing, winning by 384 votes June '01; she asked for help for local Marconi employees threatened with redundancy July '01; she failed to secure an emergency adjournment debate on the sacking of 570 local Marconi workers from a site on which £12m had been spent July '01; she complained about constituents' difficulties in registering with an NHS dentist Oct '01; complaining about threatened local redundancies for which she was asking further Trade and Industry help, she

Copyright (C)Parliamentary Profile Services Ltd   *13*

Mrs Annette BROOKE New MPs of '01

was stopped by the Speaker for reading out her long request without a specific question Nov '01; she complained that Labour had followed Tory spending plans on education too long and that "our teachers and head teachers are suffering undue stress" Nov '01;
Born: 7 June 1947;
Family: She does not disclose her parents' names or jobs; married with two grown-up daughters;
Education: Romford County Technical School; LSE (BSc (Econ) Hons; Hughes Hall, Cambridge University (PGCE);
Occupation: Partner in family-owned small company dealing in rocks and minerals; ex: Lecturer in Economics at Open University and Talbot Heath School, Bournemouth '71-94;
Traits: Parted reddish-brown hair; specs; broad smile; coy about family names and jobs and her own age;
Address: House of Commons, Westminster, London SW1A 0AA; 138 Lower Blandford Road, Broadstone, Dorset BH18 8NZ;
Telephone: 0207 219 3000 (H of C); 01202 696523;

Chris(topher John) BRYANT Labour RHONDDA '01-

Majority: 16,047 (47.2%) over Plaid Cymru 5-way;
Description: The archetypal former twin mining valleys - Rhondda Fach and Rhondda Fawr - which in 1886 provided Labour's first MP: William ('Mabon') Abraham, who took the Labour tag from 1910; opposition to sitting Labour MPs, normally miners, used to come from Communists; recently, it has come from Plaid Cymru which sensationally captured the seat in the Welsh Assembly election of '99; the closing of the last pit in '90 has left it with serious male unemployment (8%) and depopulation; it still has three first-class male choirs and the best brass band;
Position: On Culture, Media and Sport Select Committee '01-; ex: Hackney Borough Councillor '93-94; Chairman, Christian Socialist Movement;
Outlook: A fervent pro-European and PR enthusiast; the "openly gay former Anglican vicar" and Christian Socialist author who has captured "this archetypal Welsh Valleys constituency" (Tom Baldwin, TIMES); this followed on his little-noticed success in the slicing of Sir Ray Whitney's former Wycombe majority of 17,000 down to 2,370 in '97; "the first Anglican priest to take a seat in this House for 200 years" (CB); retains a powerful preacher-like speaking style;
History: His family was Conservative; "between 1969 and 1972, when I was young, I lived in Spain...under Franco"; he was a Tory at his public school; at Oxford he "sat alongside William Hague on Oxford University's Conservative Association's Committee" (Tom Baldwin, TIMES); "I came from a Tory family, but I saw the light when I went to theological college and saw the damage their policies were doing" (CB); he joined the Labour Party '86; "my Bishop told me that if I sat on my hands and was quiet for 15 years, I was clever enough to get all the perks that he had as a bishop - dining with Cabinet Ministers, visiting the House of Lords"; "to me that isn't what Christianity is about"; he became the first Anglican clergyman to

renounce his Orders under the Clerical Disabilities Act 1870 to qualify to sit in the Commons; he said, "if Jesus were around now, he might also be standing"; he later admitted he used a phoney Scottish accent when telephone canvassing for the Kincardine & Deeside by-election Nov '91; he served as Frank Dobson's Agent '92-93; when Chief Whip on Hackney Council he "chucked out" some Labour councillors, costing Labour control of the council '94; a former local curate, he was selected to tackle Ray Whitney's 17,000 majority at Wycombe Oct '95; he managed to reduce this to 2,370 on a 13.6% anti-Tory swing May '97; he "withdrew from [the] 1998 NEC ballot to make way for [the] official leadership slate" (RED PEPPER); he was hoping to be selected for Cardiff South, where he still had family connections, if Alun Michael had remained in the Welsh National Assembly and gave up his Commons seat; unexpectedly, he was selected for Plaid-threatened Rhondda, until '99 one of Labour's safest and most traditionally Welsh seats, to succeed retiring MP Allan Rogers May '00; he had to try to overcome the suspicions of him by traditional Labour voters that he had once been a Conservative; a former jailbird, Paul Rees, threatened to kill him; he criticised the Plaid candidate, Leanne Wood, for attacking Labour and the Conservatives as "British nationalist parties" May '01; he was elected for Rhondda by a majority of 16,047 despite a 7% pro-Plaid swing, losing almost 9,000 Labour votes from the previous election June '01; in his Maiden speech, with its brilliant description of the constituency, he, like its first Labour MP William Abraham, urged the disestablishment of the Church of England and the representation of all faiths in the House of Lords June '01; he urged more police officers for Wales, to combat drugs June '01; he urged "universal access" to digital TV July '01; he was named to the Culture, Media and Sport Select Committee July '01; he spoke in favour of EU enlargement as promised in the European Community (Amendnent) Bill; he clashed with Tory and Labour Eurosceptics on the exact application of EU legislation July, Oct '01; on the fringe of the Brighton annual conference he urged PR for local government, pointing out that, with first-past-the-post, Welsh councils exaggerated the Labour vote, leaving Conservatives and LibDems under-represented Sep '01; he insisted that the further development of a common market within Europe required entering new areas of co-operation Oct '01; baited Eric Pickles on the clash with EU rules of his Food Labelling Bill Nov '01; he suggested making "Gibraltar, like the Canary Islands, an autonomous region of Spain", giving them "an opportunity to live as full and forthright members of the European Union" Nov '01;
Born: 11 January 1962, Cardiff
Family: Son, Rees Bryant, IT specialist, and Anne Gracie (Goodwin), make-up artist; he has a "largely unpolitical partner";
Education: Hurst Grange, Stirling; Cheltenham College; Mansfield College, Oxford University (BA in English '83; MA); Ripon College, Cuddesdon (MA Cert Theol '86); Isedet, Buenos Aires;
Occupation: Free-lance author/biographer: Reclaiming the Ground: John Smith; an Appreciation; Stafford Cripps, the first Modern Chancellor; Glenda Jackson, the Biography (two editions 1999, 2000); Possible Dreams: A Personal History of the British Christian Socialists (1996); ex: BBC's Head of European Affairs '98-00; London Manager, Common Purpose '94-96; Local Government Officer '93-94; Labour Party Organiser '91-94; Youth Chaplain, Diocese of Peterborough '89-91; Curate, All Saints, High Wycombe '86-89;
Traits: Tall; close-cropped blond hair; slim face; pallid countenance; expressionless; "clipped middle-class English accent" (Barrie Clement, INDEPENDENT) "exotic" (Patrick Hannan, BBC Wales); "his piety can grate" (DAILY TELEGRAPH); forceful speaker;
Address: House of Commons, Westminster, London SW1A 0AA; 133 Shepherdess Walk, London N1 7QA; isolated Welsh farm;
Telephone: 0207 219 3000 (H of C); 014443 730865 (home); 01443 687697 (constituency

Chris(topher John) BRYANT

New MPs of '01

office); bryant-cj@hotmail.com;

Andy (Andrew) BURNHAM   Labour   LEIGH '01-

Majority: 16,362 (46.4%) over Tory 5-way;
Description: The former Lancashire coalfield where light industry is replacing mines in Leigh, Atherton and Hindley; it has long been also a textile town, the spinning jenny having been invented there; a safe Labour seat since '22; in '95 minor boundary changes did not alter its impregnable Labour majority: Atherton's Hindsford ward was lost to Eccles, in exchange for Lightshaw ward from Makerfield;
Position: On Health Select Committee '01-; Treasurer, all-party Rugby League Group '01-; ex: Special Advisor to Culture Secretary Chris Smith '98-01;
Outlook: The local boy - he grew up in Culcheth - who made good in 'the smoke' and came back to claim the local seat; an informed opponent of football hooligans; a pro-European who "has an abiding belief in the core values of our party" (Chris Smith); "a committed trade unionist" with "a strong belief in workers' rights and improving our public services" (Rodney Bickerstaffe); one of four former Whitehall party staffers in the '01 Labour intake;
History: He joined the local Culcheth and Glazebrook Labour Party at 15, "just after the miners' strike to fight for a better deal for working people in the area" '85; he later admitted he had been the "naive researcher" who had made the first mobile phone call to breach the tranquility of the Commons Oct '96; as Political Adviser to Chris Smith, he claimed credit for "targeting more money from the National Lottery on former coalfield areas, leading to a doubling of the number of Lottery grants in the Leigh area, getting free TV licences for people 75 and over, benefiting nearly 6,000 people in Leigh, securing £750m of Lottery money for new playing fields and sports facilities in schools in the most deprived communities" '98-01; he was supported in his efforts to secure the seat by Cabinet Office Minister Ian McCartney, who sat for neighbouring Makerfield; after Millbank, over local objections, insisted on including London-based aspirants, he was selected to replace retiring veteran MP Lawrence Cunliffe at ultra-safe Leigh Mar '01; he retained the seat with a 16,362 majority despite a 3.5% pro-Tory swing on a reduced turnout June '01; in his Maiden speech supporting the European Communities (Amendment) Bill, he claimed "many people of my generation in the northwest feel proud of their regional roots but also feel part of Europe"; he then disclosed that "Ingersoll-Rand has announced that it is considering relocating its manufacturing operation for portable compressors from Hindley Green to the Czech Republic, resulting in the loss of 250 jobs"; he said that he had to restore the public's faith in politics by showing that "Parliament does listen and deliver good news as well as bad" July '01; he asked how many local miners had had their compensation claims settled July '01; as a former "adviser to the Department for Culture, Media and Sport during the Euro 2000 tournament" and one "with 20 years' experience of following Everton football club home and away" and an eyewitness to "the matches in France '98 and Euro 2000", he supported the Football (Disorder) (Amendment) Bill because it dealt with a "unique problem", of the "perception of some young men" - "hostile, xenophobic and racist" - "that they have a right to go overseas, flout the laws of

New MPs of '01   *Andy (Andrew) BURNHAM*

another country and cause general havoc, supposedly in the name of supporting England"; he was afraid that the Bill would not work effectively unless the "spotter" system used by the National Criminal Intelligence Service for detecting troublemakers was applied more effectively, especially abroad Oct '01; he again urged a railway station for Leigh, perhaps bringing to it Manchester's Metrolink service Oct '01; he called on the EU to help its "oldest economies" to prevent the loss of local plants like Ingersoll-Rand in Hindley Green to lower-wage countries like the Czech Republic Oct '01; "More than 2,500 claims by former pitmen in my constituency are still unsettled" Nov '01; he backed the rights of women NCB canteen workers for equal pay Nov '01;
Born: 7 January 1970, Liverpool
Family: Son, Kenneth Roy Burnham, Telecoms Engineer, and Eileen Mary (Murray); m '00 Marie-France/'Frankie' (Van Heel); 1s 'Jimmy'/James '01;
Education: St Aelreds RC High School; Newton-le-Willows, Merseyside; Fitzwilliam College, Cambridge University (MA Hons in English '91);
Occupation: Ex: Political Adviser to Culture Secretary Chris Smith '98-01; Administrator of Football Task Force '97-98; Parliamentary Adviser to NHS Confederation '97; Labour' Northwest Campaign Organiser '97; Researcher for Tessa Jowell and Labour's Shadow Health team '94-97; TGWU '95-, UNISON '00-;
Traits: Dark, parted hair; solid look; excellent cricketer: he played cricket for Atherton and football for Lowton and Golborne;
Address: House of Commons, Westminster, London SW1A 0AA;
Telephone: 0207 219 8250 (H of C); 07770 431430 (mobile);

David (Wilson Boyd) BURNSIDE   **Ulster Unionist**   **ANTRIM SOUTH '01-**

Majority: 1,011 (2.3%) over DUP 6-way;
Description: Formerly the second safest Ulster Unionist seat which the DUP had not fought for 17 years but was narrowly captured by the Rev William McCrea in September '00; a four-fifths Protestant stronghold and prosperous commuting area north of Belfast, containing its international airport; it has lost bits to North Belfast, West Belfast, East Antrim, Upper Bann and Lagan Valley; it was bequeathed to the late Clifford Forsythe by former party Leader James (recently Lord) Molyneaux when he went on to contest tougher new Lagan Valley;
Position: On the Select Committee on the Environment, Food and Rural Affairs '01-; Founding Patron of Friends of the Union '85-; on the Ulster Unionist Council '85-; Press Officer, Vanguard Unionist Party '74-77;
Outlook: A new Ulster Unionist hard-liner to rival Jeffrey Donaldson in opposing the Good Friday Agreement unless buttressed by decommissioning and an unhampered RUC; it was his motion which won the UUP's support for keeping the name and image of the RUC; an early 'Young Turk', he has been belatedly learning the flesh-pressing political techniques in the wake of criticisms of his standoffish postures in the by-election in which he was defeated by McCrea; he insists he is "not a career politician" nor a representative of the "Protestant Sinn Fein"; he initially made his name as chief of staff to Lord King in running British Airways

which he thinks was "one of the most successful privatisations in the Thatcher years"; this partnership foundered on BA's 'dirty tricks' campaign against the fledgling Virgin Atlantic Airways, resulting in his sacking by the British Airways board;
History: He refused to resign from the Ulster Defence Regiment after warning that "the people will have to take steps to defend themselves" against the "Communist threat"; "I fought my case on the basis of my freedom as an individual outside service in the Ulster Defence Regiment to state my opinions"; his appeal to be reinstated failed but he received an honourable discharge '75; he worked with William Craig and David Trimble in the Vanguard Unionist Party, of which he was Press Officer '74-77; as British Airways' Director of Public Affairs, working in tandem with Lord King, he was happy to build up a supportive group of MPs by providing free or upgraded flights but drew the line at being exploited by Neil and Christine Hamilton: "Neil and Christine Hamilton were once invited to Taiwan by British Airways, back in the days when Lord King was Chairman; the Hamiltons flew 1st class, naturally, and BA took care of all the bills, which is how they like[d] to travel; towards the end of their stay, they asked if they could come back via Hongkong; the airline was happy to agree; they then asked if British Airways would pay their Hongkong hotel bill; British Airways declined that kind offer; no sooner had the Hamiltons arrived in Hongkong than Neil Hamilton telephoned John King's office; Christine Hamilton had contracted food poisoning during the flight from Taiwan; they would now have to prolong their stay in Hongkong, and in the cirumstances, British Airways would surely wish to cover their hotel bill;...At that time John King's chief of staff was David Burnside...a tough Ulsterman [who] was unamused by the Hamiltons' tricks; he immediately phoned Hamilton, and told him that Lord King would be appalled when he heard what had happened to Christine Hamilton; BA hated the thought of any passenger catching food poisoning on any of its flights, let alone in 1st class; the matter would have to be investigated; fortunately, one of the world's leading experts on food poisoning worked in Hongkong and was a consultant to BA; he would be straight round to examine Christine Hamilton; but even before he reached the hotel, she had made a remarkable recovery; there was no further mention of hotel bills" (Bruce Anderson, INDEPENDENT); Burnside's collaboration with Lord King was less successful in their 'dirty tricks' campaign against Virgin Atlantic Airways; after Lord King retired, Burnside was dropped allegedly with a £500,000 payoff, which he described as "wildly inaccurate"; he unsuccessfully contested Antrim North in the Northern Ireland Assembly elections Oct '82; he opposed the Anglo-Irish Agreement Dec '84-Jan '85; he was a Founder-Patron of the Friends of the Union '85; he was elected to the Ulster Unionist Council '85; he was backed by the UUP in his motion to tie a return to government to the RUC's retention of its name and badge May '00; he was chosen to fight the Antrim South by-election June '00; his narrow defeat by 822 votes (37.95% to 35.25%) at the Antrim South by-election by DUP hard-liner Rev William McCrea underlined the fading of Unionist support for the Good Friday agreement; he blamed defeat on the failure of decommissioning and the repugnance of RUC reforms Sep '00; after ten months, he ousted the DUP firebrand Rev McCrea from Antrim South by 1011 votes, having said he had voted for the agreement, including decommisioning but not for the "shameful treatment of the RUC"; he promised to "rebuild Unionism" June '01; in his Maiden speech he insisted he was not a "career politician", nor were the Ulster Unionists the "Protestant Sinn Fein"; he promised to speak on local constituency issues and those which "affect the whole of the United Kingdom" June '01; he asked when rewards would be given to Northern Ireland's democrats and sanctions applied to "terrorist-related parties": "Sinn Fein-IRA and Loyalist paramilitary parties" July '01; he accused the Government of a "dereliction of duty" in trying to "wind down the [RUC's] fulltime reserve and the RUC's operational capacity at a time when the Provisional IRA - I stress the Provisional IRA, not Real or Continuity IRA - is engaged in

New MPs of '01 *David (Wilson Boyd) BURNSIDE*

procuring arms from continental Europe and the United States of America to rearm" July '01; with fellow hard-liner Jeffrey Donaldson, he assailed the Blair-Ahern 'take it or leave it' plan to rescue the Northern Ireland peace agreement as another "fudge" July '01; he insisted that the Sinn Fein-IRA should be "punished" for the IRA's refusal to disarm by being excluded from the power-sharing Executive Aug '01; he intervened in the second recall of Parliament to attack the "double standard" of attacking Afghanistan-based terrorists but not those based in Northern Ireland Oct '01; he urged giving the restoration of agriculture a higher priority Oct '01; he justified the Protestant 'Loyalist' paramilitaries not giving up their arms on their "alienation" by the Parades Commission; he then shifted to:"Was what we gained symbolically from the IRA worth sacrificing the RUC for? No!" Oct '01; he backed continued helicopter surveillance of north Belfast Oct '01;
Born: 24 August 1951, Ballymoney, Co Antrim
Family: He declines information on his parents' names and occupations and his first wife's name; m 2nd '99 Fiona (Rennie); has a daughter from his previous marriage;
Education: Coleraine Academical Institution '63-70; Queen's University, Belfast (BA in Politics and Ancient History)'70-73;
Occupation: Chairman, New Century Holdings Ltd '95-, and David Burnside Associates Ltd (his international PR company) '93-; ex: Director, of The EUROPEAN (when owned by Robert Maxwell) '90-91; Executive Director of British Airways, in charge of Public Relations and Marketing (he was sacked by the BA board allegedly with a £500,000 payoff ("wildly inaccurate" [DB]) after the failure of the "dirty tricks" campaign against fledgling Virgin Atlantic Airways) '84-93; Director of Public Relations, Institute of Directors '79-84;
Traits: Short grey parted hair; "pugnacious" (TIMES); "hard-nosed" (GUARDIAN); "a tough Ulsterman" (Bruce Anderson, INDEPENDENT); he enjoys fishing, shooting and motorcycling; formerly a heavy drinker (was fined £1,000 and banned for three years after being found drunk in his car by Lancashire police after a spectacular drinking bout with Owen Oyston);
Address: House of Commons, Westminster, London SW1A 0AAl
Telephone: 0207 219 8493 (H of C);

Alistair (James Hendrie) BURT   Conservative   BEDFORDSHIRE NORTH EAST '01-

Majority: 8,577 (19%) over Labour 4-way;
Description: The '97-new seat composed of Tory-voting affluent commuting villages and market towns along the A1 from North Bedfordshire and Mid Bedforshire, including Biggleswade and Sandy; a historic centre of brickmaking; on '92 projections it was expected to produce an ultra-safe Tory majority of 20,000 instead of its '97 outcome of less than 6,000;
Former Seat: Bury North '83-97
Position: Shadow Minister for Higher Education '01-; on the International Development Committee '01-; ex: Chairman and Founder-Director, The Enterprise Forum '98-01; Minister of State '95-97, Under Secretary '92-95, for Social Security; Secretary, Parliamentary Christian Fellowship

Alistair (James Hendrie) BURT

'84-97; PPS to Kenneth Baker '85-90; on European Standing Committee B '91-92; Vice Chairman, Conservative MPs' European Affairs Committee '91-92; Secretary, Northwestern Conservative MPs '84-88; Vice Chairman, Tory Reform Group '84-87; Secretary, Conservative MPs' Energy Committee '83-85; Haringey Borough Councillor '82-84;
Outlook: Relocated retread version of the intelligent, ultra-churchy, pro-EU moderate in the Tory Reform Group: "in the Conservative Party frame I am generally seen...as being broadly Centre-Left"; ex-Heathman, later a born-again loyalist Pollyanna and Kenneth Baker boy, then a Heseltinie; then a deft junior Minister until the Tories' and his defeat; in his final Ministerial years as Social Security Minister, he nursed the hated 'hot potato' of the Child Support Agency, resulting in hostile slogans on his garden walls and two attacks on his home; formerly an enthusiast for a "positive image" of the northwest; socially-concerned; religion-obsessed ("I don't believe that God would vote for any of the parties; he doesn't do things that way; he set Christians up in all political parties"); anti: hanging, Sunday trading, embryo experimentation, abortion ("I have a basic interest in the right to life, and that stems from my religion; the created child inside the body has a right to be heard and considered"); pro: balanced arms cuts, Israel, refuseniks;
History: He grew up in a non-activist Conservative family; found it "amazingly exciting" when local Tories "came round and put a board up on our tree"; "I got hooked on the fun of it all" Oct '64; joined Bury and Radcliffe YCs '74; became member of Oxford University Conservative Association but "I gave politics a miss at university because I could not easily make the transition from real politics - going out with the local Conservative Association, winning votes from folk in terraced streets in an industrial town - to Oxford University student politics" '74; was tempted by the SDP because of disenchantment with the Thatcher Government at that time, but joined the Hornsey Conservative Association '81; was elected to Haringey Council where he found "good Labour councillors and good officers" "trying their best to deal with an outer London borough with inner London characteristics" overtaken by "more militant elements of the local Labour Party" May '82; urged more money on health care and less on NHS administration at Tory conference Oct '82; slammed Labour MP Frank White's "ideological whim" of suggesting the state should absorb Bury Grammar School, his old school May '83; warned that position of Chief Constable James Anderton would be put in jeopardy if Labour were returned to power June '83; won Bury North June '83; urged sensible defence with balanced reduction of all arms and arms spending July '83; opposed return of capital punishment on all counts July '83; visited Berlin in party of Conservative MPs, two of whom were accused of giving Nazi salutes Aug '83; was hostile to NGA activities in Bury, Stockport and Warrington Nov '83; urged shorter speeches from MPs Jan '84; abstained on curbed housing benefits Feb '84; in debate on miners claimed that Labour closed more mines than Tories Mar '84; refused to support the Government's introduction of a free market in the provision of spectacles May '84; complained that miners' strike would lose many jobs May '84; in debate on Queen's Speech said: "the shift from manufacturing to service industries has not been kind to the Northwest"; "unemployment is abysmal and it is time the Government recognised the pain that honourable Members must endure in their constituencies when they deal with the problem" Nov '84; urged UK to work with EEC partners to improve UNESCO Nov '84; although he knew it "had done good things" he backed the abolition of the Greater Manchester Council Dec '84; backed Parliamentary motion attacking PLO Dec '84; was named PPS to Kenneth Baker Jan '85; in article written before his appointment, he complained of growth of unemployment and called for more investment in industry Feb '85; warned that the Tories could be gravely damaged if their concern about unemployment was not expressed more clearly Mar '85; criticised Greater Manchester Council for stopping concessionary fares to children travelling to private schools July '85; urged investigation of self-extinguishing

cigarettes to curb furniture fires Aug '85; his offer to resign as Kenneth Baker's PPS was refused after he abstained against Government's Shops Bill to permit Sunday trading Apr '86; visited Zimbabwe and South Africa under sponsorship of Timothy Trust ("brothers in Christ") May '86; in Commons said "we proclaim that the love of Jesus Christ was never more necessary than it is in South Africa today"; Britain had to put on more pressure without going to full economic sanctions June '86; went to USA under official sponsorship Aug '86; reintroduced Enoch Powell's former Unborn Children (Protection) Bill, opposing embryo experimentation, after coming fourteenth in the Private Members' ballot Dec '86; backed a Bill to limit public smoking Dec '86; expressed the hope that the next Budget would do more to help bridge the north-south divide, which would probably end when people voted with their feet to relocate in the salubrious north Mar '87; in a loyalist speech on the northwest's economic performance, claimed that the '79-83 decline in employment had been reversed between '83 and '86 as a result of the development of new industries July '87; urged Ulster Secretary Tom King to set his face against the pressure for the return of hanging - which would provide martyrs for the IRA - or allowing the Enniskillen murders to undermine the Anglo-Irish Agreement Nov '87; supported the Government's flat-rate poll tax because there was no better alternative, the rate-capping which preceded it having punished unfairly even moderate local councils like Bury's Dec '87; voted for David Alton's abortion-curbing Bill Jan '88; introduced Bill to require installation of smoke detectors in all private houses Feb '88; acclaimed impact of enterprise economy on jobs in Bury and the northwest Mar '88; urged more regional museums to show treasures found in the north but monopolised by London Apr '88; claimed firms in northwest would benefit from uniform business rate Apr '88; co-sponsored motion calling for freedom of religion in the USSR Oct '88; voted for Nicholas Bennett's Bill to privatise BR Nov '88; again introducing a Bill requiring installation of smoke detectors in homes, inadvertently set off a smoke detector's alarm Feb '89; said unemployment in Bury - where the flying shuttle had been invented - was down from 13% in '83 to 6%, largely by switching to specialised manufacture May '89; was a Teller against the Church of England measure allowing the ordination of divorced men July '89; backed pushing through Mrs Thatcher's Bill for football identity cards before the Taylor Report on Hillsborough July '89; expressed concern that some breweries behaved badly towards their tenants in debate on Landlord and Tenant Bill debate, disclosing he was "a consultant to the firm of solicitors which acts for the National Licensed Victuallers Association" Dec '89; defended student loans because grant system could no long cope with expanded higher education Dec '89; asked about investigation and failed prosecution of Kevin Taylor by Greater Manchester Police Jan '90; was again a Teller against ordination of divorced men Feb '90; visited Berlin as guest of Konrad Adenauer Foundation to observe East German elections Mar '90; again opposed embryo research Apr '90; with others in all-party Parliamentary Pro-Life Group, protested alleged BBC bias against opponents of abortion and embryo experimentation Apr '90; visited Caddanabia, Italy for conference with German Christian Democrats as guest of Konrad Adenauer Foundation May '90; again visited South Africa to see Christian workers, as guest of Timothy Trust May '90; urged more generous support for vaccine-damaged children June '90; supported losing Tory candidate in hopeless Bootle by-election Sep '90; visited France as guest of French government Nov '90; was cut adrift by Kenneth Baker when he backed Michael Heseltine for Leader, against Mrs Thatcher Nov '90; defending grant-maintained schools, announced he was replacing promoted Robert Key as a parliamentary representative of the Assistant Masters and Mistresses Association Nov '90; was named to European Standing Committee B Jan '91; urged an early interest rate cut Jan '91; arranged a game for the MPs' team, the 'Westminster Wobblers', at Trafford Park Feb '91; introduced Empty Properties Bill to allow unoccupied private residential property to be transferred to housing associations

Alistair (James Hendrie) BURT

Mar '91; said the real lesson of the Gulf War was the need for closer European collaboration Apr '91; insisted NHS expenditure in Bury had grown considerably Apr '91; visited Israel with Conservative Friends of Israel May '91; insisted NHS waiting lists were coming down, particularly in Bury July '91; was criticised by Labour MPs for blaming Labour-controlled Bury Metro for losing £6.5m in BCCI when councils of all political colours had also lost money by accepting Bank of England approval July '91; was named to Committee on Sittings of Commons July '91; visited Moscow for International Freedom of Press Conference as guest of Konrad Adenauer Foundation July '91; took an intermediate position between Army's plans for more training grounds at Holcombe Moor and local protesters July '91; after seeing the PM privately with ten other pro-EC Tory MPs, publicly told PM Major that "he carries the support of the vast majority in this House and in the country in his refusal to rule out a single currency on our terms at some future time", adding: "is he not finally giving this country the role that it lost with the empire?" Nov '91; urged Commons business end always at 10 PM Nov '91; with Sir Norman Fowler and Peter Temple-Morris on same pro-EC slate, successfully contested vice chairmanship of Conservative MPs' European Affairs Nov '91; enthused about Maastricht and a single European currency Nov '91; accused Labour of being soft on inflation Feb '92; somewhat unexpectedly, retained seat with majority down from 6,911 to 4,764, a swing to Labour of 2.1% Apr '92; was named Under Secretary for Social Security Apr '92; predicted doubling of single mothers' support from former absent former partners when Child Support Agency came into effect Nov '92; urged promotion of responsible fatherhood rather than discouraging single mothers as part of a coherent family policy to steer the work of all Whitehall departments May '93; complained that firms often made "outrageous" demands on staff, forcing them to work excessive hours; his wife, Eve, also complained that his Ministerial work allowed him "only four hours a night during the week and has to come home to have a proper sleep" June '93; said he was "deeply concerned by allegations of fraud in housing benefit" by foreigners June '93; said it was an "open abuse" for foreigners to enter, claiming to be self-supporting but then claiming £17m in benefits July '93; promised social security fraudsters would be curbed by computer coding July '93; he became the Sponsor Minister for Manchester and Salford, giving him responsiblity for the Tories' City Challenge programme in Bolton, Blackburn, Manchester-Moss Side and Wigan Aug '94; he was promoted Minister of State and Minister for Disabled People, responsible for taking through the final stages of the Disability Discrimination Act 1995, July '95; he attended the Atlanta Paralympic Games '96; he was censured by the Whips for his letter in the DAILY TELEGRAPH criticising Margaret Thatcher Jan '96; with Michael Heseltine, he was given responsibility for co-ordinating the Government's response to the aftermath of the IRA bomb that destoyed Manchester's city centre; he also helped to launch the competition to redesign the afflicted area Feb '96; he lost Bury North in the Labour landslide which produced a 11.2% swing to his Labour successor, David Chaytor, who won by a 7,866 majority May '97; Burt co-founded and became Chairman of The Enterprise Forum, to keep the representatives of some 50 companies in touch with Tory shadow Ministers '98; he served as a UN election monitor in South Africa '99; he was selected to succeed Sir Nicholas Lyell in his safe seat, Bedfordshire NE June '00; he retained the seat with a majority of 8,577, an almost 3,000 increase over Sir Nicholas Lyell's '97 majority, thanks to a 2,000 drop in the Labour vote, representing a 3.6% pro-Tory swing June '01; he voted for Ken Clarke in the Leadership contest June-July '01; he was named to the International Development Committee July '01; in his debut as shadow Minister for Higher Education, he contrasted the Tory success in increasing higher education from one in eight of the populace to one in three to the stagnation and heavy debt burdens of a Labour Government having to junk its financing of students Oct '01; he complained the Labour Government were not straight-forward on university access

New MPs of '01 *Alistair (James Hendrie) BURT*

Nov '01; he urged relief for hard-pressed manufacturing Nov '01;
Born: 25 May 1955, Bury, Lancashire
Family: Son, James Hendrie Burt, Rightwing Conservative Bury GP, and Mina Christie (Robertson); m '83 beautiful Eve Alexandra (Twite), ex-Assistant to the Jockey Club Disciplinary Committee, former Chairman Hornsey YCs, formerly his Commons secretary; 1s, Matthew James Hendrie '87, 1d, Hazel Miriam '86;
Education: Bury Grammar School (head boy; "I was a late developer; I was never in the top stream, and at one stage I was thought not to have a chance of university entrance, but my sixth form teachers did a very good job on me"); St John's College, Oxford (BA Hons in Law);
Occupation: Executive Search Consultant with Whitehead Mann Group Plc '97-01; Solicitor: Consultant, to Vallance Lickfolds '83-92, formerly employed full-time by Watts, Vallance and Vallance, solicitors at John St, London '80-83; was articled to Slater, Heelis and Company, Manchester '78-80; Parliamentary Adviser: to Assistant Masters and Mistresses Association '90-92, British Fibreboard Packaging Association '88-92;
Traits: Slight; diminutive; youngish; front-combed hair; spectacles; "dapper"; trouser-splitter (HOUSE MAGAZINE); sensitive; super-churchy; "sleeps only four hours a night during the week" (his wife Eve); art-interested (Friend of Tate Gallery, Friend of Royal Academy); sportsman (recently a jogger and London Marathon runner - in '89 he took 6 hours 20 minutes running in an elephant's head, but raised over £2,000 for charity); was a cross-country runner at school, ran in Lancashire Championships '71; played in 1st XI football at college '74-77, and on Commons team which was worsted by Lobby by 3-0 in '92; "a (Right) wing with good dribbling skills" (DAILY TELEGRAPH); "my favourite way of relaxing", "is on a Friday night with my wife; we have a plate of pasta, a bottle of wine and a video and then fall asleep";
Address: House of Commons, Westminster, London SW1A 0AA; 6 Summerfield Drive, Wootton, Beds MK43 9FE;
Telephone: 0207 219 3000 (H of C); 01234 764255/764277 Fax (home); 01767 313385/316697 Fax (constituency); planetburt@compuserve.com;

David CAIRNS   Labour   GREENOCK & INVERCLYDE '01-

Majority: 9,890 (34.8%) over LibDem 5-way;
Description: The original home of James Watt and Captain Kidd, now tough working-class shipbuilding towns on the beautiful Firth of Clyde, suffering heavily from male unemployment which reached 25% in '85-88; it has begun to recover, mainly thanks to a thriving electronic sector; IBM, which has been there for over 50 years, has been joined by National Semiconductor, FCI and others;
Position: Merton Borough Councillor (Chief Whip '99-) '98-; ex: Co-ordinator, Christian Socialist Movement '94-97;
Outlook: A former priest from a local working-class family who is the first former Catholic priest to take his seat in the Commons, after special legislation to permit this; he had previously been the main energising force in the Christian Socialist Movement; "imaginative and energetic" (Chris Bryant MP); "very loyal, but open about his own feelings; could be very good if he recovers from his political connection with the sisters (McDonagh)" (RED PEPPER);

Copyright (C)Parliamentary Profile Services Ltd

History: He was born into a Labour-supporting family; he received a prize from his local Labour MP, Dr Dickson Mabon, a week before the latter deserted to the SDP '81; as an RC priest, "I was always politically-minded but as a priest I was not allowed to be politically active under Catholic regulations; you cannot have clerics being overly political when members of their congregation support other parties"; he was provoked into leaving the church by his experiences as a priest in Clapham: "it was the type of place where the very rich and very poor live next to each other; it became very clear that political action was going to be part of the solution"; he left the priesthood to become full-time Co-ordinator of the Labour-supporting Christian Socialist Movement Oct '94, he joined the Labour Party '96; he became Political Researcher to Merton & Morden MP Siobhain McDonagh '97; he was elected to Merton Borough Council May '98; he was named its Chief Whip '99; he was selected as candidate to replace retiring veteran Labour MP Norman Godman Apr '00; Godman backed him but said he would have preferred the nomination to go to "a woman with good honourable Old Labour qualifications" Feb '01; his boss, fellow-Catholic Siobhain McDonagh, sister of the Labour Party's then General Secretary, initially launched a predecessor of the Removal of Clergy Disqualifications Bill as a 10-minute Bill to remove the 200-year-old ban on Catholic priests sitting in the Commons; relaunched by the Government in Jan '01, it was carried through by Mike O'Brien, a Home Office Minister, becoming law just before the election May '01, enabling him to take his seat in the Commons if elected; with a 3.8% swing to the LibDem, he secured a majority of 9,890, 3,000 down from his predecessor's margin June '01; he endorsed the Nice Treaty in his Maiden speech as opening up new European markets; he said he was the first local MP to come from the constituency itself, and the first in 50 years not to have a doctorate; he went out of his way to congratulate Tory MP John Bercow for his "intellectual clarity and courage" in supporting the Removal of Clergy Diqualification Act, although his boss, the shadow Home Secretary, Catholic convert Ann Widdecombe, was an opponent and sat "well within handbagging distance" July '01; in the wake of the terror attack on New York and Washington, he officiated at a CSM prayer meeting on the fringe of the Brighton annual Labour conference, evoking St Francis of Assisi Oct '01; he insisted to Chancellor Brown that "to tackle residual and longterm unemployment it is important not only that the Employment Service and the Benefits Agency work together but that all the other agencies in the field, chiefly the Inland Revenue, the Careers Service and local authorities also work in partnership" Oct '01; in the debate on the Bill to ratify the Nice Agreement he said British business was anxious to see EU enlargement Oct '01;
Born: 7 August 1966, Greenock
Family: Son, John Cairns, engineer, and Teresa (Harkins), cleaner;
Education: St Patrick's, Greenock; Notre Dame High School, Greenock; Gregorian University, Rome; Franciscan Study Centre, Canterbury;
Occupation: Ex: Political Researcher, to Siobhain McDonagh MP '97-01; Co-ordinator, Christian Socialist Movement '94-97; RC Priest, at St Mary's Church, Clapham '91-94;
Traits: Short; portly; dark, parted, retreating hair; heart-shaped round face; specs; friend of Chris Bryant; shares his pastoral skills;
Address: House of Commons, Westminster, London SW1A 0AA; 5 Sir Michael Street, Greenock PA15 1PQ; 48 Clive Road, Colliers Wood, London SW19 2JB;
Telephone: 0207 219 3000 (H of C);

These profiles show our monitoring is top-notch; check with us on 020 7222 5884.

Mrs Patsy CALTON   **Liberal Democrat**   **CHEADLE '01-**

Majority: 33 (.1%) over Conservative 4-way;
Description: The suburban seat south of Manchester with the greatest proportion of 'top people' in the northwest; in '01 it became the country's most marginal seat; it was previously a stronghold of Liberal voting in the '60s, when Dr Michael (later Lord) Winstanley held it on somewhat different boundaries; its strongest Liberal ward was removed to form Hazel Grove in '74; in '83 it lost Wilmslow and acquired Bramhall; in '95 1,500 voters were added from Wythenshawe; recent local controversies have centred on the unfinished Eastern Link Road to nearby Manchester Airport;
Position: On the Administration Committee '01-; Stockport Metropolitan Borough Councillor (Deputy Leader '98-01, Chairman of Social Services '99-01) '94-;
Outlook: An impressively-thoughtful locally-resident former chemistry teacher and veteran LibDem candidate for this seat who was narrowly third-time lucky; her success was due to her exploitation of the "unfairness" of inadequate local government grants and over-high council tax in an area polluted by an unfinished road to Manchester Airport;
History: She was selected to contest Cheadle but lost the seat to the Tory incumbent Stephen Day by 15,778 votes, on a 4.5% swing to the Tories, having lost 3,000 LibDem votes garnered by her predecessor Apr '92; she was elected to Stockport Metropolitan Borough Council May '94; on an 11% swing, she reduced Stephen Day's majority to 3,189 May '97; she became Deputy Leader of Stockport MBC '98; she was re-selected to contest Cheadle; she captured Cheadle, ousting Stephen Day, one of the last two Tory MPs in the northwest, after 14 years; she scraped through with a majority of 33 votes June '01; her Maiden speech about Cheadle "where I have lived and brought up my family for the past 27 years" was a rerun of her election campaign; it was a rant about only a third of the Manchester Airport's Eastern Link Road having been built, about over-high council taxes and inadequate local government and educational grants and disproportionate spending on refuse disposal July '01; she was in the Capitol, in Washington, when the terror plane struck the Pentagon Sep '01; in the first Parliamentary recall she expressed sympathy for the pro-Muslim views of Labour Leftwinger George Galloway and warned against a crusade against Islam; she urged a targeted, proportionate response to terror Oct '01; she backed the Sure Start programme for early-years education, urging more in-service training in the field Oct '01; she expressed concern about the depression caused in local women diagnosed with cervical cancer Oct '01; she blamed low representation of women in the Commons on its behaving like a male club Oct '01; she led a motion urging equal compensation for owners of static prefabs whose removal from nearby roads would cost over £5,000 Nov '01;
Born: 19 September 1948;
Family: She does not disclose her parents' names or jobs; married '69 Clive Calton; 2d, 1s;
Education: Wymondham College, Norfolk; UMIST, Manchester;
Occupation: Ex: Teacher '71-01: of Chemistry (recently head of department) in an 11-18 comprehensive) Stockport '87-01, Human Biology, Stockport '84-86, Chemistry, Manchester '71-79 (NASUWT);
Traits: Parted blonde tonsure with dark roots; rounded face; specs; pleasant smile; sensible;

Copyright (C)Parliamentary Profile Services Ltd

Mrs Patsy CALTON *New MPs of '01*

practical; undramatic style;
Address: House of Commons, Westminster, London SW!A 0AA; 4 The Avenue, Heald Green, Stockport, Cheshire;
Telephone: 0207 219 3000 (H of C); 0161 282 6143;

David (William Donald) CAMERON   Conservative   WITNEY '01-

Majority: 7,973 (16.2%) over Labour 6-way;
Description: Solidly-Conservative Witney (formerly Mid-Oxfordshire), in the heart of West Oxfordshire, is made up of the market town of Witney itself, with its famous blanket factory and industrial estates, plus Chipping Norton, Woodstock and Carterton (with RAF Brize Norton next door); it also has 70 growing villages; the commuter dormitory of Kidlington, just north of Oxford, was removed in '95; the leaders of the Levellers were rounded up and shot in Burford's churchyard; William Morris lived and is buried at Kelmscott Manor; Winston Churchill was buried at Bladon and born at Blenheim Palace, awarded to John Churchill, Duke of Marlborough for his victories in the War of the Spanish Succession; for 23 years it was the well-upholstered seat of Douglas Hurd who bequeathed what was thought likely to be a 20,000 majority to his successor Shaun Woodward, who managed to make it only 7,028; what was infinitely less-expected was Woodward's '99 defection to Labour;
Position: On the Home Affairs Select Committee '01-; ex: Special Adviser: to Home Secretary Michael Howard '93-94 and to Treasury Ministers Norman Lamont and Michael Portillo '92-93; Head of Political Section at Conservative Research Department '90-92;
Outlook: Shaun Woodward's more suitable replacement: an Old Etonian hereditary Conservative opposed to "further significant European integration"; "bright, ambitious and well-connected" (Rachel Sylvester, DAILY TELEGRAPH); "brings all the professionalism to politics of one who has worked in both Whitehall and television" (Michael Gove, TIMES); one of the rump of 14 Old Etonians;
History: His first political affiliation was to the Conservative Party; he joined the Conservative Research Department '88 becoming Head of its Political Section '90, briefing the PM twice weekly before question times and daily during election periods; he also wrote pamphlets on local government, energy and the Labour Party; he served on the Conservatives' general election team, Apr-May '92; as Special Adviser to Treasury Ministers he worked on the Budget '92-93, then on criminal justice legislation for Home Secretary Michael Howard '93-94; he helped to toughen the sentencing regime through the Criminal Justice Act 1994, '93-94; he was selected for the new seat of Stafford Jan '96; he lost Stafford to Labour's David Kidney on an anti-Tory swing of 10.7% May '97; he was selected for Witney, in the wake of Shaun Woodward's defection to Labour Apr '00; he retook the seat by a majority of 7,973 on a pro-Tory swing of 1.87% June '01; in his witty Maiden speech, he described himself as one of the "bad guys" who, as Special Advisor to the Treasury and Home Office in John Major's time, was "always in a rush to get legislation through the House in order to prove that the Executive were delivering their programme; however, experience shows that too many Bills were passed too quickly, often with too little scrutiny and to little concrete effect"; he handled

26   *Copyright (C)Parliamentary Profile Services Ltd*

New MPs of '01 *David (William Donald) CAMERON*

his predecessor, Shaun Woodward, with delicate irony as still a "constituent, and not insignificant local employer, not least in the area of domestic service; we are, in fact, quite close neighbours; on a clear day, from the hill behind my cottage, I can almost see some of the glittering spires of his great house" June '01; he expressed concern about the area cost adjustment for West Oxfordshire, which "could add £100 to my constituents' council tax bills" July '01; he complained that his constituency's Cotswold Wildlife Park had been "badly affected by foot and mouth and had to close" but had failed to secure advice or decisions from the Government July '01; he declared his support for Michael Portillo July '01; he felt "uneasy" that, under an anti-hooligan Bill, a football fan could be stopped from leaving the country just because a policeman did not like the look of him Oct '01; he urged greater speed in amending the Human Rights Act 1998 Oct '01; he urged the Health Minister to allow the sale of closed Burford cottage hospital so that it could reopen as a private local health facility Oct '01; he urged an early statement on "the shambles of the four-year tests on sheep's brains that turned out to be cow's brains" Oct '01;
Born: 9 October 1956, London
Family: His maternal great-great grandfather was W G Mount, the Conservative MP for Newbury 1885-1900; his great grandfather was W A Mount, the Conservative MP for Newbury 1900-06, 1910-22; son, of Ian Cameron, stockbroker, and Mary (Mount) a magistrate descended from Tory MPs; m '95 Samantha (Sheffield), the daughter of Lincolnshire landowner Sir Reginald Sheffield and a step-daughter of Viscount Astor; she is head of design at the stationery firm of Smythson of Bond Street;
Education: Heatherdown School, Ascot; Eton '79-85; Brasenose College, Oxford University (1st Class BA in PPE) '85-88;
Occupation: Director of Corporate Affairs, Carlton Communications Plc '94-01; Special Adviser, to Treasury Ministers '92-93, to Home Secretary Michael Howard '92-94; In Conservative Research Department '88-92, Head of its Political Section '90-92;
Traits: Oval face; dark hair; high forehead; "Hugh-Grantish good looks...witty - writes accomplished column for GUARDIAN ONLINE"; "despite Berkshire roots, Notting Hill polish may make him seem too metropolitan for some" (Michael Gove, TIMES); enjoys country sports; a keen bridge and tennis player;
Address: House of Commons, Westminster, London SW1A 0AA; 10 Bridge Street, Witney, Oxon; 3 Finstock Road, London W11 6LT
Telephone: 0207 219 3000 (H of C); 0207 460 1846 (home); 0207 663 6431 (work); cameron@parliament.uk;

WADING IN FILES:
Apart from the boiled-down versions which appear in these books and on our computers, we have shelves and shelves full of information built up over our over forty years of existence. Since we are not run by accountants, we are not compelled to purge the best bits by having junior assistant librarians culling our files. If you want to write the biography of ex-MP Sir John Stokes, it will only cost you £30 to see his file. There you will find that he was so pro-Franco during the Spanish civil war, that Balliol put up its own anti-Franco candidate against him for President of the Oxford University Conservative Association. This win was the springboard for Ted Heath's political career. Postwar, having held this position helped him overcome the deep prejudice among Conservative selectors who resisted choosing as the candidate for a winnable seat the son of a carpenter and a housemaid.

Greg(ory) CAMPBELL   Democratic Unionist   LONDONDERRY EAST '01-

Majority: 1,901 (4.8%) over UUP 5-way;
Description: A two-thirds Protestant rural seat in the County Londonderry with no part of the divided, mainly-Catholic city of Londonderry; it was created in '83 after the hiving off of Londonderry city as a safe seat for Catholic SDLPer John Hume; it encompasses the towns of Coleraine and Limavady, with Magherafelt transferred out in '95; it relies mainly on farming and tourism;
Position: On the Select Committee for Transport, Local Government and the Regions '01-; Northern Ireland Assemblyman (Minister for Regional Development '00-01) '98-, '82-86; Londonderry City Councillor '81-; ex: in Northern Ireland Forum '95-98;
Outlook: The more hard-line DUPer who unexpectedly ousted veteran MP William Ross, a hard-line UUPer, after failing in '97; a class-conscious spokesman for the 'poor whites' of Protestant Northern Ireland from a "working-class...family" whose "social conditions were poor" with "outside toilets and a lack of bathroom facilities" and who "enjoyed none of the benefits of the so-called [Protestant] Unionist ascendancy"; he demands redress for the situation in which his "community is angry, disillusioned, discrimnated against and marginalised" (GC);
History: He joined the DUP '71; he was elected to Londonderry City Council May '81; he was elected to the Northern Ireland Assembly Oct '82; he was elected to the Northern Ireland Forum June '96; he contested Londonderry East against Willie Ross, losing by 3,794 to the UUPer May '97; he was elected to the Northern Ireland Assembly June '98; having served as the DUP's Security spokesman, was named Minister for Regional Development July '00; he won Londonderry East from Willie Ross on a swing of 7.4% by a majority of 1,901; he said his victory showed "the Unionist community in Northern Ireland" "were disillusioned with the Good Friday Agreement" and therefore had sent a "no surrender" message June '01; promised to resign as a Northern Ireland Minister if the UUP Ministers also pulled out June "01; in his rather bitter Maiden speech he deplored the fact that in the last 30 years of the 'Troubles' in Northern Ireland, the republicans had "pocketed the political gains that the violence brought for their community", with HMG continually appeasing the Catholics; this left the Protestant community "angry, disillusioned, discrimated against and marginalised, not only since the Belfast agreement but for decades before"; "I am here to work for the revitalisation of that community" to end the situation where "[Protestant] Unionists feel their second-class citizenship acutely"; "the part of Northern Ireland that I represent is disadvantaged" June '01; he deplored as "unsatisfactory" the attempt to bring the Catholic quota in the RUC up to half its recruits because for many years the republican community had been intimidating and hostile to the RUC and "the political representatives of many people in the republican community were associated with the criminal gangs who attacked members of the [police] authority"; in contrast to the welcome for "some minute political parties, with no more than 2% support in Northern Ireland" who were welcomed on police authorities, the DUP's repeated offers to serve had fallen on deaf ears July '01; he demanded transparent, continuous IRA decommissioning but yielded his Assembly post as Minister for Regional Development to DUP colleague Nigel Dodds in the wake of the IRA first major step Oct '01;

New MPs of '01 *Greg(ory) CAMPBELL*

Born: 15 February 1953, Londonderry
Family: Son, of James Campbell, Royal Navy seaman, and Joyce (Robinson); m Frances (Patterson); 1s, 3d;
Education: Londonderry Technical College;
Occupation: Self-employed businessman '94-; Civil Servant '86-94, '76-82; "I started work as a shop assistant in 1969";
Traits: Parted, greying auburn hair; long, thin face; specs; wears colourful clothes; outspoken; enjoys soccer and music;
Address: House of Commons, Westminster, London SW1A 0AA; 25 Bushmills Road, Coleraine, Northern Ireland BT52 2BP;
Telephone: 0207 219 3000 (H of C); 0208 70327/328 Fax;

Alistair (Morrison) CARMICHAEL   Liberal Democrat   **ORKNEY & SHETLAND '01-**

Majority: 3,475 (20.8%) over Labour 5-way;
Description: Scotland's northernmost seat; although recently dominated by oil, it is the UK's 5th most prosperous agricultural and fishing seat, with prosperous agriculture in Orkney and fishing, knitwear and crafts in Shetland; Liberal for a century, except for 1900, '35 and '45, it was Jo Grimond's perch '50-83 and the safest LibDem seat for Jim Wallace in '97; until recently, SNP has had little backing;
Position: On the Scottish Affairs and International Development Select Committees '01-; Director, Aberdeenshire Women's Aid '00-; ex: Convenor, Gordon Liberal Democrats '98-00; Chairman, Scottish Liberal Students '84-85;
Outlook: A Scottish newcomer who sounded a pacifist, pro-Arab note in the wake of the terrorist attacks on New York and Washington; favours disestablishment of Church of England; the solicitor who only once before fought a Commons seat - quite disastrously against Norman Buchan - who succeeded in holding Jim Wallace's safeish abandoned Parliamentary seat;
History: He became Chairman of the Scottish Liberal Students '84; he was the Liberal/Alliance candidate for Paisley South against Norman Buchan, securing 15.1% of the vote, a drop of 9% from '83, June '87; he became Liberal Democrat Agent for Banff & Buchan '98; he became Convenor of the Liberal Democrats in Gordon '98, Agent for Gordon '99; he was selected to hold Jim Wallace's relinquished Commons seat Feb '00; he retained the seat by a majority of 3,475, reducing it to the LibDems' 14th safest seat June '01; in his Maiden speech he launched a sharp attack on the Crown Estate Commission's intention of taking £1m in "stealth taxes" from "the fish farming industry in Shetland alone", pushing some businesses into the red; he also protested the Crown Estate Commission's intention of levying £100-164,000 annually for the privilege of laying a fibre optic cable on the sea bed June '01; he asked why a constituent who was a Dutch national could vote for her member of the Scottish Parliament and for the Orkney Islands Council and for the European Parliament, but not for the House of Commons June '01; he urged that the sale of houses made surplus by the Defence Department's closing down of RAF Saxa Vord be offered locally and "will not be left to the

Alistair (Morrison) CARMICHAEL

mercy of property developers" July '01; at the LibDem conference in the wake of the outrages in New York and Washington, he dismissed the debates in the previous one-day recall of Parliament as cliche-ridden, except for the speeches of Menzies Campbell, Peter Mandelson and, to his surprise, pro-Arab George Galloway; he warned that the world faced disaster unless it understood and eliminated the causes of terrorism: "poverty leads to war which leads to poverty"; "we have bombed and shot ourselves to he brink of disaster"; "war challenges our liberalism"; "if we fail to meet that challenge, those who died will have died in vain" Sep '01; he welcomed a wave and tidal power testing centre proposed for Stromness, Orkney Nov '01; he was named to the International Development Select Committee, replacing Nigel Jones Nov '01; he urged the removal of all Anglican bishops from a reformed Lords: "in the 21st century we should have representation from all faiths and denominations or from none at all" Nov '01;
Born: 15 July 1965, Islay
Family: Son, Alistair Carmichael, hill farmer, and Mina (Mackay); m '87 Katheryn Jane (Eastham), a vet; 2s: Sandy '97, Simon '01;
Education: Islay High School, Argyll; Glasgow University, but did not graduate '82-84; Aberdeen University (LLB '89-92, Diploma in Legal Practice '92-93);
Occupation: Solicitor, in private practice '96-; former Procurator Fiscal Depute '93-96; hotel manager '84-89;
Traits: Parted dark hair; chubby face; thin lips; Elder of the Church of Scotland '95-; enjoys amateur dramatics and music;
Address: House of Commons, Westminster, London SW1A 0AA; 39 Junction Road, Kirkwall, Orkney; Albert Building, Esplanade, Lerwick, Shetland;
Telephone: 0207 219 8307 (H of C); 01856 87 6541 (Kirkwall), 01595 69 0044 (Lerwick);

Colin CHALLEN   Labour   **MORLEY & ROTHWELL '01-**

Majority: 12,090 (31.5%) over Conservative 4-way;
Description: Its most famous son was Herbert Asquith; an altered and renamed seat replacing Leeds South & Morley which was the "plain daft" (Merlyn Rees) uniting of two wards from old Leeds South and half of old Batley and Morley; it straddles the southern boundary of Leeds; in '95 Hunslet ward was transferred to Leeds Central, leaving Middleton as the only truly Leeds ward in it; the independent West Riding towns of Morley and Rothwell were only incorporated in Leeds in '74; once dominated by mills and mines, its last mine closed in the '80s; although unemployment has declined recently, part of it suffers from multiple deprivation, with poor housing and high rates of heart disease;
Position: On the Environmental Audit Select Committee '01-; ex: Branch Secretary, Morley South CLP '97-01; Hull City Councillor (Secretary its Labour Group '91-94) '86-94; Chairman, North Hull CLP, Agent, Humberside European Elections '89;
Outlook: An idealistic Leftish author and publisher with an intriguing background as a party polemicist; he puts himself in the pragmatic regionalist "centre" of the European argument, between the Europhobes and Europhiles;
History: "At around 16 or 17 I sent off for details about the Young Communist League; I

think I tried to join but never got a reply"; "after the RAF I was for two years a member of the Liberal Party" from '76; he joined the Labour Party '84; he was elected to Hull City Council May '86; he became the Secretary of the Labour Group on Hull City Council May '91; he contested hopeless Beverley against James Cran, coming third with 18.6% of the vote, 2.1% better than the '87 Labour vote Apr '92; he became the Labour Party Organiser for Leeds '94; he became Labour Agent for Leeds North East, which was a Labour gain May '97; he was selected as Labour's candidate for safe Morley & Rothwell on the retirement of ailing John Gunnell Dec '00; he retained the seat by a majority of 12,090, over 2,000 down on John Gunnell's prior majority June '01; in his Maiden speech he attributed the drop in turnout to electors feeling "powerless"; "perhaps people feel powerless to tackle the mysterious forces of global competition which, unhindered, pick up and deposit wealth wherever the markets choose"; "real powerlessness is to be in pain, waiting too long for a hospital bed; real powerlessness is hiding at home, fearful of going out or of facing the yobs who will make our lives a misery if we challenge them; real powerlessness is sitting on a train or waiting on a platform wondering what time we might get home" June '01; he backed the European Communities (Finance) Bill endorsing the Nice Agreement, as a member of the "centre", midway between Europhiles and Europhobes; he felt the Bill made the financing of the EU more fair, made it more possible for backward regions like Yorkshire and Humber to catch up in IT and curb the tendency to spend half the EU's outlay on subsidising incompetent agriculture through the CAP July '01; he suggested that "the best Leader for the Conservative Party would be Dr Faustus, who believed that a short-term gain pays off with a long-term pain"; he asked the cost to the country if nothing was done to prevent flooding July '01; he was named to the Environmental Audit Select Committee July '01; an ex-postman, he led a motion supporting a "publicly-owned universal mail service" July '01; he complained that his constituency was being treated unfairly: it was 253rd in purchase of National Lottery tickets but 654th in receipt of Lottery funds Oct '01; he urged a debate on poverty as a breeding ground for terrorism in heavily-indebted countries Oct '01; for Leeds families with drug-abusing children, he welcomed the Home Office's programme for a robust community-based alternative to custodial sentences Oct '01; he urged Tories to apologise for privatising British Rail Oct '01; he asked PM Blair to find new ways to finance 3rd World development aid to block subsequent Tory cuts Nov '01;
Born: 12 June 1953, Scarborough
Family: His great grandfather, Stephen Chalwyn, was "driven from London by that arch-rebel, Cromwell"; son, of Steve Challen, quarry manager, and Helen (Swift);
Education: Various primary schools in north and east Yorkshire; Norton Secondary School, East Riding; Malton Grammar School; Open University; Hull University (BA Hons IIii '82);
Occupation: Self-employed Writer and Researcher 00-; Editor: LABOUR ORGANISER (quarterly) '97-; Author, Price of Power, The Secret Funding of the Tory Party (1998), 'Save As You Travel: New Directions in Mutual Ownership' (1999), 'In Defence of The Party: The Secret State, the Conservative Party and Dirty Tricks' (with Mike Hughes (1996); 'The Quarrelsome Quill: Hull's Radical Press Since 1830' (1984); ex: Labour Party Organiser in Leeds '94-00; Marketing Development Worker (part-time), Humberside Co-operative Development Agency '91-93; Self-employed Printer and Publisher '82-94; Postman '74-78; Supplier Accountant, RAF '71-74;
Traits: Tall (6'2"); full face; grey beard; retreating hair;was formerly Captain of the Hull University Judo Team '78-79 ("a series of uncomfortable positions, as I soon found out"); GSOH: "if life was fair, Elvis would be alive and all his imitators would be dead";
Address: House of Commons, Westminster, London SW1A 0AA; 2 Commercial Street, Morley, West Yorkshire LS27 8HY;

Colin CHALLEN New MPs of '01

Telephone: 0207 219 3000 (H of C); 0113 238 1312;

Derek (Leslie) CONWAY TD   Conservative   OLD BEXLEY & SIDCUP '01-

Majority: 3,345 (7.9%) over Labour 4-way; Description: A swathe of southeast London's Kentish suburbs expanded in '95 into the former Bexleyheath seat; about seven-eighths owner-occupied with only an eighth in social housing; in '01 Sir Edward Heath finally heaved his bulk out of this seat after 51 years in the area; Former Seat: Shrewsbury & Atcham '83-97; Position: Chairman: of Liaison Committee '01-, Accommodation and Works Committeee '01-; on Chairmen's Panel '01-; ex: Vice Chamberlain of HM Household '96-97; Government Whip/Lord Commissioner '94-96; Assistant Whip '93-94; Vice Chairman, Conservative MPs' Defence Committee '91-92; PPS: Michael Forsyth '92-93, Wyn Roberts '88-91; Secretary, Conservative MPs' Environment Committee '84-85; on Select Committees on: Transport '87-88, Agriculture '86-87, Administration, Accommodation and Works, Armed Forces; Chairman: British-Moroccan Parliamentary Group '87-93, British-Venezuelan Parliamentary Group '87-93; Vice Chairman, British Group, Inter-Parliamentary Union '91-93; Tyne and Wear Councillor (Leader, its Conservative Opposition '79-82) '77-83; Gateshead Borough Councillor (Deputy Leader, Opposition) '74-81; on Washington Development Corporation, North of England Development Council; on Board of Northern Arts, Newcastle Airport; on Conservative Party National Executive '72-81; National Vice Chairman, Young Conservatives '73-75;
Outlook: Sir Edward Heath's unlikely successor and a surprise Ken Clarke backer in '01; a relocated retread; a flexible Eurosceptic; a hardworking, ambitious but occasionally rebellious Geordie who took a long time to make it into the Whips' Office; having initially won an unexpectedly plum Shropshire seat, he insisted on being considered a provincial MP, perhaps because he had been a big frog in the Tyne and Wear pond; Rightish on punishment and a 'cold warrior' on defence; an enthusiastic former Territorial Major in the Light Infantry, "I am pleased to be a subject of the Queen rather than a citizen of Europe" (DC); "my scepticism about the European cause is long-standing" (DC): voted against Single European Act ("In 1985 I was one of 12 Members who voted in defiance of Mrs Thatcher's three-line Whip on the Single European Act" for which "I was made to spend even more time on the backbenches"); he also opposed the monetary union element in the Maastricht treaty, favouring a referendum; an interventionist in economics, protective about local hospitals; although locally self-publicising, he "made little impact at Westminster" before he lost Shrewsbury (Peter Riddell, FINANCIAL TIMES); served in silence on Welsh Grand Committee because he was PPS to Wyn Roberts, but resigned in protest over property element in council tax; after his Shrewsbury defeat he had a rough time until he became Chief Executive of the Cats Protection League; "some of my more cruel friends suggested that as a Government Whip I had gone from neutering Members of Parliament to neutering cats; I always argued that it was a good process for both species because it stops them wandering" (DC);

History: "I was actually brought up on a housing estate" he later told a hostile Kensington & Chelsea selection conference; he was a Labour backer until he was 12, 65; joined the Conservatives at 15, '68; at 19 he became a member of Conservative Party National Executive '72; became National Vice Chairman of the Young Conservatives '73; at 21 was elected a Gateshead Borough Councillor May '74; became Vice Chairman of Northern Area Conservative Council; contested Durham Oct '74; at 24 was elected to Tyne and Wear Council May '77; at 26 became Leader of the Tory Opposition on the Tyne and Wear Council, ousting veteran Arthur Grey Mar '79; contested Newcastle East May '79; proclaimed himself "the North's top Tory", admitting his devotion to politics had lost him his fiancee Aug '79; was selected for Shrewsbury from among 263 applicants, in succession to Sir John Langford-Holt '82; was elected June '83; opposed the building of £27m Telford General Hospital Aug '83; moved 2nd Reading of contested Shrewsbury and Atcham Borough Council (Lords) Bill Feb '84; he was one of 19 Tories who voted against suspending elections to the Greater London Council before its abolition Apr '84; tried to introduce a Bill compelling local authorities to consult local opinion before providing a waste disposal licence July '84; in Army debate, spoke up for the Territorials against the generals Oct '84; backed a reappraisal of Trident because of "worsening exchange rate between the US dollar and the £ Sterling" Oct '84; with 'wets' resisted cuts in housing benefit Oct '84; claimed that metropolitan councils, like Tyne and Wear on which he had served, had "deteriorated from a noble idea to a municipal farce" Dec '84; backed a rebel motion calling for councils to be able to spend more of their money from house sales on house building Jan '85; voted against big increases for 'top people' due to contrast with nurses' pay phasing July '85; with only 11 other anti-Marketeers, voted against the Single European Act Apr '86; was one of 30 rebel Tories who helped increase MPs' allowances for secretaries and researchers July '86; visited Jordan and West Bank as a guest of the Arab League July '86; visited Turkey as a guest of the Turkish Government Oct '86; met resistance from Mrs Thatcher when he proposed an early day motion urging a Royal Commission on national service Nov '86; urged free syringes be provided for diabetic children before drug addicts Dec '86; complained about the sale of Leyland Trucks to DAF because of the resultant movement of engines from Perkins Engines in his constituency to the Netherlands Feb '87; backed the resistance of the Shropshire Health Authority to making cuts of £2m Mar '87; visited Morocco on an IPU delegation Mar '87; urged the abolition of the West Midlands Regional Health Authority to "give us fewer administrators and more nurses" Apr '87; defended Trident missile, partly because it brought more jobs to Shrewsbury May '87; in an adjournment debate he complained about the growth of hospital spending in the Telford area at the expense of Shrewsbury cuts June '87; again deplored the financial penalties imposed by the DHSS on unemployed Territorials paid for weekend exercises Oct '87; urged Moscow to let many more Jews emigrate and to evacuate Afghanistan and other occupied territories Dec '87; voted for David Alton's abortion-curbing Bill Jan '88; voted against televising the Commons Feb '88; disclosed that, from '86, he had played a leading role in securing the release after three years of Private Ian Thain, also from the Light Infantry, who had been serving a life sentence for murdering a Roman Catholic in Northern Ireland Feb '88; justified ban on GCHQ unions by claiming TUC had "targeted GCHQ during its 'day of action'" Oct '88; defended local egg producers against Edwina Currie's salmonella charges Dec '88; was named PPS to Wyn Roberts Dec '88; in wake of President Gorbachev's visit to London, pledged UK's allegiance to Washington and NATO Apr '89; visited Barbados for CPA conference Sep '89; protested closure of baby services at Royal Shrewsbury Hospital Sep '89; backed poll tax "enthusiastically" Nov '89; introduced an amendment attacking just-deceased Dolores ('La Pasionaria') Ibarruri for a "career of political murder and intrigue" Nov '89; was named to Welsh Grand Committee Nov '89; demanded reassurances that there would be no "backdoor reductions" in infantry regiments June '90; acclaimed Government for spending £990m on supporting the elderly in Shropshire homes, as opposed to the £10m spent by the Labour Government July '90; enthused about the need for road safety, including seatbelts, disclosing he had knocked down a five-year-old 17 years before Nov '90; was named to Select Committee on the Armed Forces Bill Dec '90; resigned as a PPS to Wyn Roberts over Government's decision to have a property element in its council tax Mar '91; visited Israel as a guest of its government May '91; twitted Labour on arguments between its unilateralists and multilateralists July '91; visited Paris for briefing with Aerospatiale Ltd, as Fellow-Elect of Industry and Parliament Trust Oct '91; introduced debate welcoming Government's employment policies, particularly its reduction of strikes and condemning Labour's minimum wage proposals Nov '91; signed pro-referendum amendment to pro-Brussels Liberal Democrat motion; also co-sponsored motion opposing "monetary union as a prospective [Maastricht] treaty obligation" Nov '91; retained seat with majority up from 9,064 to 10,965, a swing to Conservative of 1.1% Apr '92; was named PPS to Michael Forsyth Apr '92; after Baroness Thatcher threatened to vote against Maastricht as "a treaty too far", retorted: "it really is too much for her to behave in this way when she used the full pressure of her Whips Office to push through [the Single European Act] a measure which has given rise to the present European difficulties" June '92; with British-Taiwanese Parliamentary Group visited Hongkong as guest of its administration and Taiwan as a guest of its government Oct '92; urged replacement of "Marxist" May Day by a bank holiday to mark the anniversary of the battles of Trafalgar, Agincourt, or Waterloo Dec '92; made another strong speech supporting the Prevention of Terrorism Act and ridiculing "wriggling" Labour for abstaining or voting against Mar '93; asked about the performance of Shrewsbury-made DROPS, the battlefield ammunition resupply carrier during the Gulf War Mar '93; congratulated John Major on his "realistic judgment" on Bosnia, avoiding "expressing emotion and anger" Apr '93; was promoted an Assistant Whip for the Midlands in mini-reshuffle on sacking of Chancellor Lamont, to whom he handed over his room in 1 Parliament Street May '93; with fellow anti-Marketeer Michael Brown as new Whips escorted anti-Marketeer Nick Winterton to vote for Maastricht July '93; for the Government, introduced the European Economic Areas Bill Oct '93; voted to restore capital punishment, especially for killers of policemen Feb '94; voted to reduce age of homosexual consent to 18, but not 16, Feb '94; in the reshuffle was promoted a full Whip or Lord Commissioner of the Treasury July '94; he was promoted Vice Chambelain or Pairing Whip June? '96; he lost Shrewsbury on an 11.4% swing to Labour's Paul Marsden, by a majority of 1,570 May '97; with 8 other former Tory MPs, including Jonathan Aitken, he came out in favour of the Leadership candidacy of Michael Howard, as "an achiever" and "the best Home Secretary since the war" June '97; having "expected at least an MP's salary for life" he was stuck with "a large mortgage, three kids at private schools" (Phillip Oppenheim) and "no income for [three months] until he became director of the Cats' Protection League"; by then he had had to sell his "medieval" six-bedroom house for £285,000; along with Michael Portillo, he was a finalist for selection for safe Kensinghton & Chelsea in the by-election after the death of Alan Clark; he was knocked out by a Portillista questioner who asked why he and his wife had not voted in the preceding June's European Parliament election in which the Tories had done so well; he was also asked how a boy from a secondary modern could cope with constituents in a "very upmarket and middle-class constituency" Nov '99; he was selected for Old Bexley & Sidcup, in the wake of Sir Edward Heath's indicated retirement Nov '00; Sir Edward Heath supported his election campaign May '01; he retained the seat by a majority of 3,345, roughly the same as secured in '97 by Sir Edward June '01; in his 'retread' Maiden speech - he wondered whether "it is possible to be a virgin twice" - he emphasised his vote against the Single European Act and appealed for CCTV and more police for Bexley, which

had suffered a 19% increase in notifiable offences the year before June '01; initially, he supported the Leadership candidacy of Eurosceptic David Davis but, on his withdrawal, switched to Europhile Ken Clarke June-July '01; he wrote to the DAILY TELEGRAPH that he still regarded Duncan Smith as "a decent man" because he had warned of his Maastricht rebellions, but he had not "declined Ministerial office in order to rebel" because he had not been offered a Ministerial post; he felt Kenneth Clarke, with whose pro-European views he disagreed, was "both genial and able; the Conservative Party would be mad not to elect him Leader" Aug '01; he complained that the Bexley Primary Care Trust was under-funded Oct '01; he worried that the families of forces going into Afghanistan might be unnecessarily worried by the thrill-seeking of the media Oct '01;
Born: 15 February 1953, Newcastle-upon-Tyne
Family: Son, Leslie Conway, District Superintendent, Parks Department, and Florence (Bailes); his father's late brother was a Labour Councillor and Mayor of Gateshead; m '80 Colette (Lamb), ex-TV makeup artist ("met his wife whilst she was powdering his nose for a television debate") and secretary; 2s Henry '82, Frederick '85; 1d Claudia '89;
Education: Sunderland Road Junior School; King Edward Street School; Head Boy at Beacon Hill Boys' (secondary modern) School; Gateshead Technical College; Newcastle Polytechnic; London Academy of Music and Dramatic Art;
Occupation: Chief Executive, of Cats' Protection League ("Britain's largest and oldest cat welfare charity" which "helps 165,000 cats a year, has 79,000 members and sites and groups in 280 constituencies" [DC]) '98-; also Managing Director, CPL Enterprises Ltd '98-; Chairman, New Millenium Hospitals Ltd '97-; ex: Owner, Lea House (formerly Lea Farm) Shropshire; the family house detached from the farm which was never his; sold for £285,000 in '98 '87-98; Director, Foreign & Colonial Development Fund '97-00; Adviser: to British Shops and Stores Association '90-93, National Association of Bookmakers '91-92; Principal Organiser, for Action Research for the Crippled Child/National Fund for Research into Crippling Diseases '74-83; Director, of Printed Marketing Aids; Executive, at Granada TV; Advertising Manager, with International Paints; Owner, of a grocer's shop; Advertising Representative, for Newcastle paper;
Traits: Blond; chubby; balding; "genial roly-poly" (Matthew Parris, TIMES); 'Bulldog'; image-conscious; can be fair-minded (but not about defence); Territorial (former Major, Officer commanding Headquarters Company and Operations Officer in Fifth Battalion [TA] Light Infantry; was commissioned from RMA Sandhurst into Royal Regiment of Fusiliers, 6th battalion; he was later transferred to Light Infantry and promoted Major; awarded the Territorial Decoration); "while he is an officer in the TA, in politics he is no gentleman" (NEWCASTLE JOURNAL); folk guitarist; banjoist; former Sunday school teacher; recently "a convert to the Church of Rome"; initially brash; recently "very serious" (Tory colleague); can still be jokey (threatened to wear "my bow-tie, flashing specs and diamante T-shirt to catch the producer's lens" after TV was introduced into the Commons); numismatist; persistent yet flexible (his flexibility was reflected in a canvassing experience in the other direction in Shrewsbury & Atcham where, when a voter refused to talk to him in brown Hush Puppy shoes, he returned next day wearing black shoes); generous host capable of staging "legendary vintage champagne entertaining, honed when he was one of the Queen's Household officers in the Government Whips' Office" (fellow ex-Whip Michael Brown, INDEPENDENT)
Address: House of Commons, Westminster, London SW1A 0AA;
Telephone: 0207 219 3000 (H of C); 0208 300 3471 (constituency); 0207 828 2157 (home); 01403 221982 (work); derek@derek-conway.demon.co.uk;

Jon CRUDDAS   Labour   DAGENHAM '01-

Majority: 8,693 (31.5%) over Conservative 6-way;
Description: The long, thin seat dominated by Ford's Dagenham stretching north from the Thames; made up mainly of council-house dwellers who have Ford's as their main employer; before '97 it was only marginally safe for Labour; in '95 it acquired another 1,700 voters in a minor boundary change;
Position: Deputy Political Secretary to PM Tony Blair '97-01; Chief Assistant to Larry Whitty General Secretary of Labour Party '94-97;
Outlook: One of the least-known of those long close to power because, as a reticent academic type, unlike others, he never exploited his position to stir things up; this would have been easy for him because of the long-established contacts with the Parliamentary press gang of his popular wife, Anna Healy; "close to Cabinet Office Minister Ian McCartney and strongly backed by the TGWU" (RED PEPPER);
History: He supported Labour at school; he joined the Labour Party '81; he went to work as policy adviser to the Labour Party's Policy Directorate '89; "ingratiated himself with young Employment Spokesperson T Blair while assuring colleagues and trade unionists he couldn't stand him" (RED PEPPER); he joined the TGWU '90, becoming a branch chairman in '92; he became Chief Assistant to the Labour Party's General Secretary Larry Witty at Walworth Road headquarters '94; "as head of then Labour Party General Secretary Larry Whitty's office in 1994 [he] illicitly helped Blair win [the] Leadership election against Prescott and Beckett, but continue[d] to persuade unions and some on the Left he is on their side" (RED PEPPER); the EVENING STANDARD wrote: "party insiders predict that because of his close relationship with Blair he will be the lynchpin between the party HQ and Westminster" '94; he became Deputy Political Secretary to the new Prime Minister, Tony Blair May '97; he was selected for Dagenham in succession to the ailing, retiring Judith Church with the support of his union, TGWU, which, it was claimed, offered to redecorate the local constituency headquarters if "their man" was selected May '00; he retained the seat by a majority of 8,693 despite a 7.8% pro-Tory swing June '01; he was one of the sponsors of a motion supporting the "employment rights of school ancillary workers" July '01; he insisted that he had been wrongly cited as one of "the majority of London Labour MPs" to back the Blair Government's public-private Tube investment plans; "I did not see the statement and I did not sign it; I was not very happy; I am still not very happy"; he said he shared the doubts of other MPs who believed the Government should have continued to negotiate for a compromise on PPP rather than ram it through July '01; he proposed that motor car manufacturers be required to pay owners 75 pounds for their old cars and then scrap them Aug '01;
Born: 7 April 1962, Helston, Cornwall
Family: Son, of Pat and John Cruddas, sailor; m '92 Anna Healy, longtime Labour Party functionary as Parliamentary Press Secretary, recently Special Adviser, successively to Jack Cunningham, Mo Mowlam and then Lord (Gus) Macdonald; 1s Emmett '93;
Education: Oaklands RC Comprehensive, Portsmouth; Warwick University (BSc, MA, PhD '81-88); Visiting Fellow, Wisconsin University '87-88;
Occupation: The Prime Minister's Deputy Political Secretary '97-01; Chief Assistant to the Labour Party General Secretary Larry Whitty '94-97; Policy Adviser, Labour Party Policy

Directorate '89-94; TGWU '89-00 (Branch Secretary '92-94);
Traits: Stooped, scholarly, quiet, reticent; "ambitious" (RED PEPPER); likes golf, angling;
Address: House of Commons, Westminster, London SW1A 0AA; Civic Centre, Dagenham, RM10 7BN; 76 St George's Rd, Dagenham RM9 5JT; 221a Stephendale Rd, London SW6;
Telephone: 0207 219 3000 (H of C); 0208 984 7854; 0208593 0854;

'Tony' (Thomas Anthony) CUNNINGHAM   Labour   WORKINGTON '01-

Majority: 10,850 (25.9%) over Tory 4-way;
Description: A Lake District seat and thus hard-hit by foot-and-mouth; its Labour majority comes from the Cumbrian coastal industrial belt; Workington's council estates house workers from its steelworks and formerly from Maryport's now-defunct docks; it includes part of the Sellafield nuclear power plant and the shut former Volvo/Leyland bus plant; in '95 9,000 voters were drafted in from rural Aspatria and Silloth wards formerly in Penrith and the Border;
Position: Ex: MEP for Cumbria and North Lancashire '94-99; Allerdale Borough Councillor (Leader '92-94) '87-94; Mayor of Workington '90-91;
Outlook: A widely-experienced low-profile local politician who has replaced high-profile 'incomer' Dale Campbell-Savours; is especially interested in the 3rd World, where he worked as a teacher;
History: He joined the Labour Party '83; he was elected to the European Parliament for Cumbria and North Lancashire, becoming Labour's spokesman on the 3rd World saying: "I am hoping...to help to drive forward the [Development] committee to increase funding and to strive to make sure that that funding goes to the poorest people in the poorest countries" June '94; he wrote a major report on landmines for the European Parliament '95; he unsuccessfully contested the Northwest Region for the European Parliament June '99; selected to succeed ailing, retiring Dale Campbell-Savours, despite a 6.9% pro-Tory swing, he retained the seat, by a majority of 10,850, almost 9,000 below Campbell-Savours previous one June '01; he was briefly on the Joint Committee on Human Rights but replaced by Kevin McNamara, much his senior July '01; he urged the involvement of local people in plans for rural recovery in foot-and-mouth-hit Cumbria Oct '01;
Born: 16 September 1952, Workington
Family: Son, of Bessie and late Daniel Cunningham; m '85 Anne Margaret (Gilmore); 1d; 1steps; 1stepd;
Education: Workington Grammar School; Liverpool University (BA Hons in History and Politics '75); Didsbury College (PGCE '76);
Occupation: Ex: Chief Executive, of Human Rights (human rights organisation) '99-00; MEP for Cumbria and North Lancashire '94-99; Teacher '76-94: at Alsager Comprehensive '76-80, Mikunguni Trade School, Zanzibar '80-82, Netherhall School, Maryport '83-94 (NUT);
Traits: Thinning hair; specs; beard; sounds idealistic;
Address: House of Commons, Westminster, London SW1A 0AA; The Labour Club, South William Street, Workington, Cumbria; 17 Carlton Road, Workington, Cumbria CA14 4BX;
Telephone: 0207 219 3000 (H of C); 01900 605799/603895;

Paul (Andrew) DAISLEY   **Labour**   **BRENT EAST '01-**

Majority: 13,047 (45%) over Conservative 7-way;
Description: A diverse northwestern London suburb, with growing middle-class and declining working-class areas; its shrinking Irish population is centred in Kilburn and Cricklewood; it also has Jewish, Asian, West Indian, Albanian and other minorities; it is 37% non-white; its many incompetent, feuding hard-Leftists among its activists helped Labour lose council elections until recently;
Position: Brent Councillor (Chief Whip '91-93, Leader '96-01) '90-01;
Outlook: Ken's friendly replacement, "previously considered a model Blairite" (Hugh Muir, EVENING STANDARD); with some justice, he describes himself as the "council leader responsible for transforming Brent into a model Labour authority"; his profile is low except locally, where he has gained kudos for his stand against the "gangsters" of Harlesden;
History: He joined ASTMS '76, MSF '80. the Labour Party '82; he was elected to Brent Council May '90; he became Chief Whip of the Labour Group on Brent Council '91, Leader of its Labour Group '94, Leader of Brent Council '96; he was selected "against stiff competition" (Hugh Muir, EVENING STANDARD) to replace Ken Livingstone on the latter's election as Mayor of London; the four-sided contest involved throwing out 100 postal ballots; the selection of another white candidate for an ethnically-mixed seat was attacked as a "disgrace" by Kingsley Abrams, Vice Chairman of the Black Socialist Society, who blamed it on institutional racism Sep '00; he called on Tony Blair to re-admit Ken Livingstone to the Labour Party, from which he had been excluded for contesting the mayoralty as an Independent against Labour's official candidate, Frank Dobson; "we should be grown-up; Ken has shown during his time in office that he wants to build bridges; he has gone out of the way to be conciliatory and that is not a bad start" Oct '00; Ken Livingstone promised to campaign for him May '01; he retained the seat with a majority of 13,047, a percentage almost identical with that previously achieved by Livingstone, on a 15% lower turnout June '01;
Born: 20 July 1957, Acton, London
Family: He declines to disclose his parents' names or jobs; his Partner is Lesley Jordan '84-;
Education: Littlemore School, Oxford; Abingdon College, Berkshire;
Occupation: Consultant; former Financial Director of Daisley Associates '84-96; Accounting Officer, Texaco '76-84 (MSF);
Traits: Beefy; square face; he enjoys badminton and football, rooting for Leicester City;
Address: House of Commons, Westminster, London SW1A 0AA; 102 Liddell Gardens, London NW10 3QE;
Telephone: 0207 219 3000 (H of C); 0208 969 2730/4550 Fax;

We reach the uncovered parts of MPs the press no longer notice, because the correspondents leave the Press Gallery too early.

Wayne DAVID Labour **CAERPHILLY '01-**

Majority: 14,245 (37.3%) over Plaid Cymru 5-way;
Description: The town of Caerphilly (cheese and castle) plus parts of the Rhymney Valley (declining coal, steel and transport); a more diverse economy is emerging, with many of its workforce employed outside the constituency;
Position: On the European Scrutiny Committee '01-; Vice President, Cardiff Branch, UN Association '89-; ex: Leader, European Parliamentary Labour Party '94-98; on Labour Party NEC '94-98; MEP '89-99;
Outlook: A Welsh pro-European Kinnockite trying his third legislative chamber to find a better deal for deprived Welsh areas; he gives the impression of not having been fully repatriated from Brussels; "a committed European and internationalist" (WD), his reputation suffered a battering when he lost Rhondda to the Plaid in the '99 Welsh Assembly elections;
History: He was brought up in a Labour-supporting family; his grandfather was a miner and his father a teacher and local Labour councillor; he joined the Labour Party at 16, '73; he called for a EU-wide ban on leg-iron traps July '88; he was elected to the European Parliament for South Wales; on being elected Treasurer of the British Labour MEPs he promised a more constructive pro-European attitude June '89; he opposed the war to oust Saddam Hussein from Kuwait, warning with other Labour MEPs that "such a war would be a great disaster", preferring "conflict resolution" by economic pressure Nov '90; he warned that EMU might not work for "peripheral areas" like Wales Dec '91; with 21 other Labour MEPs, he suspended his membership in the Tribune Group over its plan to publish an anti-Maastricht pamphlet without having consulted them Oct '92; with other Labour MEPs he informed Michael Heseltine his closing of 31 mines was based on short-term thinking Jan '93; he complained the Major Government was diverting money from local authorities, mostly Labour, towards quangos over which it had more control Oct '93; he was re-elected to the European Parliament for South Wales Central June '94; he was elected Leader of the European Parliamentary Labour Party to replace Pauline Green, elected to lead the European Socialist Group June '94; he disowned the revolt among Labour MEPs against Tony Blair's dropping of Clause 4, saying: "This is part of making Labour acceptable to the City and to industry; we want to build links with industry and to move away from the traditional assumpion that business must always support the Conservative Party and the trade unions are automatically linked to Labour" Nov '94; he suffered badly when he was beaten by the Plaid Cymru candidate in the elections to the Welsh Assembly in the long safe-for-Labour constituency of Rhondda May '99; he was selected for Caerphilly to replace retiring Ron Davies July '00; despite a 10.5% swing to Plaid Cymru, he retained the seat with a majority of 14,245, over 11,000 below the pre-exposure majority of Ron Davies June '01; in his Maiden speech he pointed out that "there are still coal tips in the constituency that need to be removed; the award of miners' compensation must be speeded up"; he also urged a new hospital June '01; he was named to the European Scrutiny Committee July '01; he urged much better scrutiny of European Union institutions as a way of repairing its "democratic deficit"; he warned the Conservatives against opposing Europe-wide political parties; "I am proud to be a member of the Party of European Socialists as well as of the Labour Party" July '01; he enthused about the '99 Berlin Council of the European Council, especially its contribution of £1.2b over the next seven years for south and west Wales July

Wayne DAVID

'01; he endorsed the Treaty of Nice July '01; he welcomed new jobs coming to his constituency as a result of the decision on a new Army communications system July '01; he intervened repeatedly in support of the ratification of the Bill enacting the Nice Agreement Oct '01;
Born: 1 July 1957, Bridgend, South Wales
Family: His grandfather was a miner; son, of Haydn David, teacher and councillor, and Edna (Jones); m '91 Catherine (Thomas);
Education: Cynffig Comprehensive School, Bridgend; University College, Cardiff (BA Hons in History; PGCE); Swansea University; Fellow, Cardiff University;
Occupation: Policy Advisor, to Wales Youth Agency '99-01; MEP '89-99; Tutor-Organiser, Workers Educational Association '85-89; Teacher, Brynteg Comprehensive '83-85;
Traits: Lean face; thining hair; droopy moustache;
Address: House of Commons, Westminster, London SW1A 0AA; Ty Cathway, Bryn Rhedyn, off The Rise, Tonteg, Pontypridd CF38 1UG;
Telephone: 0207 219 8152 (H of C); 01443 217810/217811 Fax;

Parmjit DHANDA **Labour** **GLOUCESTER '01-**

Majority: 3,880 (8.1%) over Conservative 5-way;
Description: The 'barometer seat' of '97 because Labour allegedly had to win it to win a one-seat majority; it acquired its marginal reputation when Tory Sally Oppenheim won it from Labour's Jack Diamond in '70; Douglas French inherited a 12,000 majority in '87, halved to 6,000 in '92; in '95 it lost 3,400 voters in suburban villages to Stroud; the re-capture of the seat by Labour's Tess Kingham was soon overshadowed by her increasingly public disenchantment with Westminster; the constituency's ethnic minority is 6%, the national average;
Position: Hillingdon Borough Councillor '98-; on Labour NEC's Working Party on Equal Opportunities '97-;
Outlook: Highly competent and ambitious young politician of Sikh origins who has found a crucial new role as a spokesman against targeting ethnic minorities in the wake of Afghanistan-based terrorism; he also draws on his municipal exprience to urge tougher deals between local councils and the private entrepreneurs over out-of-town shopping hubs; previously he tried climbing various political trees, including a local council and the European Parliament; to achieve this, he has used union and party (including the Co-operative Party) connections; "slick, professional and with the common touch" (INDEPENDENT); "placed high on [the] South East regional list for [the] 1998 Euro-elections, so presumably seen as reliable by Millbank" (RED PEPPER);
History: He joined the Labour Party '88; he became Agent for Ealing '96; he became Labour Agent for West London, Hampshire and Wiltshire '96; he was elected to Hillingdon Borough Council May '98; he contested the South East seat in the European Parliament, coming fifth out of eleven on the Labour list June '99; as a member of USDAW's Parliamentary Panel, he was selected to contest Gloucester after disillusioned mother-of-three Tess Kingham decided not to contest the seat again '00; he denied claims he was threatening to sue a Gloucester paper, THE CITIZEN, when its columnist suggested that Labour's selection of "a foreigner" in

New MPs of '01   *Parmjit DHANDA*

constituents' eyes meant Labour could "kiss goodbye" to their seat Apr '01; he retained Gloucester despite a 3.1% pro-Tory swing with a majority of 3,880, a drop of over 4,000 on Tess Kingham's '97 majority June '01; in his Maiden speech he called attention to a 30 million pound new hospital development, a new college of higher education and a state-of-the-art tennis centre coming to Gloucester June '01; he criticised Leftwing Labour MP Ann Cryer's suggestion that Asian immigrants be tested for English, warning that "speaking English isn't the be-all and end-all" July '01; at a conference-fringe meeting he urged local councils to drive harder bargains with developers of out-of-town shopping hubs, forcing them to fund community facilities such as health centres, polling stations and free bus transport Oct '01; in the second recall of Parliament he told how sharply most Muslims criticised terrorism - "a crime against religion and a crime against all of us" - and therefore must be protected against anti-Muslim terrorism Oct '01; he secured an adjournment debate to express concern about limits on access to sport on TV Oct '01;
Born: 17 September 1971;
Family: His grandfather was proud to wear his turban and beard while fighting "for King and Country" in wartime Burma; he does not otherwise disclose family names or jobs;
Education: Mellow Lane Comprehensive, Hayes, Middlesex; Nottingham University (Hons BEng in Electrical Engineering '93, MA in IT);
Occupation: Assistant National Organiser, CONNECT (union for professionals in communications) '98-; ex: Labour Agent for West London, Hampshire and Wiltshire '96-98 (MSF);
Traits: Tall (6'2"); very slim; dark brown skin; British-born of Sikh origins; declassed London accent; personable; enjoys football, Rugby, cricket, chess;
Address: House of Commons, Westminster, London SW1A 0AA; 1 Pullman Court, Great Western Road, Gloucester GL1 3ND; 36 Berwick Avenue, Hayes, Middlesex UB4 0NG;
Telephone: 0207 219 3000 (H of C); 0208 581 8330 also Fax (home); 0961 173862 (mobile); ps@dhanda.freeserve.co.uk;

Jonathan (Simon) DJANOGLY   **Conservative**   **HUNTINGDON '01-**

Majority: 12,792 (26.1%) over LibDem 4-way;
Description: The Tories' safest seat in '97, when still that of John Major, becoming their 16th safest in '01; it kept its old name but had been greatly altered and made more compact: centred on the old county town of Huntingdon, plus the other market towns of Godmanchester, St Ives and St Neots, with their connecting artery, the Great Ouse River; it contains 12,500 from the southern half of the old seat, plus the return of 29,000 from around the overspill town of St Neots, back from SW Cambridgeshire; it embraces the US airbases of Alconbury and Molesworth, which housed Cruise missiles;
Position: On the Trade and Industry Select Committee '01-, on Statutory Instruments (Joint Committee) '01-; ex: Westminster City Councillor '94-01; Vice Chairman, Westminster North Conservative Association '93-95;
Outlook: Thoughtful young successor to John Major, despite a name "more like a nightmare in Scrabble than a surname" (Matthew Parris, TIMES): "a Rightwinger", "heir to a large

Jonathan (Simon) DJANOGLY New MPs of '01

family fortune" "with close links to the Conservative Way Forward group which is strongly anti-European" (James Landale, TIMES);
History: His first political affiliation was to the Conservative Party in Oxford East Jan '85; he became Chairman of the Oxford Polytechnic Conservative Association '86; he was elected Chairman of the Maida Vale branch of the Westminster Tories, capturing all three local seats in May '90; he became Vice Chairman of the Westminster North Conservative Association '93; he was elected to Westminster City Council May '94; on the Council he rose to Chairman of Planning Applications and Traffic '95, chairman of Contracts '96, Finance '97, Social Services '98, Environment '99; as its Tory candidate he contested Oxford East against Labour's Andrew Smith, winning 22% of the vote on an anti-Tory swing of 9.1%, which he later said was "better than the national [10%] and county average" May '97; he was selected to contest Huntingdon on the impending retirement of ex-PM John Major; as a Rightwing anti-European, he beat off the challenges of David Platt, a former aide to Chris Patten, and Stephen Castle, an Essex businessman July '00; he retained Huntingdon despite a 7.9% swing to the LibDems with a majority of 12,792, over 5,000 below John Major's '97 majority June '01; in his Maiden speech on the Homelessness Bill he opposed as a "grave error" the building of too many new houses in his market towns. which would be "as great an error as was made by planning policies which over the years led to the depopulation of many of our nation's inner cities, with the subsequent disastrous impact on businesses and balanced social environments"; too much strain would be put on hospitals and schools; he urged tax incentives to encourage private developers to bring empty private properties back into use July '01; he was named to the Trade and Industry Select Committee, to the Statutory Instruments (Joint Committee) July '01; he backed Iain Duncan Smith in all the ballots for Leader July '01; he was one of 14 new Tory MPs who together wrote to the DAILY TELEGRAPH endorsing Iain Duncan Smith as a Leader who "can unite the party on Europe" Aug '01; he strongly opposed the Bill enacting the Nice Agreement as leading "to a regressive Europe", compounding its "introspective, exclusive, rich-member-club mentality"; "after enlargement the UK's position is likely to deteriorate"; he urged the EU embrace the global economy and restructure its institutions accordingly Oct '01; he complained that "an asylum stop-off site in Great Gransden" in his constituency was being planned without consulting local people Oct '01; he backed the Marine Wildlife Conservation Bill for ending a "disjointed" and "haphazard" approach to the sea Oct '01; he said businessmen felt that "many bright but non-academic young people would be better served by a decent apprenticeship system" Nov '01;
Born: 3 June 1965, London
Family: Son, of Sir Harry Djanogly CBE, textile company director, and Carol (Gold); m '91 Rebecca (Silk), company director; 1s Joseph '95, 1d Beth '97;
Education: Greenhome, Nottingham; University College School, London; Oxford Polytechnic (BA Law and Politics '87); Guildford College of Law;
Occupation: Solicitor: youngest Partner '98- in SJ Berwin & Co (corporate finance) London '88-; Director and Founder, Audio Books Direct Ltd (direct-mail casette books, co-founded with wife) '94-;
Traits: Young-looking ("looks about 14" - Matthew Parris, TIMES); long-faced; Jewish; his oft-mispronounced name sometimes comes out as 'Dangly' or 'Jan Godly', but is actually pronounced 'Jan-og-lee'; he enjoys sports, the theatre, reading biographies;
Address: House of Commons, Westminster, London SW1A 0AA; Archer's Court, 8 Stukely Road, Huntingdon PE29 6XB;
Telephone: 0207 219 3000 (H of Commons); 01480 453062 (constituency); jonathandjanogly@hcca.org.uk;

Nigel DODDS   **Democratic Unionist**   **BELFAST NORTH '01-**

Majority: 6,387 (15.6%) over Sinn Fein 6-way;
Description: A changed, predominantly-Protestant constituency with a substantial (37%) Catholic minority; it contains the Protestant working-class areas of Oldpark, Crumlin and Shankhill - with the problems of the extremely deprived - as well as some more pleasant residential parts: Antrim Road, Belfast Castle and Cavehill; Catholics are concentrated in the Ardoyne and New Lodge areas and their numbers are rising as the Protestants decline; there were more killings here during the Troubles per head of population than anywhere else: "we have lost more than 600 people in the constituency as a result of terrorist violence" (ND); this was also the site of the ugly baiting by Protestant extremists of school-going Catholic children in Sep '01; before the '83-01 era of UUPer Cecil Walker, the seat was held by DUPer John McQuade '79-83;
Position: Belfast City Councillor (Mayor '88-89, 91-92) '85-; DUP Party Secretary '98-;; Northern Ireland Assemblyman (Minister for Social Development '01-, '99-00) '98-; ex: on Northern Ireland Forum '96-98;
Outlook: An infinitely articulate and hyperactive DUP replacement for ultra low-profiled UUPer Cecil Walker; one of the most liked and respected of DUPers whose entry into Westminster was previously delayed by pacts among Protestant political parties not to fight each other; "a reputation for hard work and commitment" (David McKittrick, INDEPENDENT);
History: He was elected to Belfast City Council May '85; he became Belfast's youngest-ever Mayor '88; he was named Secretary of the Democratic Unionist Party Apr '93; he was elected to the Northern Ireland Forum June '96; he survived an IRA attack when a gunman opened fire on his bodyguards while he was visiting his ill son Andrew in hospital Dec '96; he stood down as the DUP candidate for Belfast North to give UUPer Cecil Walker a clear run for the Protestant and Unionist vote there May '97; he was awarded an OBE for his work in local government June '97; he was elected to the new Northern Ireland Assembly June '98; he was selected as the DUP candidate for Belfast North Aug '99; he attacked his UUP opponent, incumbent Cecil Walker as the Unionist MP with the "worst record", having spoken only once in four years May '01; he accused UUP Leader David Trimble of misleading the voters by telling them the DUP would be handing seats to nationalists; he had said DUP voters should put their transfer votes in the PR count in the Assembly to like-minded Unionists May '01; achieving a majority of 6,387, he swept Cecil Walker out of office after 18 years, despite his 13,000 previous majority, pushing him into 4th place June '01; in his Maiden speech he spoke of the political tensions, terrorism and unemployment in his new constituency; "yesterday, I had the sad task of having to stand in a local Protestant church in my constituency that has been a target of arsonists", he said, demanding more policing June '01; in the debate on the Electoral Fraud (Northern Ireland) Bill, he preferred photographic identification but opposed an exclusion zone around polling booths July '01; he told Northern Ireland Secretary John Reid that "one of the main causes of concern in Northern Ireland has been the ongoing process of concessions to the IRA and Sinn Fein, with little or nothing in return" July '01; he claimed that RUC morale was being "undermined" by the Patten Report and the Belfast agreement which meant that the Northern Ireland Policing Board would "comprise members of the Sinn

Fein-IRA"; he insisted that fear of IRA intimidation was the main reason for Catholics not joining the force July '01; he quoted the Chief Constable of the RUC as saying that "the IRA orchestrated and organised violence in Ardoyne in my constituency", demanding to know why the Government negotiated with the "IRA-Sinn Fein" but excluded "representatives of the Democratic Unionist Party, which has more votes and more seats in the House" July '01; he kept a low profile during the horrendous scenes of local Protestant extremists harrassing Catholic children en route to school Sep '01; he emphasised the threat to Northern Ireland jobs of Shorts' laying off of thousands of aircraft workers and BA cutting its flights to Belfast Oct '01; in the wake of IRA decommissioning, he resumed his post as Minister for Social Development in the Northern Ireland Assembly, along with Peter Robinson Oct '01; he complained of the slowness with which the Government were bringing in tighter procedures to avoid electoral fraud Oct '01; he accused Northern Ireland Secretary John Reid of an attempt "to cheat, to rig the processs by the Government and the pro-Agreement parties", "getting David Trimble back into government by the back door" "rather than going for fresh elections" Nov '01; he was active in DUP's last-minute efforts to block David Trimble's resumption of his role as First Minister Nov '01; he alleged that, far from decommissioning, the Provisional IRA was involved in "shooting attacks on the RUC in Duncairn Gardens, the shooting of a Protestant man on the Limestone Road and a shooting attack on the Ardoyne on Saturday a week ago" Nov '01;

Born: 20 August 1958, Londonderry
Family: Son, Joseph Dodds, customs officer, and Doreen (McMahon); married; two s, one d;
Education: Portora Royal School, Enniskillen; St John's College, Cambridge University (1st Class Hons BA in Law); Institute of Professional Legal Studies, Queens University, Belfast;
Occupation: Barrister '81-; Secretary to the DUP '93-, Assistant to Rev Ian Paisley MP; in European Parliament's Secretariat '84-96;
Traits: Dark, parted, retreating, thinning hair; lean, lined face; has "a reputation for being both dour and extreme but...[also] has...a reputation for hard work and commitment" (David McKittrick, INDEPENDENT); "the only likeable man in the DUP" (political opponent quoted in BELFAST TELEGRAPH);
Address: House of Commons, Westminster, London SW1A 0AA; 210 Shore Road, Belfast BT15 3QB;
Telephone: 0207 219 3000 (H of C); 028 90 774 774/777 685 Fax; 028 9077 4774;

Pat(rick) DOHERTY   Sinn Fein   WEST TYRONE '01-

Majority: 5,040 (10.4%) over UUP 3-way;
Description: Northern Ireland's additional new seat in the west: a rural, predominantly (63%) Catholic seat made up of the handsome county town of Omagh - bombed by the Real IRA in '98 - and less-lovely Strabane; three-quarters was taken from Mid-Ulster, with the area around the town of Strabane coming from Foyle; it was rated a three-way marginal between the UUP-SDLP-Sinn Fein on the basis of the vote in this area in the '96 Forum election; this showed the SDLP slightly ahead of Sinn Fein, both on 28% with the UUP trailing a poor third with 18%, and the DUP in fourth place; in '97, the

UUP's Willie Thompson won with only 35% of the vote; in '98 Sinn Fein topped the polls in the constituency in the Northern Ireland Assembly elections, taking 41% of the vote to win the seat in '01;
Position: Northern Ireland Assemblyman for West Tyrone '98-; Vice President, Sinn Fein '88-; ex: National Organiser '85-88, Director of Elections '84-85 of Sinn Fein;
Outlook: "A sharp politician and committed republican; he was a central backroom figure when Sinn Fein first made its serious drive into politics; now he is out in front as the party makes its most significant breakthrough in nationalism" (Darwin Templeton, BELFAST TELGRAPH); the surprise victor of the '01 election, crucially beating Brid Rodgers of the SDLP when she was expected by the press to win more of the seat's predominant Catholic vote because of her high profile as an able Agriculture Minister at Stormont during the foot-and-mouth crisis; her popularity in the press was outweighed by Sinn Fein's formidable local electioneering machine which concentrated on this seat and Fermanagh & South Tyrone; in this seat Sinn Fein chalked up 2,200 postal and proxy votes; before the election he slightly under-estimated his vote as 18,000; as with his three Sinn Fein colleagues he has not taken the Loyal Oath entitling him to a seat in the Commons;
History: He returned to his family's Donegal home in '68 after spending his first two decades in Glasgow, where he was born; he first became a Sinn Fein activist in '70; he became Sinn Fein's Director of Elections '84, its National Organiser '85; he was elected Vice President of Sinn Fein '88; he was leader of the Sinn Fein delegation to the Dublin Forum for Peace and Reconciliation '94; he came a close 3rd, after the SDLP's Joe Byrne in West Tyrone in the general election May '97; he won West Tyrone in the Northern Ireland Assembly elections June '98; he was accused by DUPer Peter Robinson in the Assembly of being a member of the 7-man Provisional IRA's Army Council, which he denied Apr '01; he predicted his better machine would prevail over the SDLP: "there is no SDLP machine on the ground; you don't win elections in the three or four weeks before an election; you win them in the years beforehand; you build support and, in an election, you reap that support" May '01; he won the seat on a 7% swing by a majority of 5,040, forcing the SDLP into 3rd place behind the incumbent Willie Thompson; he increased the Sinn Fein vote by 10%; Mrs Rodgers' SDLP vote declined by 3.3% June '01;
Born: 18 July 1945, Glasgow
Family: Son of a Donegal man who emigrated to find employment in Glasgow; his brother Hugh served decades in prison as a member of the IRA's Balcombe Street gang; he married Mary; two s, three d;
Education: In Glasgow; school names undisclosed;
Occupation: Founder-Director of local Credit Union '92-; Site Engineer '75-;
Traits: Parted full head of dark hair; jowly square face; specs; "with his soft burr and relaxed country manner, he cuts an almost grandfatherly figure" (Darwin Templeton, BELFAST TELEGRAPH); he "cuts an awkward figure; he looks like a shambolic science teacher"; "born in Glasgow, but says he feels all-Irish and has assumed an accent to match" (Alison Hardie, SCOTSMAN); "in person he resembles a primary school headmaster rather than a godfather of terrorism; he is genial, apparently completely open and smiles readily" (David McKittrick, INDEPENDENT); he enjoys building stone walls;
Address: House of Commons, Westminster, London SW!A 0AA; 12 Bridge Street, Strabane, County Tyrone BT82 9AE; lives in Carrigart, County Donegal;
Telephone: 0207 219 3000 (H of C); 028 7188 6464/6466 Fax;

Sue DOUGHTY   Liberal Democrat   GUILDFORD '01-

Majority: 538 (1.1%) over Conservative 5-way;
Description: The virtually-unaltered county town which has been associated with Conservatism since Disraeli's time, despite a Liberal win there in 1906; before '97 it was the least safely-Tory of all the 11 Conservative seats in Surrey; the one-time home of Charles Dodgson (Lewis Carroll) and Alan Turing, it is partly a commuting city, but big enough to be a commercial centre on its own and the home of Surrey University; a middle-class seat with a high proportion of professionals, it has lost some of its stuffiness under its LibDem-controlled council, which has encouraged a 'yoof-culture' with wine bars and themed pubs proliferating; its only change in '95 was the shift of a village into neighbouring Surrey Heath; if '97 voting had followed the '92 pattern it should have produced a majority of 13,000 for the Tory victor; instead it gave him 4,791; even this was not safe from the successful LibDem assault in the 'standstill election' of '01;
Position: Chairman, LibDems Reading East Constituency Association '96-98;
Outlook: The 'Guildford Girl' who seemingly emulated 'Orpington Man' Eric Lubbock in conquering a previously historically Conservative redoubt; she felt her success was partly due to the anti-European attitude of the Tories: "this is a very prosperous place and the local businesses and the bankers who live in the rural retreats know that the Euro is a very good idea"; her opponent attributed her success to her greater attraction for "aspiring young professionals"; his supporters among them "stayed at home" because "they didn't think we had anything to offer them" (its previous Tory MP Nick St Aubyn); she later attributed her success to the appeal of her crusade against the building of a giant incinerator as threatening the environment;
History: She contested London in the European Parliamentary election June '99; selected for Guildford, she campaigned strongly against building a large incinerator in the middle of Guildford Apr-May '01; she appealed to voters on a highly-personal level, citing her son at university whose friends had been over-burdened by debt; she was very concerned abut how her 80-year-old father was going to get by on his paltry pension; like a number of other LibDem candidates, she sent out a seemingly-handwritten mailing addressed to individual voters June '01; she won the seat by the narrow majority of 538 on a 4.8% pro-LibDem swing, with a 11.7% drop in turnout June '01; the first Liberal MP for Guildford since 1906, she made a very pro-European Maiden speech, urging her constituency to emulate Cologne in the compulsory separate recycling of bottles and welcoming imminent EU directives to increase recycling of electronic and electrical waste; she again attacked the planned building of a giant incinerator dominating Guildford July '01; by the Bournemouth conference of the LibDems she had decided that her success was due to her anti-incinerator crusade, which had "won Guildford for the Liberal Democrats" because "we put the environment at the heart of [local] government"; the Labour Government's "short-termism" made it "fall down time and again" and deaf to demands for "sustainable waste management" Sep '01; she insisted it was "more realistic to promise improvements in public service and help for students by accepting that taxes may have to rise, than by pretending that they will be cut" Oct '01; she supported the Labour Government's anti-terrorist campaign, but its bombing of Afghanistan "to a certain extent with reluctance" because of civilian suffering Nov '01; she led a motion's amendment

Copyright (C) Parliamentary Profile Services Ltd

insisting that Guildford and Surrey opposed building any homes beyond those planned by SERPLAN Nov '01;
Born: 13 April 1948, Yorkshire
Family: Married to David Vyvian Orchard; 2s, 2 stepdaughters;
Education: Mill Mount Grammar School, York; Northumberland College of Education (Art Certificate '69);
Occupation: Free-lance journalist; ex: Consultant Project Manager with Norwich Union '00-01; Management Consultant '99-00; IT Project Manager, Thames Water '89-98; Independent Consultant, ("worked for major utilities, 'big five' firms, law practices) '82-88; O&M Analyst, Wilkinson Match '76-77; Work Study Analyst: CEGB '75-76, Northern Gas '71-75; Teacher, in East Riding of Yorkshire '70-71;
Traits: Reddish-brown hair; heart-shaped face; specs; sharp chin; nice smile;
Address: House of Commons, Westminster, London SW1A 0AA; 96 London Road, Guildford, Surrey GU1 she lives in Shalford;
Telephone: 0207 219 3000 (H of C); 01483 572699/568700 Fax;

Peter **DUNCAN**   Conservative   **GALLOWAY & UPPER NITHSDALE '01-**

Majority: 74 (.2%) over SNP 5-way;
Description: Britain's most agricultural seat: little-changed and sparsely-populated in remote southwestern rural Scotland; the old counties of Kirkcudbright and Wigtown plus part of Dumfriesshire, with their mountains, glens, lochs and forests and equally beautiful placenames; embracing over 1,500 square miles, it is the 6th largest seat in the UK; its tourism and sheep flocks suffered from foot-and-mouth; it was first captured by the SNP '74-79 before being retaken by Ian (recently Lord) Lang '79-97, then again SNP-snatched by Alasdair Morgan '97-01;
Position: On the Select Committee on Scottish Affairs '01-; Chairman, Cunninghame North Conservatives '99-;
Outlook: The Eurosceptic "political virgin" on whose "shoulders will be carried the burden of Scottish Tory aspirations at Westminster for the next few years" (Robbie Dinwoodie, SCOTSMAN) because he succeeded very narrowly where would-be retreads Sir Malcolm Rifkind and Raymond Robertson failed: a talented local businessman and apprentice politician who was 2001's only Tory to re-enter Parliament from Scotland, overcoming the 5,624 majority inherited from the SNP's incumbent Alasdair Morgan by his young researcher and would-be successor, Malcolm Fleming;
History: He joined the Conservative and Unionist Party '82; "he voted No-No in the devolution referendum but when this stance was lost, he accepted the 'settled will' of the people and decided to become active in politics again, becoming Chairman of Cunninghame North Conservatives in 1999" (Robbie Dinwoodie, SCOTSMAN); he was selected in good time to try to recapture Galloway & Upper Nithsdale for the Tories Jan '00; he consulted Ian Lang, who told him "Do it your way" Jan '00; he argued in favour of a new kind of community politics, engaging people in local issues; in the election campaign both he and his SNP opponent supported the upgrading of the Euro-route from Ireland to Gretna, which runs

Peter DUNCAN *New MPs of '01*

through the constituency, so that the ferry terminal at Stranraer, the region's biggest employer after the council, did not lose out to the Welsh who were busy upgrading to dual carriageway their route from Holyhead to England Apr-May '01; he very narrowly retook the seat by 74 votes on a 6.8% swing from the SNP June '01; his graceful and witty Maiden speech was widely admired June '01; he was named to the Select Committee on Scottish Affairs July '01; having voted for Duncan Smith in the first ballots, he was one of 14 new Tory MPs who together wrote to the DAILY TELEGRAPH endorsing Iain Duncan Smith as a Leader who "can unite the party on Europe" Aug '01; he defended the conflict in Afghanistan as "a just war", but urged keeping the "high level of support that exists in the country" Oct '01; he worried about "blatant gerrymandering" by the Boundary Commission which would report in 2002 Oct '01; he asked "what will the Government do to reverse the decline into devastating poverty of Scotland's rural communities?" Nov '01;
Born: 10 July 1965, Kilwinning, Ayrshire
Family: Son, of late Ronald Duncan, textile businessman, and late Aureen (Anderson); m '94 Lorna (Forbes), fundraiser for a charity; 1s Gavin '94, 1d Hannah '96;
Education: Ardrossan Academy; Birmingham University (Commerce);
Occupation: He runs the family textile business in Gatehouse, set up by his great-great grandfather in 1820, '99-; was previously in the retail furniture trade '88-99;
Traits: "A strapping big Ayrshireman" (Robbie Dinwoodie, SCOTSMAN); very full-faced, with heavy jowls and underchin (I have "somewhat cruelly been compared" to the profile of "the world-famous belted Galloway" - Peter Duncan);
Address: House of Commons, Westminster, London SW1A 0AA;
Telephone: 0207 219 8235 (H of C);

Annabelle EWING **SNP** **PERTH '01-**

Majority: 48 (.1%) over Conservative 5-way;
Description: The former Perth & Kinross seat, shorn in '95 of 7,500 voters in Kinross (removed to Ochil); apart from Perth and smaller Crieff and Auchterader, it consists of vast tracts of rolling farmland and hills; as Kinross and West Perthshire it once provided the blue-chip base for Sir Alec Douglas-Home '63-74, then as a Tory-SNP marginal, a precarious seat for the eccentric Sir Nicholas Fairbairn '74-95; on his death it fell to the SNP in May '95, until Roseanna Cunningham transferred her loyalties to the Scottish Parliament;
Position: On the SNP's Standing Orders and Agenda Committee;
Outlook: A younger representative of the dynasty dominating the SNP who would really rather join her mother, brother and sister-in-law in Holyrood rather than an 'ambassador' to a Westminster the SNP does not really believe in; her finger-tip majority seemed to reflect this lack of enthusiasm; "has great integrity and commitment and it is allied to properly-controlled ambition"; "that ambition encapsulates keeping the family flag flying, but it is mainly because she is passionate about Scotland and what she perceives to be its present second-class role within the UK and Europe; she wants desperately to change that" (Close observer cited by Jim McBeth, SCOTSMAN);

48 *Copyright (C)Parliamentary Profile Services Ltd*

History: The daughter of Winnie Ewing, she was 7 years old when her mother, Winnie, won Hamilton Nov '67; she joined the SNP at 15 in '75; she contested the Hamilton South by-election for the SNP, 32 years after her mother's sensational win there; the by-election was triggered by the departure of its incumbent Labour MP, George Robertson, to become NATO chief; she increased the SNP vote to 34%, just 556 votes (2.9%) behind Labour, representing a threatening pro-SNP swing of 22.6% Sep '99; she was selected to fight Perth on the impending departure to Holyrood of Roseanna Cunningham '00; hardly mentioning the SNP's independence target, she campaigned on local issues, defending the Perth Royal Infirmary against the threat posed by the loss of its maternity and paediatric departments May '01; she very narrowly retained the seat with a 48 majority - the Commons 2nd smallest - down from '97's 3,141 margin June '01; she asked when an amendment to the Housing Benefit Regulations would be brought into force July '01; she asked whether, as reported in the Scottish press, the UK Government might not "continue to pay attendance allowance with respect to Scottish pensioners following the implementation in the Scottish Parliament of the proposals on free personal care for the elderly" Oct '01; she urged more generous treatment for carers than proposed Oct '01;
Born: 20 August 1960, Glasgow
Family: Daughter, of Winnie Ewing, SNP President and MSP for Highlnds and Islands, and Stewart Ewing, Chartered Accountant;
Education: Craigholme School, Glasgow; Glasgow University (LLB); Bologna Center of Johns Hopkins University; Amsterdam University;
Occupation: She has practised as a lawyer, in Brussels and in Glasgow: Ewing and Company, Glasgow (a small legal practice "which has developed a reputation as a champion of the poor and unrepresented" - GLASGOW HERALD) '98-; ex: Freelance Lawyer, doing European Commission work '97; Special Counsel, with McKenna and Cuneo, Brussels '96; Contract Partner '93-96, Associate '89-92, Akin Gump, Brussels; Associate: of Lebrun de Smedt and Dasssesse, Brussels '87-89; in the European Commission Legal Service '87; Apprentice Lawyer, with Ruth Anderson and Company '84-86;
Traits: Dark tonsure; full face; specs; "a natural resilience"; "that air of confidence in public which is bred into lawyers"; "better looking and more vivacious than her campaign portrait would suggest" (Jim McBeth, SCOTSMAN); has "neither the sass nor the charisma of her mother" (Jonathan Freedland, GUARDIAN); "a good speaker" (GLASGOW HERALD); has admitted she does not feel British at all;
Address: House of Commons, Westminster, London SW1A 0AA; 7 Munro Avenue, Stirling, FK7 5RA;
Telephone: 0207 219 3000 (H of C); 0141 423 1765/422 1222 Fax (home); 01786 463054; ewing@globalnet.co.uk;

AN EXTENSION OF MPS
MPs have developed an added dimension, called researchers. Until recently only more sophisticated MPs used them. Or were used by them. One former Northwest MP, suddenly seemed fascinated with Trans-Pacific trade, according to questions in his name. These were planted by his research assistant, an American PhD-aspirant, writing his dissertation with the help of answers provided by UK civil servants. Recently the number of questions has increased by a third, as researchers vie with lobbyists and cause groupies. One now has to distinguish between MPs' questions and those planted on them. Our monitoring does so.

{Christopher) Paul FARRELLY   Labour   NEWCASTLE-UNDER-LYME '01-

Majority: 9,986 (25.8%) over Conservative 5-way;
Description: A fringe-Potteries north Staffordshire seat which has remained consistently loyal to Labour since 1919; traditionally a mining and market town, its last pit shut at the end of the 1990s, being replaced by growing light industries; it embraces Keele University but is just below-average in professional-middle class representation and above-average in the number of social-housing dwellers;
Position: Chairman, of North Staffordshire's NHS 'Care for All' campaign (care for the elderly) '98-;
Outlook: A local boy who made good at Oxford, in the City and Fleet Street, returning to his working-class roots; his politicisation was due to the brutal sacking of his gas pipe-laying father by privatised British Gas; he shares "traditional Labour values" and is pledged "to work hard for the needs of ordinary people";
History: Coming from a Labour-supporting family, with an inspiring activist grandfather, he joined the Labour Pary in '87; in the Hornsey & Wood Green CLP, he became Constituency Organiser, Secretary, and Vice Chairman '88-95; as the Labour candidate for hopeless Amersham and Chesham he avoided being wiped out by tactical voting; while still coming 3rd, he increased the Labour vote by 78% from 5,758 to a record 10,240 May '97; on the announced impending retirement of Llin Golding, whose late husband's biography he was writing, he was selected to fight for Labour in his home town of Newcastle-under-Lyme Junw '00; he retained the seat with a majority of 9,986, a fall of over 7,000 from Llin Golding's '97 majority on a 15% lower turnout, still the second biggest majority since '45, June '01; with 123 other Labour MPs he voted against the composition of Select Committees June '01; in his skilful Maiden speech, he spoke of the difficulties of local working-class kids continuing their education after 16, unlike himself: "I was the first of my family to go to university - in Oxford" July '01; he welcomed the Export Control Bill as "a new weapon in our armoury to restrain the merchants of death" including those wreaking death and destruction in the Congo where "other African states that should know better are systematically looting a country that is already on its knees", with Zimbabwe as "one of the vultures" Nov '01;
Born: 2 March 1962, Newcastle-under-Lyme
Family: "My [maternal] grandfather was one of the first Labour Party members in Newcastle and a staunch trades unionist"; his paternal grandfather was a "rabbit-trapper from county Meath"; son, of Tom Farrelly, Irish-born gas pipe-laying foreman, and Anne (King), nurse; "my mum left school at 15 and my dad, in Ireland, at 12"; m '98 Victoria (Perry) architect; 1s 'Joe' '99; 1d Aneira '01;
Education: St Mary's Primary, Newcastle-under-Lyme, Wolstanton County Grammar; Marshlands Comprehensive, Newcastle; St Edmund Hall, Oxford University (BA Hons in PPE);
Occupation: Author: forthcoming Hard Labour: John Golding's Battles Against Militant; ex: City Editor, The OBSERVER '97-01; Deputy Business and City Editor, INDEPENDENT ON SUNDAY '95-97; Reuters Correspondent and News Editor '90-91; Manager, Corporate Finance, Barclays De Zoete Wedd (specialising in project finance, mergers and acquisitions) '84-90;

Traits: Dark hair, retreating hairline, high widow's peak; long oval face;
Address: House of Commons, Westminster, London SW1A 0AA; Waterloo Buildings, Dunkirk, Newcastle-under-Lyme ST5 2SW; 7 Langford Road, Seabridge, Newcastle-under-Lyme ST5 3JZ;
Telephone: 0207 219 8391 (H of C); 01782 619 724; 01782 610834; 0468 113315;

Mark FIELD   Conservative   CITIES OF LONDON & WESTMINSTER '01-

Majority: 4,499 (13.2%) over Labour 5-way;
Description: The elite constituency with the City and Westminster, Mayfair and Belgravia, expanded in '83 by 20,000 voters from the southern part of abolished Marylebone; it '95 a further 10,000 were added from the abolished Westminster North seat;
Position: Kensington & Chelsea Councillor '94-; Chairman, Benefits Review Board '98-; ex: Deputy Chairman, Islington North Conservative Association '89-91
Outlook: Rightwing Eurosceptic (Conservative Way Forward) and Portillo supporter; he resembles Portillo in also being half-foreign, with a German refugee mother; "regarded as a high-flyer" (Michael White, GUARDIAN); an opponent of tight rules on MPs' outside earnings: "if you're earning several hundred thousand a year in the City are you going to give it up for £47,000 a year in the Commons?";
History: He joined the Conservative Party at 20, '84; he served as PA to John Patten for two years from '85; he became Secretary of the Oxford University Conservative Association '85; having run COUNCIL BRIEFING documenting the Hodge regime in Islington, he contested a council seat in Islington North May '90; in CROSSBOW he attacked AIDS campaigns as a waste of taxpayers' money and wanted mandatory tests instead: "many charitable trusts set up to help counter AIDS in the mid-1980s became little more than gay rights fronts" '91; he became chairman of his Cheyne ward in the Conservative Association of Kensington & Chelsea June '92; he was elected to Kensington and Chelsea Council May '94; was the runner-up in the selection for Colchester Nov '95; was in the final three in the selection for Reading East Feb '96; on the resignation of Tim Eggar, he was selected as the candidate for Enfield North, majority 9,430, from among 150 applicants, including former MPs and MEPs May '96; in the DAILY TELEGRAPH he was listed with fellow candidates as favouring negotiating entry into the Euro on a noncommital basis, the least Eurosceptic option on offer Dec '96; he lost Enfield North to Labour's Joan Ryan by 6,822 votes on an anti-Tory swing of 16.1% May '97; he was among the final three short-listed for the Eddisbury by-election June '99; with a small group of strongly Eurosceptic Tories, he worked to ensure that no Europhile candidate succeeded in winning the selection for Kensington & Chelsea on Alan Clark's death, aiding the emergence of Michael Portillo as the Tory candidate Oct '99; with the backing of the "pro-Portillo" Conservative Way Forward (Michael White, GUARDIAN), was selected to succeed Peter Brooke as the Tory candidate for Cities of London & Westminster Dec '99; in the election campaign he suffered the disadvantage in daytime canvassing of facing Filipino servants instead of their voting masters and mistresses when he knocked on Belgravia doors May '01; he retained the seat by a majority of 4,499 votes, almost identical with that secured in

Mark FIELD *New MPs of '01*

'97 by his widely-popular predecessor, Peter Brooke June '01; in his well-received Maiden speech, he disclosed that the fate of his German maternal antecedents had emphasised the importance of the middle class engaging in politics; he also complained that the Labour Government's concession of devolution had "upset the equilibrium of the United Kingdom and it will be difficult to restore" June '01; insisted that Stephen Byers' "misleading statements" exposed in a GUARDIAN article suggested a "cancer of cynicism in his department"; he said London Underground's "third world" infrastructure was "falling apart" and London's massive wealth contribution required increased transport like the Crossrail project Oct '01; while anxious to improve the environment in central London, he was "increasingly concerned by the alarmist views that are all too often expressed in the environmental debate by unscrupulous lobbyists and scientists" Oct '01; he objected to the swallowing up of the antique City magistrates courts by the new London-wide bench Oct '01; "as a former small businessman" he felt they paid too much in tax (64%) apart from serving as "unpaid tax collectors" Nov '01;
Born: 6 October 1964, Hannover (British Military Hospital)
Family: "My [maternal] grandfather...was from a well-to-do Silesian family and became a doctor"; "my grandfather regretted to his dying day that he had rather looked down on politics, as had many others of his generation, as that was the vacuum that, along with the discredited Weimar republic and the great economic crisis in Germany in the 1920s, let in, to a large extent, National Socialism"; son, of late Major Peter Field, professional soldier, and Ulrike (Peipe); "my mother was born in the early months of the last World War in 1939 in a little village outside a large town called Breslau - now called Wroclaw - which subsequently became part of Poland"; "my mother was twice a refugee by the age of 15, fleeing first from Breslau to Leipzig and then, finally from east to west Berlin before the days of the Berlin Wall"; "I was born in Germany and brought up in the home counties"; m '94 Michele (Acton), a Director of stockbrokers HSBC;
Education: Reading School, Berkshire (then a grammar); St Edmund Hall, Oxford University (MA Oxon in Jurisprudence); School of Law, Chester;
Occupation: Founding Partner of Kellyfield Consulting (specialist employment recruitment consultancy firm, "with turnover trebling and profits increasing five-fold in the last four years" to 2000; "within a few months of the general election in June ['01] I was bought out") '92-01; ex: Director, Portobello Business Centre (buisness development agency) '96-98; Solicitor, with Freshfields (international law firm specialising in international corporate transactions) '88-92; Publisher, with small company in Sheffield (sold in '91) '86-88;
Traits: Youthful good looks; oval-faced, thin lips; modishly cut swept-back hair; tentative; "I am a keen cricketer, having played to county level as a schoolboy";
Address: House of Commons, Westminster, London SW1A 0AA; 67 Elizabeth Street, London SW1W 9PJ; 90 Ebury Street, London SW1W 9QD;
Telephone: 0207 219 3000 (H of C); 0207 219 8160 (work) 0207 730 5787 (home); 0207 730 8181/4520 Fax (association);

DOORSTEPPING JOURNALISTS

We accept that one of the weaknesses in this volume is paucity of information about the parents of politicians. We find it valuable to know whether the father of an MP is a multi-millionaire property developer or a plumber. But some MPs claim that their parents fear press intrusion. Any pressman with experience of doorstepping journalists or aggressive photographers can understand some trepidation. But our jury is still out on whether this is the main reason for withholding such information.

Adrian (John) FLOOK   Conservative   TAUNTON '01-

Majority: 235 (.4%) over LibDem 4-way;
Description: The unaltered seat containing the county town of Taunton plus four wards of West Somerset District, stretching across Exmoor to the Devon border; it has eight hunts, two of the country's three packs of deer hounds and 1,000 dairy farms; the town is increasingly dependent on service jobs, due to the decline of local manufacture; its voters inclined to vote for the Liberal Democrats in district, county and Euro elections before '97, when they also elected LibDem Jackie Ballard as their MP;
Position: On the Select Committee on Culture, Media and Sport '01-; Wandsworth Councillor '94-; ex: Deputy Chairman, Battersea Conservative Association '94-96;
Outlook: Deft PRman who was the narrow beneficiary of his LibDem opponent's knee-in-the-groin campaigning techniques against hunting; a pro-NATO Rightwing Eurosceptic (Associate Member, of Thatcherite 'Conservative Way Forward'); a self-proclaimed "member and keen supporter of the Countryside Alliance (attended both the Rally and the March)" but in private is not over-enthusiastic about fox-hunting;
History: He joined the Conservative Party at 15, '78; he stood as a Consrvative in his school's mock election, and won '79; campaigned for Chris Patten in Bath in the election '79; he became Vice Chairman in charge of the Battersea Conservatives' fundraising '90; he was a campaign aide to John Bowis, who retained marginal Battersea Apr '92; became Treasurer of Battersea Conservatives '93; became Deputy Chairman of Battersea Conservative Association '94; he became more strongly Eurosceptic after Helmut Kohl's fourth German victory, when Kohl said "Now we can begin to build a federal Europe" Oct '94; he was elected to Wandsworth Borough Council May '96; as the Tory candidate in Labour's ultra-safe mining seat of Pontefract & Castleford, he came 25,725 votes behind Labour's Yvette Cooper, having lost half his Tory predecessor's vote but held the anti-Tory swing to 6.6% May '97; once selected for Taunton, he began to sink local roots, organising the Taunton Half Marathon for the Somerset Leukaemia Group and joining the Somerset County Cricket Club and Taunton Rugby Football Club; at his party's conference he demanded a better deal for farmers Oct '00; "winnable" Taunton was one of William Hague's election tour stops May '01; in Flook's effective rural campaign, although no enthusiast for fox-hunting, he listened sympathetically to its advocates; he narrowly retook the seat from Jackie Ballard by 235 votes on a 2.2% pro-Tory swing; Jackie Ballard announced she was quitting politics June '01; in his Maiden speech he emphasised the extent of the rural crisis and the impact on tourism in his constituency, including its towns; he urged more and younger people to get involved in voluntary work for problems like homelessness July '01; he was named to the Culture, Media and Sports Select Committee July '01;
Born: 9 July 1963, Bristol
Family: Son, of Julian Flook, wine merchant, and late Anne (Richardson) Physiotherapist, the daughter of Francis Richardson of Eastern Electricity who "had to stand up to Wedgwood Benn in the mid-'70s" (AF);
Education: Grittleton House School, Wiltshire; King Edward's School, Bath '74-82; Colonel By High School, Ottawa; Mansfield College, Oxford University (MA in Modern History '85);

Adrian (John) FLOOK *New MPs of '01*

Occupation: Financial PR Consultant: Account Director, with Financial Dynamics (financial PR)'98-; Director, Julian Flook (family's wine merchants' firm): ex: Stockbroker, with Branston & Gothard '96-98; Merchant Banker: with S G Warburg and Societe General ("where I specialised in advising investors on UK and European stocks and shares") '85-96;
Traits: Parted dark hair; heart-shaped face; young-looking; "dapper, articulate, intelligent and charming" (Andrew Vine, YORKSHIRE POST); "I've a reputation for being a terrier; once I get my teeth into something I don't let go" (AF); collects water colours by local artists (eg Barrie Temple, Terry McKivragan); plays tennis, watches Rugby;
Address: House of Commons, Westminster, London SW1A 0AA; 37 Simpson Street, Battersea, London SW11 3HW; 64 Trull Road, Taunton TA1 4QL;
Telephone: 0207 219 3000 (H of C); 0207 978 4534; 01823 286106 (office); 01823 330726 (home);

Dr Hywel FRANCIS   **Labour**   **ABERAVON '01-**

Majority: 16,108 (53.4%) over Plaid Cymru 7-way;
Description: An unchanged, mainly English speaking South Wales seat between the Bristol Channel and the Welsh mountains, embracing Port Talbot and dominated by the declining but still-important steelworks of Abbey and Margam; in '97 it was Labour's 19th safest seat, with a 21,571 majority; it was the birthplace of Dic Penderyn ("the first martyr of the Welsh working class" [HF]) and of William ('Mabon') Abraham ("the great champion of the Welsh miners" [HF]); it was Ramsay Macdonald's seat when he was first Prime Minister;
Position: On the Select Committee on Welsh Affairs '01-; ex: Special Policy Advisor, to Welsh Secretary Paul Murphy '99-00; National Convenor of 'Yes for Wales' campaign '97; Vice President, Welsh Labour History Society; Chairman, Paul Robeson Cymru Committee; Trustee, Bevan Foundation;
Outlook: Scion of Wales' political Establishment as Dai Francis's academic son who has been a strong campaigner for Welsh devolution; immersed in Swansea University for 35 years, he has belatedly emerged into Parliamentary politics, shaken by the '84-85 maltreatment of his father's miners; "Pal of virtually everyone in the Labour Taffia, it would be difficult to get more connected than this boy" (WALES WATCH website); "far too nice to lmake waves" (BLACK SHEEP);
History: "The date of 7 June was...the date when I was outside the House [of Commons] with tens of thousands of people from mining communities all over Britain, seeking...justice" June '84; he joined the Labour Party at 44, '90; he was National Convenor of 'Yes for Wales' campaign '97; he was a candidate on the National List for election to the Welsh National Assembly '99; he joined ISTC, the dominant union in Aberavon '00; was selected to succeed Sir John Morris on his retirement, with the support of the ISTC and other unions '00; he retained the seat, despite a 6.06% swing to Plaid, with a 16,108 majority, down 5,000 from Sir John's '97 lead, due to an 11% reduction in turnout; it moved from being the 8th to the 3rd safest Labour seat in Wales June '01; in his Maiden speech he emphasised the need for fuller citizenship rights for the disabled: "fewer than one in 10 people with a severe learning

54   *Copyright (C)Parliamentary Profile Services Ltd*

New MPs of '01 *Dr Hywel FRANCIS*

disability are in work and more than 1m people with disabilities want to work" June '01; he was named to the Select Committee on Welsh Affairs July '01; he claimed that "our learning country will be achieved only if we base it upon the principles of equity, lifelong learning and citizenship" Oct '01;
Born: 6 June 1946, Dulais Valley
Family: Son, of Dai Francis, former General Secretary of South Wales NUM, and Catherine (Powell); m '68, Mair Georgina (Price); 2s (1 dcd), 1d;
Education: Llangatwg Secondary, Neath; Whitchurch Secondary, Cardiff; Whitchurch Grammar, Cardiff; Swansea University (BA in History '68, PhD '78);
Occupation: Fellow, National Policy Centre for Public Policy, University of Wales, Swansea '00-; ex: Special Adviser, Welsh Secretary Paul Murphy '99-00; Professor of Continuing Education '92-99, Director, of Continuing Education '87-92, Lecturer in Continuing Education at University of Wales, Swansea (AUT) '74-87; Senior Research Assistant, University of Wales, Swansea '72-74; Assistant, TUC's Organisation Department '71-72;
Traits: Parted grey hair; rounded face;
Address: House of Commons, Westminster, London SW1A 0AA;
Telephone: 0207 219 3000 (H of C);

Mark FRANCOIS   **Conservative**   **RAYLEIGH '01-**

Majority: 8,290 (19.4%) over Labour 4-way;
Description: A new name for what is essentially the pre-'97 Rochford seat, shorn of 10,000 voters in Rochford itself; it remains staunchly Conservative, embracing newly-expanded suburban commuter towns northwest of Southend in semi-rural Essex, including its historic town of Rayleigh (population 15,000), five villages from old Chelmsford, Maldon and South East Essex; "stretching from the outskirts of Chelmsford in the West to Foulness in the East" (MF), adjacent to Bradwell nuclear power station;
Position: Ex: Basildon District Councillor '91-95;
Outlook: A new defence-orientated Rightwing Eurosceptic friend of John Bercow and Iain Duncan Smith; although half-Italian, he is strongly against a European "super-state" and a "European army"; an ex-Territorial officer in the International Institute for Strategic Studies '99- and the Royal Institute for Defence Studies '91-;
History: While living in Bristol, he debated against the CND in Westcountry schools; he became Chairman of the Bristol University Conservative Association '84; he was elected to Basildon District Council by capturing a marginal seat from Labour, becoming Vice Chairman of Housing May '91; he contested Brent East against Ken Livingstone, opposing the Euro while Ken urged a single European currency; he came second with 22.3% of the vote on a 14.4% anti-Tory swing May '97; he was a finalist in the selection for Castle Point Oct '99; he was a finalist in the selection for Kensington & Chelsea, the runner-up to Michael Portillo Nov '99; he was a finalist in the selection for East Devon Apr '00; selected for safe Rayleigh Apr '00; he retained it by a majority of 8,290, over 2,500 down on that of its former Tory MP, Dr Michael Clark, due to a UKIP candidate and a 13% drop in turnout June '01; in his Maiden, he said he favoured "enlargement of the European Union in principle, but not at any price"; he

Copyright (C)Parliamentary Profile Services Ltd

Mark FRANCOIS   *New MPs of '01*

expressed "affection" for Ireland, which had rejected the Nice Agreement; he insisted "we will not be subsumed by a foreign super-state that ignores our traditions and undermines our laws"; he then intervened in a pro-EU Labour MP's speech to express his distaste for a "European army" July '01; voted for Iain Duncan Smith from the first ballot in the Tories' Leadership contest July '01; was one of 14 new Tory MPs who together wrote to the DAILY TELEGRAPH endorsing Iain Duncan Smith as a Leader who "can unite the party on Europe" Aug '01; he complained that the waste of £200,000 of public funds had been buried in a website Oct '01; he claimed that "our wish to move towards higher numbers of LPG-powered vehicles in the UK...could represent another example of the Conservative Party being ready to learn from the positive experience of our European partners" Oct '01; he warned that the takeover of Railtrack would limit private investment in transport Oct '01; he warned against the Export Control Bill damaging the defence industry employing 300,000 people and necessary to defend the realm Nov '01; he warned against the LibDem-run Chelmsford Council building too many houses Nov '01;
Born: 14 August 1965, Islington, London
Family: Son, of Reginald Francois, engineer, and Italian Anna (Carloni); m '00 Karen (Thomas) '00, having proposed "while overlooking Galway Bay";
Education: Nicholas School, Basildon (Captain, its Rugby First XV) '76-83; Bristol University (Hons BA in History; a contemporary of Lembit Opik; "a favourite student of the High Tory Bristol historian John Vincent" [Michael Gove, TIMES]) '83-86; King's College, London (MA in War Studies) '87-88;
Occupation: Ex: PR Consultant/Director, Francois Associates '96-01; PR Consultant/Director, Market Access International '88-95; Graduate Management Trainee, with Lloyds Bank in the City '87;
Traits: "Short and brown-haired" (Matthew Parris, TIMES); heart-shaped face; long chin; as short as his longtime friend, John Bercow; In the TA '83-90, a Lieutenant '85-90;
Address: House of Commons, Westminster, London SW1A 0AA; 25 Bellingham Lane, Rayleigh Esssex SS6 7ED (constituency);
Telephone: 0207 219 3000 (H of C); 01268 742004/741833 Fax (constituency); 01266 641040; chairman@rayleighconservatives.org.uk;

Michelle GILDERNEW   Sinn Fein   **FERMANAGH & SOUTH TYRONE '01-**

Majority: 53 (.1%) over UUP 4-way;
Description: The UK's 12th most agricultural seat, sharing a long, troubled border with the Republic; its main market towns, Dungannon and Enniskillen, are traditional garrison towns; it has a 51% Catholic majority, but political victories depend on how which community splits or abstains; Catholics Frank McManus '70-74, Frank Maguire '74-81 and Bobby Sands '81 have won the seat; but from '83 on Catholics were unable to agree on a single candidate against its incumbent MP, Ulster Unionist Ken Maginnis; this changed when Maginnis tried to hand over to James Cooper and many young Catholics went over to Sinn Fein in '01;
Position: Northern Ireland Assemblyman (Deputy Chairman, Social Development Committee

New MPs of '01 *Michelle GILDERNEW*

'99-) '98-;
Outlook: A fast-rising young Sinn Fein spokeswoman; the first female Sinn Fein MP since Countess Markiewicz was elected in 1918; the first republican woman to be elected in Northern Ireland since Bernadette Devlin (now McAliskey); a female scion of a well-known republican campaigning family who pushed up Sinn Fein support by 6,000 votes, narrowly nosing out James Cooper, who had been bequeathed a majority of over 13,000 by Ken Maginnis; her victory pushed Sinn Fein ahead of the SDLP - in both share of the vote and share of the seats - to become the largest nationalist party in Northern Ireland; "one of the reasons she was able to achieve such a significant swing from SDLP voters is because she is seen as being on the 'soft' end of Sinn Fein - a talented politician without any IRA reputation" (Chris Thornton, BELFAST TELEGRAPH); despite her triumph, because of Sinn Fein's block on taking an oath of loyalty to the Queen, her main focus remained as Sinn Fein's representative on the Northern Ireland Assembly's Social Development Committee;
History: "Thirty-three years ago, two years before Michelle was born, her family was at the centre of a sit-in at Caledon, County Tyrone, that effectively launched the civil rights movement" (Chris Thornton, BELFAST TELEGRAPH) '68; having joined Sinn Fein in her youth, becoming its Press Officer in '97, she was elected to the Northern Ireland Assembly June '98; she became the Sinn Fein's representative on the Social Development Committee '99; selected to fight UUP-held Fermanagh & South Tyrone, she proclaimed: "There will be no decommissioning in a partitionist Ireland" May '01; she won the seat by the narrow margin of 53 votes over James Cooper, the new UUP candidate who claimed "clear and irrefutable evidence of electoral malpractice" over a polling station in Garrison remaining open after 10 pm; she told delirious supporters, "Sinn Fein has won west of the Bann; we are a republican party; we are always seeking a united Ireland and our day has come!" June '01; the electoral protest by her Ulster Unionist opponent, James Cooper, was rejected in Belfast's High Court by Lord Chief Justice Sir Robert Carswell who insisted that any polling station disturbances had only a small effect on the outcome Oct '01;
Born: 1 January 1970;
Family: Daughter of "a well-known republican campaigning family" (BELFAST TELEGRAPH); she does not disclose family names or jobs;
Education: University of Ulster, Coleraine;
Occupation: Press Officer for Sinn Fein '97-;
Traits: Reddish-brown hair; high forehead; fine teeth; specs; articulate, if not in Westminster;
Address: Northern Ireland Assembly, Stormont, Northern Ireland;

KEEPING PARLIAMENTARY SECRETS
A rueful MP claimed, with some truth, that the best way to keep something secret is to make a speech about it in the Palace of Westminster. He was commenting on the emptiness of the Press Gallery (except for HANSARD writers and the Press Association). Long gone are the days when serious newspapers carried a full or half-page summarising Parliamentary debate. Of late, Westminster has been used as a source of news stories. In our old-fashioned way, we read HANSARD daily and watch the Commons and Lords on the Parliamentary Channel. Parliamentary debaters are very self-revealing in debate. And we don't mean only Kerry Pollard MP, in whose Maiden he disclosed that until 12 he had to drop his trousers regularly to prove that Kerry was not a girl's name.

Copyright (C)Parliamentary Profile Services Ltd

Paul (Alexander Cyril) GOODMAN   **Conservative**   **WYCOMBE '01-**

Majority: 3,168 (7%) over Labour 6-way;
Description: A Chilterns seat, including Disraeli's Hughenden, which has been Tory since '24 except for '45-51; half its voters are in evenly-balanced High Wycombe, which has light industry including furniture manufacture and a sizeable (13%) Asian population; it has the largest proportion of Muslims of any Tory-held seat; but as many voters live in affluent commuter villages including Marlow; in '83 it lost 20,000 voters, mostly to Aylesbury; the only '95 loss was the transfer of Little Marlow to Beaconsfield;
Position: PPS, to David Davis '01-; ex: on Policy Committee of Conservatives' National Union '83-84, on Executive of National Union '82-84; Chairman of Federation of Conservative Students '83-84;
Outlook: An MP broader than his recent connections as a leading Tory journalist who co-ordinated the efforts of Conservative leaders and their leading press supporter-instigator, the DAILY TELEGRAPH; he was part of the small team advising William Hague and, before that, Francis Maude on major speeches while responsible for both the opinion pages and political direction of the DAILY TELEGRAPH; has quickly shed this and been shown to be sensitive to the concerns of his local ethnic minorities; recently in favour of gradual decriminalisation of drugs; "inclusive - increased support in [the] Tory seat with [the] largest Asian vote" (Michael Gove, TIMES); not overly partisan ("his "intellectual style could do with a few rougher edges" -Michael Gove, TIMES); in the Commons he can now confront former opponents in the '70s and '80s student movement, including Jack Straw and Peter Mandelson who predated him as student leaders;
History: After joining the party, he became Chairman of the York University Conservative Association, thus helping to make his name in student politics, partly as one of the two "token Tories" on the executive of the National Union of Students '81; he was named a member of the National Union Executive Committee of the Conservative Party '82; he became National Chairman of the Federation of Conservative Students '83, a "Heathite Chairman...during the Thatcherite 1980s" (Michael Gove, TIMES); he contested Richmond Town ward for the Richmond Borough Council May '86; during the general election he was an aide to Tom King May '87; he contested Limehouse ward in the elections for Tower Hamlets Borough Council May '98; he became a member of Iain Duncan Smith's and David Willetts' policy committee on welfare reform '98; he became a member of Francis Maude's speech-writing team '98; he became a member of the small journalistic team advising William Hague on his major speeches '99; he wrote an amusing DAILY TELEGRAPH feature on how British public life was dominated by former leading student politicians Apr '99; on the impending retirement of Europhile Sir Ray Whitney, he was quietly selected as the candidate for Wycombe, without any of the fanfare of Boris Johnson in neighbouring Henley Aug '00; he pointed out to tolerant Steve Norris that he had many Kashmiris in his constituency who believed in strict family values Oct '00; because Wycombe "contains one of the highest proportions of ethnic minority voters of any Tory-held constituency in Britain" he read "with contempt" Robin Cook's allegation that the Tories had introduced racism into the election campaign Apr '01; in his campaign he concentrated on securing the votes of ex-Tories who had not voted in '97 or the

58   *Copyright (C)Parliamentary Profile Services Ltd*

2000-plus who decamped to the Referendum Party in protest against the Europhilia of the previous Tory MP May '01; he succeeded in winning a slightly larger majority of 3,188, despite a UKIP candidate and an 11% drop in turnout, which represented a 1.26% swing from Labour to the Tories June '01; in his Maiden speech he urged Tories to recapture from Labour Disraeli's 'One Nation' ideal, emphasising the "poverty of hope" and "social exclusion" of the sons of single mothers with "no male model other except the slightly older men who are active in the local drugs economy" June '01; he was one of 14 new Tory MPs who together wrote to the DAILY TELEGRAPH endorsing Iain Duncan Smith as a Leader who "can unite the party on Europe" Aug '01; in the second recall session, said he was "slightly concerned" that his Muslim minority, while horrified by the terrorist attacks on New York and Washington, had a different perspective Oct '01; he was named PPS to David Davis MP, Conservative Party Chairman Oct '01; he pointed out that his Kashmiri Muslim constituents "apply to Kashmir the same standards that they see the West apply to Northern Ireland and the Middle East" Oct '01; he asked how the Government could legislate against religious hatred "without a definition of religion in the Bill" Oct '01; he worried that the decision on Heathrow's Terminal 5 would be sneaked out Oct '01;
Born: 17 November 1959, London
Family: Son, Abel Goodman, film producer/director, and Irene (Rubens); m '99 Fiona (Gill), solicitor;
Education: Tower House School, London SW14; Cranleigh School, Surrey '72-77; York University (BA in English) '78-81;
Occupation: Comment Editor, DAILY TELEGRAPH '95-01; ex: Reporter, SUNDAY TELEGRAPH '92-95; Leader Writer, DAILY TELEGRAPH '92; Home Affairs Editor, CATHOLIC HERALD '91-92; RC Novice, Quarr Abbey, Isle of Wight '88-90; Researcher, for Tom King MP '85-87; PR Exexcutive, Extel Consultancy '84-85;
Traits: Dark, parted hair; oval face; small eyes; mousy-looking; a "cerebral Mr Bean lookalike" (TIMES); "Mr Bean's stand-in" (Dennis Skinner); diffident manner; "not consumed by wordly ambition" (Michael Gove, TIMES); a convert from Judaism to Roman Catholicism, having served as a novice in a monastery for two years;
Address: House of Commons, Westminster, London SW1A 0AA; 150A West Wycombe Road, High Wycombe, Bucks HP12 3AE (constituency);
Telephone: 0207 219 3000 (H of C); 0207 7538 6416 (work); 01494521777/310042 Fax (constituency); dtcomment@telegraph.co.uk;

ANOREXIA OR OBESITY
Profiles, like politicians, can be very slim or very full-bodied. This can depend on how varied and colourful is the past of the MP concerned, or the quality of the newspapers reporting them. Some politicians are paranoid about disclosing anything beyond the bare minimum and then complain if second-hand information beyond the bare essentials turns out to be less than accurate. Others turn to their libel lawyers as an expensive threat. We adhere to the quaint idea that if people have decided to plunge into the glass fishbowl of politics they are not entitled to wear wetsuits. After all, most wrongdoing has been exposed by the media's investigative journalists, very little by politicians themselves.

Chris(topher) GRAYLING   Conservative   **EPSOM & EWELL '01-**

Majority: 10,080 (21.6%) over Labour 4-way;
Description: A solidly Conservative 'inner Surrey' commuter seat, the Tories' 22nd safest in '97 and 34th safest in '01; it stretches from the outer London suburbs to the Surrey 'stockbroker belt'; it contains the renowned horse-racing feature of Epsom Downs, as well as Toyota's headquarters; in '95 it lost 11,000 pro-Conservative voters from Banstead and gained 10,000 even more pro-Tory voters from Ashstead; a '92-style result should have produced a 20,000 majority in '97 instead of the 11,000-plus which occurred;
Position: On the Select Committee on Transport, Local Government and the Regions '01-; Merton Borough Councillor '98-; on National Council of Bow Group '91-; ex: Vice Chairman, Wimbledon Conservative Association '90-93;
Outlook: An active and thoughtful Eurosceptic PRman who has found a well-upholstered seat after heavily losing marginal Warrington South in '97; he says that "working for the BBC and hating its bureaucracy" had a radical influence on his political thinking;
History: He joined the Young Conservatives; he contested marginal Warrington South, losing to Labour by over 10,000 votes on a 12.3% notional anti-Tory swing May '97; he was elected a Merton Borough Councillor May '98; he was beaten by George Osborne when he sought selection for Tatton Mar '99; selected for ultra-safe Epsom & Ewell from among very many applicants, he retained it by 10,080 votes, just below that won in '97 by Sir Archie Hamilton June '01; in his Maiden speech he criticised the NHS decision to "downgrade" Epsom General Hospital; he also complained about the local shortage of school places June '01; he criticised the Government's "failure to meet their targets for recruitment and retention" in the armed forces July '01; he returned to the dire shortage of teachers in his constituency July '01; he was named to the Select Committee on Transport, Local Government and the Regions July '01; he was one of 14 new Tory MPs who together wrote to the DAILY TELEGRAPH endorsing Iain Duncan Smith as a Leader who "can unite the party on Europe" Aug '01; in the second recall of Parliament he urged tough action combined with humanitarian aid plus security to secure the "rights of society as a whole", possibly identity cards and getting rid of people "who are a genuine threat to our society" Oct '01; he asked Secretary of State Stephen Byers whether he had "secure funding" to complete the rest of the 10-year-plan to modernise railways, whose use had increased by 17% a year Oct '01; he worried about proposals for a Central Railways proposal to build a freight line Oct '01; he opposed "too many bureaucratic guidelines" in early-years education, barring "gifted amateurs" like his wife who had helped four-year-olds to read and use computers Oct '01; in opposing the Bill to enact the Nice Agreement, he claimed that PM Blair could not be supporting the Americans had a European Army been in place; he claimed he was a "firm pro-European" but against "a European megalith" Oct '01; he insisted the expected "debt burden" was a huge disincentive for poorer students contemplating higher education Oct '01; with Toyota's UK headquarters in his constituency, he asked how car-manufacturing newcomers could avoid the burden of recycling the cars of their older competitors Nov '01; he tried unsuccessfully to probe the Treasury about its pressure on Railtrack decisions Nov '01; he praised the independence provided to US universities by their endowment foundations; "it cannot be right to saddle

today's students with the extremely high levels of debts that they carry through into their professional lives" Nov '01;
Born: 1 April 1962, London
Family: Son, John Grayling, marketing executive, and Elizabeth (Arculus); m '87 Sue/Susan (Dillistone) former magazine editor; 1s Matthew '98, 1d Laura '95;
Education: Jordons School; Gayhurst School; Royal Grammar School, High Wycombe; Sidney Sussex College, Cambridge University (BA '84, MA in History);
Occupation: European Marketing Director, of Burson-Marstellar '97-; Author: The Bridgewater Heritage (1983), The History of Joseph Holt (1985); ex: Divisional Director, of SSVC, the company that ran British Forces Broadcasting '95-97; Director: Workhouse Ltd '93-95, Charterhouse Prods Ltd '93; TV Executive: BBC Select Business Development Manager '91-93; Channel 4 Business Daily Programme Editor '88-91; BBC News Producer '86-88, Trainee '85-86;
Traits: Dark blond fringe; balding hairline; full-faced; a keen occasional golfer;
Address: House of Commons, Westminster, London SW1A 0AA; 212 Barnett Wood Lane, Ashtead, Surrey KT21 2DB (constituency); 11 Parkwood Road, Wimbledon, London SW19 7AQ (home);
Telephone: 0207 219 3000 (H of C); 01272 270144 (home); 0208 947 9491 (home); 07788 074998 (work); chris.gayling@btinternet.com; grayling@dial.pipex.com;

Matthew (Roger) GREEN   **Liberal Democrat**   **LUDLOW '01-**

Majority: 1,630 (3.8%) over Conservative 5-way;
Description: Old small towns - Ludlow, Bishop's Castle and Bridgnorth - set in the Welsh Marches of southern Shropshire: the onetime capital of England and Wales; "a very lovely and unspoilt part of rural England" (its ex-MP Christopher Gill); it is Britain's 15th most agricultural seat; 9,000 voters were added from The Wrekin in '83 but returned in '95; on '92 projections, the '97 election should have produced a 12,250 Tory majority instead of the 5,909 garnered by Tory MP Christopher Gill; what really shook things up was his storming out of his party and the constituency on the eve of the '01 election, also attacking coloured immigration;
Position: On the National Executive of the Liberal Democrats' Parliamentary Candidates' Association; ex: South Shropshire District Councillor '94-95;
Outlook: The LibDems' unexpected West Midlands 'golden boy', "the first Liberal Democrat Member ever to represent Ludlow and, I believe, the first Liberal to do so since 1886" (MG); the surprise result of Europhobic Tory Christopher Gill's disgusted revolt against his party and constituency;
History: He joined the Liberal Democrats; he was elected to South Shropshire District Council May '94; he was selected to contest Wolverhampton South West, where the Tories' Nicholas Budgen MP, was being challenged by Labour's Jenny Jones '96; in the election won by Jones, he came in 3rd, with 8.2% of the vote, slightly below that taken by his '92 LibDem predecessor May '97; he was selected to contest Ludlow, where the '97 LibDem candidate had come in 2nd with 30% of the vote to Christopher Gill's 42% '00; on the eve of the election,

Matthew (Roger) GREEN *New MPs of '01*

Christopher Gill announced he would stand down and resign from the Conservative Party because it would not pull out of the EU Jan-Apr '01; during the election, Green managed to increase the LibDem vote by 5,000 to 18,620 while the vote of his hapless Kent-based Tory opponent declined by almost 3,000 to 16,990, giving him his 1,630 majority on a swing to the LibDems of 8.3% June '01; in his Maiden speech he complained that his rural constituency's farming economy "has been in decline in the past five years and foot-and-mouth nearly finished it off"; he also complained about the chronic under-funding of rural areas in education and roads July '01; he was one of the LibDem sponsors of a motion urging the scrapping of student fees July '01;
Born: 12 April 1970, Shropshire
Family: He has not disclosed his parents' names and jobs; married to Sarah, self-employed businesswoman;
Education: Priory School, Shrewsbury; Birmingham University;
Occupation: Managing Director of his own West Midlands media relations and training consultancy '96-; Publisher, of WHO'S WHO OF THE LIBERAL DEMOCRATS (1998); ex: Sales and Marketing Manager for timber firm '81-96;
Traits: Dark hair; full, heart-shaped face; prominent chin; enjoys Rugby, cricket, hill-walking, rock-climbing;
Address: House of Commons, Westminster, London SW1A 0AA; 9 Church Walk, Much Wenlock, Shropshire TF13 6EL;
Telephone: 0207 219 3000 (H of C); 01952 727306; matthewgreen@cix.co.uk;

David HAMILTON Labour **MIDLOTHIAN '01-**

Majority: 9,014 (31.4%) over SNP 6-way;
Description: The old Midlothian seat south of Edinburgh minus the Calders and Livingstone New Town; now based on the largely defunct Midlothian coalfield (including Bilston, once the scene of bitter strike clashes) with its small working-class communities and growing sunrise industries; "thousands were employed in only a dozen industries, and now dozens are employed in 1,000 industries; that shows that small micro-industries have developed throughout the area" (DH); three-fifths of its workers travel to Edinburgh to work; in '95 it lost 13,000 voters in Penicuik to Tweeddale, Ettrick and Lauderdale;
Position: Midlothian Councillor '95-; CoSLA Spokesman on Economic Development and Tourism '95-; ex: Chairman of the Lothians Strike Committee '84-85;
Outlook: The blackballed strike leader of the Lothian miners who has remade his career in Labour politics; proud to be a "socialist" and the first "victimised miner" to enter the Commons; pro-European because of the EU money which has helped his area;
History: He joined the NUM '75; he was a leader of the movement to prevent the closure of Monktonhall Colliery enabling it to be taken over by a private consortium four years later '83; after chairing the strike committee controlling 3,500 miners in 22 centres during the '84-85 miners' strike, the National Coal Board refused to reinstate him, despite his winning his case before the tribunal '85; he joined the Labour Party '85; he was elected to the executive, became

New MPs of '01 *David HAMILTON*

branch chairman and the CLP delegate of the Labour Party's Dalkeith branch; transferring to the Midlothian CLP, he became CLP delegate, trade union officer and trade union representative; he was elected for the Woodburn ward of Dalkeith to Midlothian Council May '95; he was selected to contest Midlothian for Labour in succession to another leading ex-miner, Eric Clarke Sep '00; he was elected in Clarke's place with a similar majority of 9,014, despite a 15% cut in turnout June '01; with 123 other Labour MPs he rebelled against the composition of Select Committees June '01; in his Maiden speech he emphasised that in his "semi-rural area" it was necessary to work with farmers, especially farm-workers July '01;
Born: 24 October 1950, Dalkeith
Family: He does not provide his parents names or jobs; m '69 Jean (Trench Macrae); 2d; 2 grandd, 1 grands;
Education: Dalkeith High School '62-65;
Occupation: Chief Executive, Craigmillar Opportunities Trust '95-00; Placement and Training Officer, Craigmillar Festival '89-95; Supervisor, Midlothian District Council, '86-89; Coalminer, '65-84; NUM '75-87;
Traits: Dark, parted hair; full face; Dalkeith accent;
Address: House of Commons, Westminster, London SW!A 0AA; 66 Gordon Avenue, Bonnyrigg, Midlothian EH19;
Telephone: 0207 219 3000 (H of C); 0131 663 5799;

Tom (Thomas) HARRIS   **Labour**   **GLASGOW-CATHCART '01-**

Majority: 10,816 (39.5%) over SNP 5-way;
Description: Glasgow's largest seat: its northern half has middle-class homes, but its dominant southern half has the massive, drug-sodden Castlemilk council estate, the largest in Europe, recently in the process of regeneration; it has Weir's, the pump manufacturers, and Hampden Park football ground; some 8,000 voters from Castlemilk were lost to Rutherglen, while Pollokshields was added from Pollok in '83; in '95 it lost Kings Park to Rutherglen and Pollokshaws to new Govan, while acquiring a few thousand voters from the Queeen's Park area of abolished Glasgow Central and some from the Arden section of Pollok; in '01 it lost its witty, rangy veteran Labour MP, John Maxton, after 22 years;
Position: Chairman, Cathcart CLP '98-00;
Outlook: A former reporter and press officer - and former local constituency chairman - who made it to Labour's backbenches;
History: He joined the Labour Party and the NUJ '84; on being named the Labour Party Press Officer for Scotland, he switched to UNISON '90; he was elected chairman of Cathcart CLP '98; he was selected for Cathcart to succeed retiring John Maxton '00; he retained safe Cathcart by a majority of 10,816, 1,400 down on Maxton's majority after a 16% fall in turnout June '01; in his Maiden speech he hoped that the drop in turnout would not result in further experiments with voting systems, which almost certainly would not improve matters; as a former journalist, he blamed the media for trivialising politics June '01; he called attention to the danger of misuse of air rifles, causing blindness and permanent brain damage July '01; he

Copyright (C)Parliamentary Profile Services Ltd

Tom (Thomas) HARRIS   New MPs of '01

intervened in the speech of DUP hard-liner Peter Robinson to point out that the majority in Northern Ireland wanted RUC reform as part of the Good Friday Agreement July '01; he urged warning people that they could be heavily fined unless they registered to vote Nov '01; made a well-received Maiden speech Nov '01;
Born: 20 February 1964;
Family: Son, Tom Harris, lorry-driver and taxi-owner, and Rita, office clerk; 1 son from previous marriage; m 2nd '98 Carolyn (Moffat), Publications Officer of the Strathclyde Police;
Education: Garnock Academy, Kilbirnie, Ayrshire; Napier College, Edinburgh (HND in Journalism '86);
Occupation: Chief Public Relations and Marketing Officer, Strathclyde Passenger Transport Executive '98-; UNISON '97-; NUJ '84-97; Public Relations Manager, East Ayrshire Council '96-98; Labour Party Press Officer for Scotland '90-92; Reporter, on PAISLEY DAILY EXPRESS '86-90;
Traits: Young-looking; light brown hair; a weakness for quotes;
Address: House of Commons, Westminster, London SW1A 0AA; Flat 2L, 6 Florida Street, Glasgow G42 9DL;
Telephone: 0207 219 3000 (H of C); tomharris.labour@virgin.net;

Dai (David) HAVARD   Labour   MERTHYR TYDFIL & RHYMNEY '01-

Majority: 14,923 (57.2%) over Plaid Cymru 7-way;
Description: The cradle of the South Wales coal and iron revolution, comprising the towns of Merthyr, Dowlais and to make up the numbers in '83, Rhymney; its last pit, Taff-Merthyr, was shut in '93; the grim legacy of mining is recalled in Aberfan and its record of having a quarter of its workers claiming sickness and disability benefit', make Merthyr 'the sickest town in Britain'; even with a new postwar manufacturing base, such as Hoover, its decline continues, with 35% male unemployment; in '97 it was still Labour's fourth safest seat, with a long-stay tradition for its MPs: Keir Hardie was its MP '00-15; Ted Rowlands, who retired in '01, was only its fourth Labour MP;
Position: On the Select Committee on Deregulation and Regulatory Reform '01-; ex: Welsh Secretary of MSF '98-01;
Outlook: "The first Labour Member elected this century and the first to have been born and brought up in the constituency that I now represent", "like Keir Hardie, I am a socialist and trade unionist" (DH); he opposes those against Labour's union links: "these are links that some would pervert, some would like to destroy and some to usurp" (DH); long linked to the MSF union, he has been a campaigner for balloting individual members by post for the Welsh Assembly and the Labour leadership, with the new Labour Party rules recently accommodating this;
History: He came "from a family of miners and steel workers": his family's political background was Liberal until the Boer War, then Labour; he had his "first experience of leadership, teamwork, representation and campaigning at the Treharris Boys Club as a 16-year-old representative on South Wales Youth Council" '66; he joined the Labour Party

New MPs of '01 *Dai (David) HAVARD*

'85; "I was the candidate co-ordinator for [Yardley] a marginal seat in Birmingham; seat regained...after 13 years" Apr '92; "I organised a one-member one-vote ballot in MSF for the Wales Labour Party leadership election" '99; he was selected to follow Ted Rowlands as Labour's Merthyr candidate, the selection meeting taking place in 'men-only' bar ("insensitive" - Clare Short) Dec '00; he retained safe Merthyr by a majority of 14,923, half that garnered by his predecessor, Ted Rowlands, due to a 12% drop in turnout which registered an 11.8% swing to Plaid, this time in second place June '01; in his partisan Maiden speech, he spoke of Merthyr's deplorable housing conditions but, as a "socialist and trade unonist" like Keir Hardie, he concneatrated his fire on those who would sever Labour's links with the unions July '01; he was named to the Select Committee on Deregulation and Regulatory Reform Oct '01;
Born: 7 February 1950, Quakers Yard, Treharris
Family: Son, 'Ted'/Edward Havard, miner, and ????? (Jones) shopworker; m '86 Julia Watts (Mackenzie), civil servant; separated;
Education: Woodlands School, Quakers Yard; Treharris Secondary Modern; Quakers Yard Grammar/Tech; Afon Taff Hall School; Warwick University (MA);
Occupation: Wales Secretary MSF '89-01; ex: Self-employed Researcher '75-79; Trade Union Studies Tutor '71-75; maintenance engineer;
Traits: Bald; heart-shaped face; trim dark beard and moustache; self-dramatising; he enjoys hill-walking, horse-riding and bird-watching;
Address: House of Commons, Westminster, London SW1A 0AA; Quakers Yard, Treharris, 74 Ty Llwyd Parc CF46 6LB; 19 Pontmorlais, Merthyr Tydfil CF47 8BU;
Telephone: 0207 219 3000 (H of C); 01443 412471 (home); 01685 387683 (constituency);

Charles HENDRY Conservative WEALDEN '01-

Majority: 13,772 (28.1%) over LibDem 5-way;
Description: A A Milne's rural Sussex Weald, with opulent commuter villages and towns such as Crowborough, Uckfield and Hailsham; it was formed in '83 from East Grinstead constituency by leaving out that town; in '97 it became the Tories' 13th safest seat; in '00 floods damaged Uckfield, Buxted and Hellingly;
Former Seat: High Peak '92-97
Position: Ex: Head of Business Liaison Unit of Conservative Central Office '97-98; Vice Chairman of the Conservative Party (Communications) '95-97; Chief of Staff to William Hague '97; PPS to Gillian Shephard '95; on Select Committee on Northern Ireland '94-97; Joint Chairman, all-party Parliamentary Group on Homelessness '92-96; Secretary: Conservative MPs' East Midlands Committee '92-97, and Social Security Committee '92-94; Joint President, British Youth Council '92-97; on Select Committee on Procedure '92-95; Special Adviser: to John Moore '88, Tony Newton '88-90; Vice Chairman, Federation of Conservative Students for Scotland '80-81; Research Officer, Bow Group;
Outlook: Longtime Eurosceptic with "a fierce loyalty to [William] Hague" (Andy McSmith, OBSERVER); has scored recently as social entertainer thanks to the wealth his divorcee wife brought from her marriage to a Moores football pool scion; an intensely partisan part-time Pollyanna who likes snuggling up to Whips; ambitious, assiduous, loquacious, loyal young

Copyright (C)Parliamentary Profile Services Ltd

London PRman-lobbyist, who has marketed himself successfully; was fortunate, at 33, to have retained the vacated Tory-held seat of High Peak after being 'blooded' twice in miners' seats; and then to secure candidacy for super-safe Wealden; always anxious to put the best Tory gloss on any subject; "competent if inconspicuous" (Andy McSmith, OBSERVER); was able to help sabotage Kevin Barron's Bill to curb tobacco advertising despite being "someone whose father died of cancer when I was a teenager, and who refused to work on a tobacco account when I was asked to do so" as a PRman-lobbyist (CH); was nevertheless a Teller for those opposing Barron's Bill to reduce children's smoking by further curbing tobacco advertising; a Centrist who has tried too hard to bait Labour to cover his own waverings over Maastricht and homelessness; close recently to William Hague, previously to Sir George Young, Tony Newton, Michael Ancram, Peter Fraser (later Baron Fraser of Carmyllie), Sir Peter Emery and, before that, to Lord (formerly John) Moore; hero-worshipped fellow MP Edward Garnier; a Bow Groupie who once tried to seem a Ridleyite, 100% in favour of deregulation and privatisation; liberal on reducing the age of homosexual consent;

History: He was brought up near East Grinstead; "I decided to go into politics when I was 10"; "my parents were involved on the voluntary side of the [Conservative] party"; he started the Political Society at Rugby School; he joined the Young Conservatives at 14, '73; became President of the Edinburgh University Conservative Association '79, Vice Chairman of the Scottish Federation of Conservative Students '80; served as Research Assistant to Scots Tories Peter Fraser and Michael Ancram, then Chairman of the Scottish Unionists, at £10 a week from '80; started the Tory Reform Group in Scotland '80; at 23 contested the hopeless mining seat of Clackmannan against Martin O'Neill; visited areas which had never seen a Tory candidate; asking why no public meetings had been scheduled, his agent replied: "Well, Charles, it is better that people wonder why you do not speak than that they wonder why you do"; came 3rd with 18% June '83; was selected for previously hopeless Mansfield Jan '86; opening the debate on transport at Tory annual conference, favoured wholesale deregulation so that local councillors' "sticky little fingers" and "narrow little minds" could no longer interfere Oct '86; with the selection for Labour of the then hard-Left candidate, Alan Meale, Hendry said: "this is the first time we can win" Oct '86; welcomed the establishment of a vote-splitting 'Moderate Labour Party' Jan '87; saw hope for Tories in the divided ex-Labour vote: "a lot of lifelong Labour supporters will vote to ensure Alan Meale loses; they will vote for the person best capable of beating him and that will be me" Mar '87; at 28 lost Mansfield to Alan Meale by 56 votes, the country's smallest majority June '87; was named Special Adviser to Tony Newton ("sometimes civil servants would come to me with a draft of a paper and ask 'how do you think this will go down?'; I was a sounding board because I knew how he thought") Jan '88; was selected for High Peak, after announced retirement of Christopher Hawkins MP, making it necessary for Hendry to retire as Special Adviser to Tony Newton Dec '89; told NEW STATESMAN that there was a growing belief among Tory candidates that "morality shouldn't be imposed by government; it's up to religious bodies to push the moral dimension" Aug '90; at annual Tory conference made a fierce attack on Derbyshire County Council leader David Bookbinder, as "the Rottweiler of local politics"; supported Michael Portillo in exploiting poll tax to make local government more accountable Oct '90; was one of the 10 prospective candidates who co-signed the pamphlet 'Bearing the Standard' which urged an end to the social divisiveness of the Thatcher years Sep '91; made a fierce attack on Derbyshire County Council's "hugely increased bureaucracy" Jan '92; retained seat with a majority of 4,819, a 4.43% swing to Labour Apr '92; after the negative Danish referendum, backed the anti-Maastricht "fresh start" motion June '92; in his witty Maiden complained of the outdated local transport structure which could not cope with High Peak's 24m visitors that year; also urged more help for the crumbling Georgian crescent in the centre of Buxton July '92; was elected Secretary of the Conservative MPs' Social Security and East Midlands committees June '92; visited Stuttgart and Budapest as guest of Konrad Adenauer Foundation Sep '92; despite his initial Eurosceptic thoughts, co-signed a letter to SUNDAY TIMES with other new MPs proclaiming their imminent support for Prime Minister on Maastricht Nov '92; welcomed new slimline Urban Regeneration Agency as a "catalyst" Nov '92; in stooge question to Prime Minister, welcomed Toyota's investment in Derbyshire as showing that "Britain was the best place for international companies to invest" while France's anti-GATT move had shown that "the French claim to be good European citizens is a total sham" Nov '92; in debate on Social Security Bill said: "first, we must support those who have been hit most by the recession; secondly, we should be targeting additional support on those most in need; thirdly, we should be keeping our election pledges, and the pledges made before the election, to the elderly, the families and others most in need" Nov '92; urged receptive Housing Minister Sir George Young to "bring into use the tens of millions of square feeet of empty office space whose owners and developers would be happy to see it used on a short-term basis to house homeless people or students" Nov '92; welcomed churches' lobby on homelessness; backed compulsory use of empty council and private houses and offices, if necessary Dec '92; again praising the new Toyota plant, urged its new model be called the 'Edwina' because of Mrs Currie's hard work in securing the plant for Derbyshire Dec '92; was named to Select Committee on Procedure Dec '92; with Donald Dewar and Simon Hughes produced report on increased number of 16-17-year-olds sleeping rough in London Dec '92; as Joint Chairman of the all-party Parliamentary Group on Homelessness, loyally defended Government's role on homelessness against criticisms from the GUARDIAN Dec '92; in social security debate admitted need to challenge such "sacred cows" as mortgage interest relief on which £5b a year was spent Feb '93; backed Government's Disability (Grants) Bill Mar '93; attacked all-night rave scheduled for his constituency Apr '93; described the Local Government Commission's plan to reform Derbyshire as an "absolute disaster" May '93; urged single parents be persuaded to share flats with other single parents June '93; tried to introduce Closure of Footpaths Bill enabling highway authorities to close footpaths during periods of severe fire risk - a year after several hundred acres of moorland had been destroyed by fire in his constituency, without authories having been able to ban hikers from tinder-dry areas May '93; visited Italy for weekend discussion as guest of Konrad Adenauer Foundation May '93; was named to Opposed Private Bill Committee to consider the British Waterways Bill June '93; was again called upon to speak when his look-alike Matthew Banks stood up Nov '93; congratulated Chancellor on his Budget Dec '93; co-complained of shortage of policemen in Derbyshire Dec '93; as a Whips' stooge, tried to bait Labour MP Andrew Bennett over the difficulties of a Tameside housing association Jan '94; on the basis of his experience in Mansfield, backed the privatisation of the remnants of the coal industry Jan '94; in debate on housing, loyally defended the Government's record and criticised the Opposition and Labour councils Jan '94; voted to reduce age of homosexual consent to 18 or 16, Feb '94; voted to restore capital punishment, expecially for killing policemen Feb '94; welcoming the Housing Corporation's Government-backed plan to enable 58,000 new houses to be built for letting, declared his interest as the "chairman of a small private sector housing company" - Home Rent 16-23 Plc; wound up his lengthy speech by saying that "no organisation has done more to damage sensible discussion than the charity Shelter; I have been in regular contact with Shelter for some years, especially as chairman of the all-party Group on Homelessness and have built up a great respect for its work; however, the publicity material that Shelter is publishing now is in breach of its charitable status" Mar '94; in the committee stage of Kevin Barron's Tobacco Advertising Bill, reassured Sir Peter Emery that "I will do all I can to ensure his grandchildren do not smoke"; one of Sir Peter's grandsons was his godson Mar '94; claimed that Tory council were better at scooping up dog mess than Labour councils Mar '94; was one of the Tory PRmen most active in tabling most of the amendments to kill Barron's Bill banning tobacco advertising, complaining the "anti-industry" Bill had been drafted by ASH (Action Against Smoking) which received Government subsidies; served as Teller against the Bill May '94; was attacked by the EVENING STANDARD for criticising Shelter, as Joint Chairman of the all-party Group on Homelessness, for being too "overtly political" because it criticised Government plans to give the homeless a lower priority for permanent council homes: "How dare Tory MPs led by the faintly ridiculous Charles Hendry...criticise Shelter, the charity for the homeless, for being 'overtly political'; Mr Hendry is by trade a public relations man, a sorry career for anyone, but one with its champagne-swilling image peculiarly inappropriate for someone dealing with as sensitive a subject as homelessness; like any organisation, Shelter has its imperfections, but it has done more to highlight the problem of homelessness in the capital and elsewhere than any other single pressure group, and it deserves the respect and support of everyone working in that field; Mr Hendry only makes himself and his party contemptible by attacking it" May '94; introduced a Bill to give TV license holders like those in High Peak a reduction in their license fees when unable to enjoy good TV reception May '94; visited Italy for seminar as guest of Konrad Adenauer Foundation May '94; was named to Select Committee on Northern Ireland May '94; said: "we shall not solve the problems of urban regeneration until we have kicked out the Labour authorities that have ruined many of our city areas" June '94; he claimed that the economy the Thatcher Government had created would enable young people to "build and earn enough to enjoy [their] social life" Aug '94; visited Hongkong as guest of its Government Information Service Sep '94; the OBSERVER claimed the eight Home Rent companies he chaired had "raised £39m from investors just before the Budget a year ago by getting around a ban on similar schemes introduced only months before; the money has been used to buy several hundred homes repossessed by one of Britain's biggest building societies, the National & Provincial" getting "up to 40% tax relief on investments" Nov '94; ended his position on Select Committee on Procedure Mar '95; entering the debate on housing, said, "I declare an interest in that I am the Chairman of a group of companies [Home Rent 16-23 Plc] involved in the private rented sector; on a non-pecuniary basis, I am Chairman of the all-party Homelessness Group, a Trustee of the Big Issue charitable trust and a friend of the National Association of Citizens Advice Bureaux" June '95; was promoted Vice Chairman of Conservative Party, with responsibility for communication July '95; married rich divorcee Sallie Moores July '95; backed Environment Secretary John Gummer's 'rejection of the right [of ramblers] to roam, proposed by the Labour Party, which would be devastating to many farming interests in my constituency" Oct '95; voted for lower mileage allowances for MPs, for a 3% cap on MPs' pay increases and against higher-rate pensions July '96; claimed that "an 18-year-old in Britain in 1996 will enjoy greater choice, live longer and lead a more prosperous life than at any time in Britain's long history" Aug '96; accused Labour MP George Galloway of failing to disclose his interest in Hawk Communications International Ltd when speaking up for a Saudi dissident Aug '96; "we have to ask ourselves whether we have a duty to the taxpayer simply to provide additional housing because people have found it convenient to move away" from home Feb '97; he said, "nothing so far has persuaded me it would be in our interests to join" a single European currency Apr '97; he dismissed the gloomy opinion polls, claiming the Tory vote was hardening; the issue of sleaze had largely dropped out of the campaign Apr '97; he lost High Peak on a 3.6% swing to Labour's Tom Levitt by a majority of 8,791 May '97; he left William Hague's 'kitchen cabinet' after having served as his chief of staff, to become Head of Business Liaison Unit at Conservative Central Office, at a similarly small retainer Nov '97; he was named as a donor (of over £5,000) to Conservative Party funds Sep '99; he joined Lord Archer's campaign to become Mayor of London Oct '99; having promised to fight against building more homes locally and in favour of re-opening the Uckfield-Lewes railway line, he was selected to succeed Sir Geoffrey Johnson-Smith, on the latter's impending retirement; he was chosen from among 180 applicants with David Cameron and Chris Grayling also making it to the short-list Mar '00; he retained ultra-safe Wealden by 13,772, virtually the same majority he had inherited June '01; in his first speech he opposed too much local house-building and urged help for farmers June '01; he initially supported the Leadership candidacy of Michael Ancram, then concealed his vote June-July '01; he urged measures to prevent a repetition of the floods that had devastated Uckfield, Buxted and Hellingly the previous year July '01; as Vice President of the Big Issue Foundation, he backed the Tory amendment to the Homelessness Bill to decant responsibility to local councils Oct '01;

Born: 6 May 1959, Sussex

Family: Son, of Margaret (Hancock) and late Charles W R Hendry, who died of tobacco-induced cancer; "my father, who was a stockbroker, died when I was 15; I was away at school which meant that I never really got the chance to know him properly"; m '95 ("to quell the rumours" [CH]) Sallie (Smith) Moores, a professional cook (author of 'Cabinet Puddings') and "an ex-wife of a member of the [Liverpool] football pools family" (DAILY TELEGRAPH); 2s, one steps, one stepd; his divorce-rich wife puts them among the top Tory entertainers;

Education: Brambletye School, East Grinstead; Rugby School '72-76; Edinburgh University (Hons BCom in Business Administration); Vienna University;

Occupation: Chairman '01-, Chief Executive and Director '99-01, of Agenda Group Ltd (corporate consultancy with Martyn Lewis); Head of Business Liaison at Conservative Central Office '97-99; Chief of Staff to William Hague '97; Chairman (at £5,000), of Home Rent 16-23 Plc (a company which owns and manages privately rented accomodation, buying up repossessed houses from National & Provincial at up to 40% tax relief) '94-99; Trustee/Patron/Vice President, Big Issue Foundation '94-; PRman: Adviser, to Fleischman-Hillard (PR consultants to: Anhauser-Busch, the US beer and leisure giant, Energis, a telecoms company) '93-94, Consultant, with Burson Marstellar (giant US PR consultancy '90-92; previously an Account Director and chief lobbyist with them) 90-92, '86-88; Ogilvy and Mather PR '83-86; Consultant, to the Oracle Company (software) '93-??; Adviser, to Andersen Consulting '92-93; Trustee: Big Issue Action '94?-; Special Adviser: to Tony Newton '88-90, John Moore '88; Research Assistant, to Michael Ancram MP and Peter Fraser MP '80-81;

Traits: Thinning brown hair; rounded face; snub nose; putty lips; "inoffensive-looking"; "bland, genial face", "on the chubby side", "a cheerful Labrador pup" (Matthew Parris, TIMES); "Hairy Hendry" (because of his hirsute body; "great tufts of hair are said to erupt from his shirt collar" - MAIL ON SUNDAY); "affable" (DAILY TELEGRAPH); "cherubic" (TIMES); a Matthew Banks look-alike (to Speaker Boothroyd's confusion): "we both look chubby and cheery and we both dress in grey suits" (CH); "a pin-striped yuppie" (Amanda Craig, SUNDAY EXPRESS) who can seem "faintly ridiculous" (EVENING STANDARD) and "sometimes takes the simple view" (DAILY TELEGRAPH); skier on annual Davos outing of Lords' and Commons' ski team in '93, had the task of righting Lord (Nigel) Lawson after his frequent falls);

Address: House of Commons, Westminster, London SW1A 0AA; 7 Chester Square, London SW1W 9HH (home); 41 Larkhall Rise, London SW4; Vigilante House, 120 Wilton Road London SW1V 1JZ (business);

Telephone: 0207 219 3000 (H of C); charles.hendry@dial.pipex.com;

Lady Sylvia HERMON   **Ulster Unionist**   **NORTH DOWN '01-**

Majority: 7,324 (19.7%) over UKUP 6-way;
Description: "A beautiful coastal constituency [running] along the top of the Ards Peninsula" (Lady Hermon); 'Ulster's Gold Coast': the most-affluent, most-Unionist seat in Northern Ireland; it is overwhelmingly Protestant, with only 8% of Catholics; mostly urban, with Holywood and Bangor among its larger communities; Bangor and its new marina - the fourth largest in the UK - is divided between the have-yachts and have-nots, a popular posh dormitory for Belfast with some very select areas favoured by the Northern Ireland Office for visiting civil servants; it is 72% owner-occupied, the highest level in Northern Ireland; but Bangor also has "the Kilhooley estate, where there are about 650 children without one play park or playground between them" (Lady Hermon);
Position: Chairman, North Down UUP Constituency '01-;
Outlook: "Mr Trimble's closest ally at Westminster" (Nichoias Watt, GUARDIAN), often serving as his stand-in; the former RUC Chief Constable's unexpectedly politically-appealing wife and former academic colleague of David Trimble; "she is attractive, intelligent and just what the party wants to project a more appealing image" (David Sharrock, GUARDIAN); "one of the few pro-Agreement MPs" who "stormed home to defeat sitting MP [hard-liner] Bob McCartney (UK Unionist Party) by more than 7,000 votes" (Aideen Sheehan, IRISH INDEPENDENT);
History: "I grew up in Fermanagh and South Tyrone, where I frequently heard the words, 'vote early and vote often'; she came from a strongly Ulster Unionist farming family; her interest in politics was kindled when her colleague, Edgar Graham, a leading Ulster Unionist, was killed by the IRA at the Law faculty '83; "having been outraged by the Chief Constable's discrimination against women in the RUC, I wrote an article criticising him bitterly for his actions, of which I sent him a copy" '87; "months of silence followed, then a 'phone call; it was a man's voice - the voice of someone claiming to be the Chief Constable, Sir Jack Hermon"; "I knew instantly that it was a hoax call, so I responded, 'If you're the Chief Constable, I'm Brigitte Bardot'; so much for female intuition and instincts; to my enormous embarrassment, he was who he said he was and I was certainly not Brigitte Bardot; so it was that we met, subsequently married and made our home in North Down"; after an accident, she decided "life is short" and joined the UUP '00; she wrote the party's response to the Patten proposals on RUC reform and David Trimble encouraged her to stand in North Down against its incumbent anti-Agreement UKUP MP Bob McCartney; in her initial effort to be selected to contest North Down against McCartney, she was narrowly defeated by anti-Agreement Peter Weir who described her as an "impostor" '00; "I was one of the Ulster Unionists who...stood in the Waterfront Hall and, despite a great deal of heckling, urged my colleagues in the Ulster Unionist Council to jump first and take Sinn Fein back into the Executive" May '00; she was selected to contest North Down for the UUP on the day the election was called; this was so unexpected that, instead of printing her unavailable photograph, papers printed that of former RUC Chief Constable Sir John Hermon; she was selected after former Mayor Leslie Cree, a staunch ally of David Trimble, pulled out after receiving an anonymous letter threatening to disclose he had fathered an illegitimate child over 30 years before; anti-Agreement Peter Weir,

who had been selected as the candidate a year before, had been suspended for voting against the UUP in the Stormont Assembly; once Lady Hermon was selected, the Alliance candidate, Dr Stephen Farry, stepped down to enhance her chances against Bob McCartney May '01; "in less than month, Catholics and Protestants, the small Jewish community in Northern Ireland and the Chinese community, Unionist voters, Alliance voters, Social Democratic and Labour Party voters, Progressive Unionist Party voters and the Women's Coalition all felt comfortable in voting for and returning me to the House with a majority of more than 7,000"; as the first of three women elected, she became the first Northern Ireland woman MP since Bernadette Devlin, a onetime near-neighbour; in Lady Sylvia's acceptance speech she said she would "be fighting for the Agreement, for all of us, I will be fighting for the people of North Down, all of them" June '01; she wound up her brilliant Maiden with an appeal: "The lives of all these [constituency] children deserve to be enriched with more investment in youth facilities the length and breadth of the consituency" June '01; she expressed disappointment in the Electoral Fraud (Northern Ireland) Bill, partly because it ignored intimidation at the poll July '01; she complained that "instead of encouraging ...essential widespread community support, the Patten commission has managed to discourage it" July '01; she welcomed as "very positive" the Gerry Adams-Martin McGuinness call on the Provisional IRA to decommission their arms Oct '01; one of the few enthusiasts for the Blair Lords' reform, she said, "I am particularly pleased that it is not a fully-elected second Chamber", apparently fearing Paisleyites might win seats there too Nov '01; the undue familiarity shown by David Blunkett's guide-dog during the SPECTATOR award ceremony was widely publicised by onlooking journalists Nov '01;
Born: 11 August 1955, Near Coalisland, Northern Ireland
Family: Daughter of an Ulster Unionist farmer named Paisley; m '88 Sir John Hermon, RUC Chief Constable '80-89; 2s;
Education: Dungannon High School for Girls; University of Wales, Aberystwyth (BA Law '77);
Occupation: Author: A Guide to EEC Law in Northern Ireland (1986); ex: Lecturer in Law, specialising in European and constitutional law at Queen's University '78-83;
Traits: Attractive straight-haired blonde; "there was more than a whiff of Lady Macbeth about Lady Hermon" (her defeated predecessor Bob McCartney); has a handsome Airedale, on whose good looks she is often complimented; she also has appeal for David Blunkett's guide-dog; enjoys fitness-training, bird-watching, proof-reading;
Address: House of Commons, Westminster, London SW1A 0AA; 77A High Street, Bangor BT20 5BD (constituency);
Telephone: 0207 219 3000 (H of C);

TAPPING INTO OUR COMPUTERS
The factual way in which we compress MPs' involvement in issues, big and small, has turned out to be a goldmine for those using our computers for searches. A client asked for a search on the Falkland Islands. To our surprise, the printer churned out over 30 pages of information which, cleaned up, yielded 10,000 words of information on all the positions taken by all the politicians involved, including the furious reactions to late Nicholas Ridley's 1980 proposal to hand the islands over to Argentina and then lease it back. We only charge £250 for such a computer search. Call us at 020 7222 5884 or Fax us at 020 7222 5889.

David (Alan) HEYES   Labour   ASHTON-UNDER-LYNE '01-

Majority: 15,518 (43.4%) over Conservative 5-way;
Description: The declining industrial seat of old textile valleys which lost 30% of its industries in Mrs Thatcher's first recession of '79-81; it still retains a shrinking ICL facility; because of its longstanding loyalty to Labour and his 22,000-plus majority, its previous MP, Robert (now Lord) Sheldon, understood its vulnerability to 'parachuting', as he ended 36 years of service; to avoid this, he therefore gave his local party enough time to select a local man by OMOV (one-member one-vote);
Position: Oldham Metropolitan Borough Councillor '92-; Manager, of local Citizens' Advice Bureau '95-01; Vice Chairman, Ashton-under-Lyne CLP '94-01; ;
Outlook: A local worthy chosen because of his long work for various sections of the local Labour movement; unlikely to excite the press, he sees his new job as extending his ability to help further local people who feel they have been unable to share in the good things in life;
History: He joined NALGO '62, becoming a steward, convenor, branch secretary and campaign organiser; he joined the Labour Party '87; he became Campaign Organiser for the Oldham West CLP; he was elected to Oldham Metropolitan Borough Council May '92, becoming Secretary to its Labour Group '94; he became Vice Chairman of the Ashton-under-Lyne CLP '94; he was selected by a majority of three as the candidate to succeed Bob Sheldon, beating Millbank favourite, Tameside councillor Kieron Quinn; he said he was "stunned by the result" Dec '00; he retained the safe seat with a majority of 15,518, over 7,000 below Sheldon's '97 majority, after a 16% cut in turnout June '01; his Maiden speech was well-received Nov '01;
Born: 2 April 1946;
Family: He does not provide his parents' names or jobs; m '68, Judith (Egerton-Gallagher); 1s 1d;
Education: Blackley Technical High School, Manchester; Open University (BA in Economics, Sociology and Urban Studies '86);
Occupation: Advice Service Manager, Citizens' Advice Bureau '95-01; Voluntary Sector Development Worker '93-95; Self-Employed, in Computer Graphics '90-93; Local Government Manager, for Education, for Oldham MBC '87-90; Trade Union Organiser, for NALGO (later UNISON) '86-87; Principal Local Government Officer, Transport, for Greater Manchester Council '74-86; Local Government Officer for Manchester City Council '62-74; (NALGO '64-86, UNISON '87-);
Traits: Dark, retreating hair; beard; spectacles; quiet; low-profile; helpful: Trustee and Founder-Member of two charities aimed at improving acces to new technology and internet by socially-excluded groups and individuals;
Address: House of Commons, Westminster, London SW1A 0AA; 30 Blandford Street, Ashton-under-Lyne, Greater Manchester OL6 7DW (constituency); 17 Partridge Road, Failsworth, Manchester M35 5NW;
Telephone: 0207 219 3000 (H of C); 0161 333 9307 (constituency); 0161 682 7744 (home); david.heyes@unisonfree.net;

Mark (Gerard) HOBAN   **Conservative**   **FAREHAM '01-**

Majority: 7,009 (15.4%) over Labour 4-way;
Description: An affluent, owner-occupied middle-class seat on the Solent coast of south Hampshire, midway between Portsmouth and Southampton; it has horticulture, varied light industry, including shipbuilding, a giant GEC factory, the Office of Population and Census and some Royal Navy establishments; altered in '83, it lost 15,000 rural voters to Winchester constituency in '95;
Position: Chairman of Conservatives' Guildford South branch '99-01; Finance Officer, Itchen, Test and Avon Euro-Constituency Council '93-95; Treasurer, Southampton-Itchen Conservative Association '89-91;
Outlook: Another Rightwing Eurosceptic newcomer: a relocated Chartered Accountant with Pricewaterhouse Coopers who is a strong believer in the free market, light regulation and low taxation; he continues to oppose joining the Euro, as he made evident in his hard-hitting '97 campaign in South Shields;
History: He comes from a traditional pro-Labour family from the coalmining area of east Durham; his politics at school were Conservative; he joined the Conservative Party at 16, '80; he was PA to Chris Chope in Southampton-Itchen '87; he became campaign manager to Chris Chope, who narrowly lost Apr '92; selected for hopeless South Shields, he was one of the Tory candidates who said they favoured ruling out joining the Euro in the next Parliament Dec '96; he contested South Shields against David Clark, coming second with 14.6% of the vote on a notional anti-Tory swing of 11.2% May '97; he stood in the Guildford borough elections May '99; he was selected for the choice seat of Fareham to succeed retiring Sir Peter Lloyd July '00; he retained the safe seat by a majority of 7,009, a drop of over 3,000, due largely to a 13% drop in turnout June '01; in his Maiden speech he displayed hostility to the Treaty of Nice, to the Government's desire to intensify house-building locally and to the danger that nearby Vosper-Thorneycroft, in whose yards "many of my constituents work", might not share in the planned build of type-45 destroyers July '01; he showed interest in schools for children with special needs July '01; he voiced the concern in Fareham, which had already been changed from a rural to a suburban constituency, about plans for further large-scale housing development without adequate infrastructure Oct '01; he urged the use of National Insurance numbers to prevent election fraud in Northern Ireland Oct '01; he asked for a Government pledge not to increase taxes Nov '01;
Born: 31 March 1964, Peterlee, Co Durham
Family: Son, Tom Hoban, general manager of an electrical wholesaler, and Maureen (Orchard); m '94 Fiona Jane (Barrett), Ceremonial Officer, Corporation of London;
Education: Our Lady of the Holy Rosary, Peterlee; St Godric's, Durham; St Leonards RC Comprehensive, Durham; LSE (BSc Econ 2:2); qualified as Chartered Accountant;
Occupation: Senior Manager '92-01, Manager '90-92 with Pricewaterhouse Coopers, international accountants; ex: Assistant Director, with PWC's predecessor Deloitte, Haskin & Sells '85-90;
Traits: Heart-shaped face; parted, retreating hair; specs; he enjoys walking, cooking and collecting prints and drawings related to wine; "computer literate"; RC by education;
Address: House of Commons, Westminster, London SW1A 0AA; 14 East Street, Fareham

Copyright (C)Parliamentary Profile Services Ltd

Mark (Gerard) HOBAN   *New MPs of '01*

PO16 0BN (constituency);
Telephone: 0207 219 8228 (H of C); 01329 822646/232585 Fax (constituency); mark@markhoban.com;

Paul (Robert) HOLMES   Liberal Democrat   CHESTERFIELD '01-

Majority: 2,588 (5.8%) over Labour 6-way;
Description: A declining coal centre from which all the mines have gone, with a steel overflow from Sheffield and a massive chemical-steel complex at Stavely; much of the engineering has also gone, including Markham Engineering, which built the Channel Tunnel boring equipment; light industries and high-tech computer firms are coming in, but not enough to reduce its higher-than-average unemployment level; it remains a major market town, with the largest open-air market in continuous use since the middle ages; in '83 it lost 10,000 voters to North East Derbyshire; in '01, after 17 years, it lost its outstanding incumbent Labour MP, Tony Benn; it was considered "classic traditional Labour heartland" (Ian Waugh, YORKSHIRE POST), before the Liberal Democrat success in '01;
Position: On Select Committee on Education and Skills '01-; Chesterfield Borough Councillor '99-, '87-95; Vice President, Local Government Association;
Outlook: One of the surprise LibDem victors of the standstill '01 election, overcoming Tony Benn's less-popular would-be successor, ex-MP Reg Race; the previous Liberal to be elected in Chesterfield was in '24; a councillor-teacher from a Sheffield working-class family, he is said to have built his support on local community groups, for example, those opposing opencast mining and the arms trade; he also supported independent small market traders;
History: He came from a working-class family living on a large Sheffield council estate; "I was the first member of my family...ever to go to university and it transformed my life; I very much doubt whether I should have been able to take that opportunity back in 1975 if my then-unemployed father and I had been faced with the prospect of yearly tuition fees and a £10,000 to £14,000 debt on graduation"; he joined the Liberals '83; he was elected to Chesterfield Borough Council May '91; he was selected to contest Chesterfield, replacing Tony Rogers (whom he had served as election agent when he had fought the seat three times before for the LibDems in '87, '92, '97) in '00; during the campaign, he remained optimistic because "for the last 15 or 16 years we have been eating away at Labour's vote" and he needed to convince only one in eight Labour voters to enable him to swap the classroom for the Commons; criticising Labour's record, he also appealled to Tory tactical voters, reinforcing this with typical LibDem bar graphs showing only they could oust Labour; since the LibDem leadership had rated Chesterfield their fifth most winnable-from-Labour seat, his efforts were reinforced by visits from Charles Kennedy and Paddy Ashdown June '01; he won the seat, ending Labour's 72-year-long reign, by a majority of 2,588, in contrast to the LibDems' lag of 5,775 votes in '97, representing a pro-LibDem swing of 8.5% June '01; in his first-rate Maiden speech he confirmed that all LibDem MPs were against President Bush's National Missile Defence proposals; he concentrated on warning education Ministers against rushing to impose new systems of testing without consulting those at the chalk-face: "I had to scrap a successful

74   *Copyright (C)Parliamentary Profile Services Ltd*

New MPs of '01 *Paul (Robert) HOLMES*

and innovative A-level course, and then, at very short notice and with no extra money to buy brand-new textbooks which had not even been written for a brand-new course, a colleague and I had to prepare and teach the new AS-level; it was February of this year before I attended an exam board course that gave me the final information on how the course would be taught and examined, yet we were already 70% of the way through teaching it and the course-work exams were imminent" June '01; he rejected the claim of Labour MP James Purnell that LibDems were only targeting "affluent Britain", pointing to his own victory in Chesterfield and LibDem control of Liverpool, Oldham and Sheffield, in letter to PROSPECT Oct '01; he urged more generous funding for early-years education Oct '01; on his experience as the head of a sixth from, where he had experienced resistance to paying for higher education from poorer students, he insisted, "if students are to be asked to pay for the benefits of higher education, they must pay post-graduate, while they ar earning and not up front, while they are studying" Nov '01;
Born: 16 January 1957, Sheffield
Family: Son, of Frank Holmes, a plumber and council caretaker, and Dorothy (Littley), home help; m, '78, Rae/Ralene (Palmer); 2s Richard '88, Oliver '90 dcd; 2d Eleanor '84, Rhiannon '92;
Education: Firth Park School, Sheffield; York University (BA Hons 2:1 in History) '75-78; Sheffield University (PGCE) '78-79; York University;
Occupation: Head of 6th Form Studies at Buxton Community School '89-01; Head of Department, Buxton '84-90; Teacher, in Chesterfield '79-84; (NASUWT)
Traits: Wavy grey tonsure; pleasant, open countenance; "solid, keen and brimming with facts" (TIMES); he enjoys running the Marathon and reading history;
Address: House of Commons, Westminster, London SW1A 0AA; 12A Old Hall Road, Chesterfield;
Telephone: 0207 219 3000 (H of C); 01246 234879;

(Alexander) Boris (de Pfeffel) JOHNSON **Conservative** **HENLEY '01-**

Majority: 8,458 (19%) over LibDem 5-way;
Description: Opulent Thames Valley seat stretching from fashionable Henley-on-Thames in the south to Thame in the north; in '83 its pro-Labour fringe in Oxford's eastern suburbs was moved to new Oxford East; in '97 it was the 20th safest Conservative seat before the eclipse and retirement of Michael Heseltine;
Outlook: Michael Heseltine's more entertaining successor: the precocious pretend 'young fogey' and former "rising star of the write" (INDEPENDENT ON SUNDAY); a Portillo-leaning pragmatic Centre-Right Tory who uses wit to conceal his less-popular liberal views; "a fox who has stuck a couple of feathers up his backside and is pretending to be a chicken" (A A Gill, SUNDAY TIMES); he does not conceal his fervently serious Euroscepticism, hardened during his Eurocrat-bashing four years in Brussels for the DAILY TELEGRAPH; in '97 he said he would "renegotiate EU membership so Britain stands to Europe as Canada, not Texas, stands to the USA"; "immensely gifted" (EVENING STANDARD); "brilliant but faintly barmy"

Copyright (C)Parliamentary Profile Services Ltd 75

(Alexander) Boris (de Pfeffel) JOHNSON   *New MPs of '01*

(INDEPENDENT ON SUNDAY);
History: "I grew up on an Exmoor farm"; he joined the Conservative Party '87; he dates his political ambitions from a Douglas Hurd speech dividing commentators from achievers '90; a few months before his Etonian chum Darius Guppy was jailed for a £1.8m insurance swindle he phoned Johnson to obtain the address and telephone number of a NEWS OF THE WORLD investigative reporter chasing him, making it clear he would have him beaten up; Johnson replied: "OK Darrie, I said I'll do it and I'll do it" '93; he claimed that while "rude" there was a "poetic truth" in Rod Richards' description of Welsh Labour councillors as "short", "fat" "slimy" and "fundamentally corrupt" Dec '94; he backed John Redwood in his contest with John Major June '95; he was rejected as a candidate for Holborn & St Pancras Feb '96; having also applied for Islington North, he was selected as the Conservative candidate for Clwyd South; he had his first Welsh lesson Feb '96; he opposed the ditching of John Major as Tory Leader, insisting "he remains, personally, a more attractive figure to many voters than his party as a whole" May '96; he said Britain had much to learn from the Chilean private pension scheme pioneered under General Pinochet Sep '96; fervently praised Rupert Murdoch as "the fellow [who] saved the British newspaper industry" Oct '96; he was one of the Tory candidates who favoured ruling out Britain's entry into the Euro during the next Parliament Dec '96; he urged Edward Heath be elevated to the Earl of Sidcup, as depicted by Wodehouse Feb '97; he lost against Labour's Martyn Jones but the anti-Tory swing of 7.7% was under the 10% average May '97; was said to be coveting contesting Sutton & Cheam, but its locally-resident defeated former MP, Lady Olga Maitland, claimed the right to fight again Mar '99; he became Editor of SPECTATOR July '99; he sacked SPECTATOR's 70-year-old Rugby correspondent, Dowager Baroness Hesketh, demoted its Deputy Editor, Petronella Wyatt and named Nicholas Soames as Wine Correspondent Dec '99; he showed interest also in contesting Huntingdon, the ultra-safe seat about to be relinquished by John Major Apr '00; beating off a challenge from David Platt, a pro-European Tory Reform Groupie, he was chosen to contest Henley in succession to the retiring Europhile, Michael Heseltine July '00; he admitted the free French state school system was superior to the British fee-paying system Sep '00; as SPECTATOR's Editor, he was caught in between its pro-Palestinian contributors and his pro-Zionist publisher, Conrad Black, and the latter's wife, Barbara Amiel Mar '01; he ridiculed claims of a Portillo-Clarke plot to oust Hague Apr '01; he opposed the ban on religious faiths being licensed to run national radio stations Apr '01; he attended the South Africa House reception for anti-Apartheid campaigners, insisting "I am a total impostor!" May '01; he claimed he had "eaten his hat" when the election was not held on 3 May, as he predicted May '01; he was included, at 50-to-1 in the betting stakes for the new Tory Leader May '01; he retained Henley by a majority of 8,458, almost 3,000 below that achieved by Michael Heseltine after a 13% drop in turnout June '01; in his witty Maiden speech, he compared himself unfavourably with Michael Heseltine, who had 247 magazines when he only ran one, adding: "It is fair to say we did not agree on every detail of European policy" July '01; he came out for Kenneth Clarke as his preferred candidate for Tory Leader June '01; he was accused by the OBSERVER of leading "the charge of the liberal bedwetters in the Bulger case" July '01; he attacked the "spinelessness" of British financial institutions for letting down Huntingdon Life Sciences, under attack by the 'animal rights' terrorists July '01; insisting that the Tories could "regenerate" themselves, he made clear this was a joke by following it up with: "Now let's go home and prepare for breakfast!" July '01; he asked about the impact of foot-and-mouth on Henley tourism July '01; he justified his support for Europhile Kenneth Clark as having "a lot up top, including hair, and no side" Sep '01; he deplored the stripping of patriotic songs from The Last Night of the Proms Sep '01; he insisted the Islamic terrorists feared the West's freedom for women Sep '01; Europe Minister Peter Hain claimed he was

New MPs of '01   *(Alexander) Boris (de Pfeffel) JOHNSON*

"living in cloud cuckoo land" when he insisted a Bill to enact the Nice Agreement was unnecessary and that "it would be perfectly possible to convene an inter-governmental conference tomorrow in Brussels to discuss enlargement issues" without the need to ratify the Nice Agreement in Bill form Oct '01; he complained that a local training scheme had been closed abruptly because the Government had belatedly woke up to the vulnerability to fraud of their Independent Learning Account scheme Nov '01;
Born: 19 June 1964, New York
Family: His great-grandfather, Ali Kemal, was the last Interior Minister of the imperial Turkish Government; his son, Osman Ali, found asylum in Britain, where he changed his name to Johnson; son, of Stanley Patrick Johnson, environmentalist, Tory MEP and "distinguished Eurocrat" (GUARDIAN), and his first wife, Charlotte Offlow (Fawcett), a "Bohemian Leftwing artist" (SUNDAY TIMES); his parents divorced when he was 14; m 1st Allegra Mostyn-Owen, d of Gaia Servadio and art dealer; divorced '93; m 2nd '93, Marina (Wheeler), a Left-leaning lawyer and daughter of BBC's ex-Correspondent Charles Wheeler; 2s, 2d;
Education: European School, Brussels; Eton (King's Scholar, Keeper of the Wall, Head Boy, friend of Darius Guppy); Balliol College, Oxford University (Brackenbury Scholar, President of the Union);
Occupation: Journalist: Editor, of SPECTATOR '99-; Columnist: for DAILY TELEGRAPH and GQ; ex: Assistant Editor and Chief Political Columnist, DAILY TELEGRAPH '94-99; Brussels Correspondent, of the DAILY TELEGRPH '89-94; Journalist on The TIMES (sacked after making up a quote from an uncle) '87-88; Trainee Journalist, WOLVERHAMPTON EXPRESS AND STAR '87; Assistant Master, Timbertop (outdoor school at which Tony Blair's guru Rev Peter Thomson was the head) '83;
Traits: Tall; tubby; mop-haired blond; "his naturally peroxide blond hair seems to be on back to front"; "his suit is a vast, filthy, shapeless thing that has room in its seat for at least two floating voters"; "wears the permanently perplexed look of an awestruck simpleton; his language is the jolly Edwardian vernacular that's part Wodehouse and part Just William" (A A Gill, SUNDAY TIMES); "bullfrog-jowled" (Simon Carr, INDEPENDENT); "nobody has ever seen Mr Johnson kempt and the suspicion grows that he sleeps standing on his head and he re-rumples his hair regularly throughout the day" (Matthew Parris, TIMES); "Dulux-dog lookalike" (EVENING STANDARD); "cosmopolitan" (OBSERVER); has a "plummy stutter" (SUNDAY TIMES); "the Jackal"; "Buffo";"speaks and writes in a melange of P G Wodehouse and the Beano...using buffoonery as a weapon" (EVENING STANDARD); "Woosterish"; he plays the innocent abroad on 'Have I Got News for You' and Radio 4 panel games and so on, but actually he's deeply serious,...particular...about making a success of his time at THE SPECTATOR" (friend); "so shambolic he can barely find his way from his Highbury home to his Bloomsbury office"; has an "irreverent, mischief-making style"; "his only wobble was when he agreed to get old school chum and convicted fraudster, Darius Guppy, the home address of a tabloid hack who was investigating him" (John Arlidge, OBSERVER); chased a youth who tried to steal his bike; an amateur painter; "I like beer and very thick cheese and onion sandwiches"; has guinea pigs called 'Duncan Smith' and 'Kenneth Clarke';
Address: House of Commons, Westminster, London SW1A 0AA; 8 Gorwell, Washington, Oxfordshire OX49 5QE (constituency);
Telephone: 0207 219 3000 (H of C); 01491 612852/612001 Fax (constituency); 0207 440 9269 (work); 0207 607 0285 Fax; boris.johnson@spectator.co.uk;

Copyright (C)Parliamentary Profile Services Ltd

Kevan JONES **Labour** **DURHAM NORTH '01-**

Majority: 18,683 (48.4%) over Conservative 3-way;
Description: A seat created in '83 out of old Chester-le-Street and parts of the former Consett constituency; it is now a largely-rural area dotted with now-pitless pit villages in the once-mighty Durham coalfield; regeneration has been slow; the Chester-le-Street part of the seat has returned Labour MPs since 1906; two wards were removed in '95; in recent years it has been a GMB seat; its middle-class Europhile MP, Giles Radice, who worked for the union, retired after 27 years, being replaced by a GMB stalwart;
Position: On the Defence Select Committee '01-; Vice Chairman '00-, Chairman '98-00, Northern Region Labour Party; ex: Newcastle City Councillor (Deputy Leader, Chief Whip of Labour Group) '90-01; Chairman: Northern Trade Unions for Labour '93-01, Labour North '94-00, Newcastle's East End Partnership '93-01; on Northern TUC Regional Council '93-01; Vice Chairman, Labour's Northern Regional Executive '93-01;
Outlook: A Newcastle-based northern GMB man of the sort who has previously provided the 'muscle' for Labour candidates, claiming a vacated GMB seat for himself; a strong supporter of regionalism and particularly a northeastern regional assembly to rebuild undermined communities in collaboration with private industry; he shares some of the pro-Europeanism of his fanatic Europhile predecessor, Giles (now Lord) Radice; a "'typical North East fixer' who helped arrange Mandelson's selection for Hartlepool" and "old friend of [former] Agriculture Minister Nick Brown" (RED PEPPER); "I do not think I am personally overtly New Labour; I have got traditional links, and believe in the federal structure of the party and in the Labour movement; but I recognise we have made great advances in the last few yars to make sure we are electable, and I am realistic on that front" (KJ);
History: He joined the Labour Party in '82 "which were dark days for the party"; he was elected to Newcastle City Council May '89; "I successfully campaigned for the re-establishment of the Northern Regional Labour Party" '97; he was "Campaign Co-ordinator in Stockton South, regaining the seat for [Dari Taylor and] Labour with a 15.6% swing from the Tories" May '97; he led the GMB's Northern Region's Asbestos Awareness Campaign which led to over £1m being recovered for victims in its first year; he was selected to replace retiring Giles Radice in Durham North Mar '01; he retained the seat with a majority of 18,683, a fall of almost 8,000, due mainly to a 12% fall in turnout June '01; in his Maiden speech he urged a balance between curbing the unethical exports of arms and maintaining the exports of the defence industries needed to maintain the economy of the northeast July '01; he was named to the Defence Select Committee July '01; in an adjournment debate he complained about the treatment meted out to a constituent, 24-year-old Christopher Rochester, who had died on the island of Rhodes, thanks partly to the poor treatment he received in the local hospital Oct '01;
Born: 25 April 1964, Shireoaks, Notts
Family: Son, of Ivor Jones, miner, and Shirley (Coddington);
Education: Portland Comprehensive, Worksop; Newcastle Polytechnic (BA Hons 2:2 in Government and Public Policy); University of Southern Maine, Portland, USA:
Occupation: Senior Organiser '99-01 (Food and Leisure) and Northern Region Political

New MPs of '01 Kevan JONES

Officer of GMB '89-01; Regional Organiser '92-99; Legal Officer, of GMB '98-00; Parliamentary Assistant, to Nick Brown '85-89;
Traits: Dimpled oval lined face, parted dark hair;
Address: House of Commons, Westminster, London SW1A 0AA; Co-operative Buildings, Plawsworth Road, Sacriston, Co Durham;
Telephone: 0207 219 8219 (H of C); 0191 1276 1952; 0374 9535921; 0191 371 8834 also Fax (constituency);

Rt Hon Greg(ory) KNIGHT   Conservative   EAST YORKSHIRE '01-

Majority: 4,682 (10.8%) over Labour 5-way;
Description: A seat created in '95 out of part of former Bridlington, keeping the fishing port and extending over the Wolds to the market towns of Driffield, Market Weighton and Pocklington; three-quarters owner-occupiers; a ninth in social housing; his controversial Rightwing Europhobe predecessor, John Townend, said: "I represent the biggest pig-producing area in the country; I certainly have more pigs in my constituency than people, but I'm glad they don't have the vote, because they wouldn't vote for me";
Former Seat: Derby North '83-97
Position: Shadow Deputy Commons Leader 01-; ex: Minister for Industry '96-97; Deputy Chief Whip '93-96; Whip/Lord Commissioner '90-93; Assistant Whip '89-90; PPS: to Lord Glenarthur '88-89, David Mellor '87; Leicester County Councillor '76-79; Chairman, Non-Profit-Making Clubs Group '87-89; Secretary, Widows and One-Parent Families Group '87-89; Leicestershire County Councillor '77-83, Leicester City Councillor '76-79;
Outlook: A relocated retread; more pragmatic than his predecessor, he switched from supporting Eurosceptic David Davis to backing Europhile Ken Clarke in the Leadership contest of '01; was "a quiet enforcer of discipline" (Colin Brown, INDEPENDENT) against Europhobes as John Major's Deputy Chief Whip; a keen collector of classic cars, he was credited with persuading Chancellor Clarke to end road tax on those over 25 years old; the many-sided, ex-Leicester solicitor and former councillor who shaved his beard to win promotion from Mrs Thatcher; a Rightwing libertarian; a Heath-baiting loyalist; assiduous attender and voter; "one who believes that we should go in for free trade as far as possible" (GK); Commons' only primatologist (monkeys and apes); "goes ape" (Tory colleague) over what he sees as a threat to the press (like John Browne's Privacy Bill and Tony Worthington's Right of Reply Bill); having ousted Philip Whitehead to win the Derby North seat - the only Tory ever to win that seat - he was initially dubbed "Silent" Knight but later opened up to defend the rule of law and monkeys; "a keen campaigner for animal welfare" (SUNDAY TELEGRAPH); "never misses an opportunity to whine about television" (Andrew Rawnsley, GUARDIAN); anti: police abuses, daubing graffiti, demonstrations;
History: He joined the Young Conservatives at 15, '64; stood as a Conservative in mock elections at his grammar school using a pop group's amplifiers to drown out opposition and others Mar '66; joined the Conservative Party in Leicester '67; became Chairman of South Leicester YCs '70, Leicester and Leicestershire YCs '72; was elected to Leicester City Council

'76, to Leicestershire County Council '77; was selected for Derby North July '82; urged a reformed and more powerful House of Lords, elected in rotation Oct '82; was elected by a 3,506 majority, ousting Labour's Philip Whitehead June '83; voted to hang terrorists and those who killed during theft July '83; urged legislation to strengthen police against trespassing itinerants July '83; in Maiden, maintained that a suspect should not be detained for longer than 24 hours Nov '83; sponsored amendment opposing televising Parliament Feb '84; supported Cycle Tracks Bill Mar '84; attacked restrictive licensing laws Mar '84; maintained that a suspect detained too long could be in danger not only from physical violence but also subject to more subtle "mental pressure" from corner-cutting policemen May '84; rebelled against Government, supporting Alliance proposal that an officer making an arrest should be in uniform (to bar agents provocateurs) May '84; co-sponsored motion urging an enquiry into collapse of state-funded Nexos June '84; sponsored debate to protect monkeys from exploitation, abuse and inadequate owners and to protect public from potential risks July '84; complained about "cowboy" garages falsely failing motorists' MOTs to create unnecessary work on their cars July '84; expressed belief that Trident would still be "good value for money" despite worsening exchange rate Oct '84; protested at statement that most cot deaths were a result of mothers smothering their babies Nov '84; supported amendment to Wildlife and Countryside Act to protect badgers against their killers Feb '85; co-sponsored Roger Gale's Bill to permit longer and more flexible opening hours May '85; warned that solicitors subsidised their court work from their conveyancing, although the actual conveyancing was done by their clerks; opposed allowing banks and building societies to carry out conveyancing May '85; again spoke against conveyancing by building societies July '85; co-sponsored Ivor Stanbrook's Bill for a compromise Sunday trading Bill May '86; rebelled to increase MPs' secretarial allowance from £13,000 to £20,000 July '86; urged opposition to efforts by compact disc manufacturers to bar emergence of digital audio tape Feb '87; was re-elected with a 6,280 majority June '87; backed Mrs Thatcher's refusal to toughen economic sanctions against South Africa Oct '87; backed abolition of right of peremptory jury challenge in Criminal Justice Bill because it created an unacceptable tilt in favour the defendant; also backed the right of appeal against an over-lenient sentence Jan '88; claimed public was getting a raw deal from the BBC-ITV "duopoly" Jan '88; asked how many marmosets had been used for chemical warfare research Feb '88; supported Tory MP Andrew Stewart's Malicious Communications Bill Feb '88; wrote: "it would be wrong to deny the accused the right to insist that the child appear in court to be cross-examined" in sex-abuse cases Mar '88; criticised Bill Walker's Scottish Whisky Bill as too "protectionist" Apr '88; tabled amendment to enable courts to confiscate animals used in dog fights Apr '88; urged tougher fines against hate mail Apr '88; urged increase in speed limit to 80mph or 90mph July '88; supported Derby and Derbyshire Business Venture Scheme Oct '88; supported Official Secrets Bill Dec '88; talked out Tory MP John Browne's Privacy Bill as "a bad Bill", unworkable and an interference with the freedom of the press Jan '89; urged Brian Clough be prosecuted for cuffing fans invading the pitch Jan '89; tried to introduce Animal Protection Bill to extend protection to wild animals and domestic pets Feb '89; strongly opposed Right of Reply Bill which he considered "a dangerous threat to press freedom" Apr '89; he voted against the Thatcher-backed War Crimes Bill Dec '89; he was promoted full Whip/ Lord Commissioner July '90; he voted to ban fox-hunting Feb '92; was re-elected with a reduced majority of 4,453 Apr '92; he was promoted Deputy Chief Whip/Treasurer of HM Household May '93; he was later accused of having offered Iain Duncan Smith the post of PPS to Jonathan Aitken or to the Lord Chancellor, to buy off his opposition to the Maastricht treaty Jan '93; negotiated with his opposite number, Labour's Don Dixon, to resume normal working relations after Labour Leader John Smith had broken them off four months before Apr '94; he told Tory MP Tim

New MPs of '01   *Rt Hon Greg(ory) KNIGHT*

Devlin to resign as a PPS because of his poor attendance and his interventions for an alleged drug dealer July '94; he was on the Government's committee to avoid 'banana skins' Jan '95; he came 10th with a 93.8% voting record Dec '94; he was hauled before the Commons authorities for having parked four cars in the MPs' free carpark: a Jensen, a Studebaker, a Rover and a Chevrolet Feb '95; he again backed a Bill against fox-hunting Mar '95; Labour polled nearly 60% in Derby's local elections May '95; "he was deeply disappointed to be overlooked for the post of Chief Whip when Alastair Goodlad was promoted over his head" (Colin Brown, INDEPENDENT); instead he was promoted a Privy Councillor July '95; he blocked the advertising of an unregistered anti-divorce group from being included on the All-Party Whip Nov '95; two untraceable secretaries of the unregistered Commmons Classic Car Club praised him highly for his "untiring efforts" to persuade Chancellor Clarke to remove road tax from vintage cars over 25 years old Dec '95; he told a constituent he was boycotting Shell because of its Nigerian activities, but informed Shell his boycott was due to its halving of its petrol's lead content, which might damage his classic cars' engines Feb '96; he made a fruitless effort to prevent the resignation from the party of Peter Thurnham by arranging a meeting with PM John Major Feb '96; he attended the summer meeting of Jonathan Aitken's Conservative Philosoophy Group where Sir James Goldsmith threatened to field Referendum Party opponents against those Tories who did not back Bill Cash's Bill to hold a referendum on renegotiating the UK's links with the EU June '96; he voted to lower MPs' mileage allowances, for a 3% ceiling on their pay rises and against a higher-rated pension July '96; as a Major-loyalist, he was promoted Minister for Industry, replacing Tim Eggar, with responsibility for competitiveness, vehicles, metal, chemicals, textiles, clothing, footwear and aerospace July '96; Whip Andrew Mitchell told investigators that he had been asked to serve on the Members' Interests Committee by Deputy Chief Whip Greg Knight Feb '97; Knight was on the 'hit list' of The Field for having voted to ban fox-hunting Apr '97; he campaigned with a specially-written pop song: 'Greg Knight's Been Working Hard for You' Apr '97; he lost Derby North on a 13.2% swing to Labour's Robert Laxton by a majority of 10,615 May '97; he produced a quarterly magazine, 'The Candidate', for aspiring Tory politicians Oct '99; he was beaten by Shailesh Vara for selection for the marginal seat of Northampton South Oct '99; although on the Approved Candidates list, he was not granted an interview in the selection process for the safe Cities of London and Westminster seat Nov '99; he was selected to replace retiring John Townend in safe East Yorkshire July '00; he stayed out of the storm around John Townend's "racist" remarks May '00; he retained East Yorkshire by a majority of 4,682 on a 2% swing to the Tories June '01; he supported Eurosceptic David Davis but switched to Europhile Ken Clarke when Davis dropped out July '01; when John Major denied he had ever offered Iain Duncan Smith a job, the latter countered that Deputy Chief Whip Knight in '93 had offered him posts as PPS to either Jonathan Aitken or the Lord Chancellor Aug '01; he asked for a statement on Rolls-Royce sackings affecting his former constituency Oct '01; in his 'second Maiden' he complimented the Labour Government for acting "responsibly" in providing a range of cleaner fuels, including LPG Oct '01; was named Shadow Deputy Commons Leader Nov '01; he claimed the aviation industry had been made more vulnerable to a world economic downturn by the Government's "increased taxation, increased red tape and increased burdens on industry" Nov '01;

Born: 4 April 1949, Leicester
Family: "Through my maternal grandmother I am entitled to wear the Fraser tartan"; "his grandfather was a miner...while his grandmother, who carried a banner on the Jarrow march, was personal assistant to James Chuter Ede, a Labour Home Secretary" (PRIVATE EYE); son, George Knight, company director, and Isabella (Bell);
Education: Thurmaston Junior, Leicester; Alderman Newton's Grammar, Leicester; College

Rt Hon Greg(ory) KNIGHT *New MPs of '01*

of Law, Guildford;
Occupation: Author, Westminster Words (a collection of witticisms and insults) (1988), Parliamentary Sauce (1992); Business Consultant '97-; since Jan '01 a Consultant to Lloyd & Associates, a legal firm specialising in immigration and asylum services; ex: Solicitor (and Police Prosecutor), who practised in Leicester ("when I used to practise in the East Midlands probably 90% of the post that I sent out on behalf of clients was in the threatening category") '73-89; Director, Lord Bug Music (music publishing company, non-salaried) '79-89; Proprietor, recording studio in Leicestershire '79-89; Director, Leicester Theatre Trust Ltd '77-85; Drummer, in pop group while a student '68-73;
Traits: Tall; dark; no longer bearded since he shaved it to secure promotion from beard-hating Margaret Thatcher; dimpled; beefy ("it is better to have a healthy appetite and be overweight"); "likeable", "approachable" (INDEPENDENT); quixotic; "overheated" (GUARDIAN); musician (was a drummer in a pop group; ex-member of Musicians Union; his telephone answering machine used to belt out a '60s rock single; ex-owner of recording studio in Leicester; wrote and produced the '83 campaign song, "Maggie Will Always Be Around"); former owner-student of monkeys (had two Brazilian Squirrel Monkeys until '88); defender of badgers; drama-lover; has shared an office with Edwina Currie - for which he was awarded the 1984 Patience of a Saint of the Year Award and a pair of industrial ear mufflers; "being alone in my view...never causes me any particular difficulty"; long a collector of classic cars: "I declare a passion for restoring, maintaining, owning and driving historic and classic motor vehicles" (GK);
Address: House of Commons, Westminster, London SW1A 0AA; 3 Tennyson Avenue, Bridlington, East Yorkshire YO15 2EU (constituency); 92 Alderney Street, London SW1V 4EZ; The Hollies, Eggington, Derbyshire DE65 6GU;
Telephone: 0207 219 8417 (H of C); 0207 834 5495; 01262 674074 (constituency); 01283 732403 and Fax (home); gregknight@aol.com;

'Jim' (James) KNIGHT   **Labour**   **SOUTH DORSET '01-**

Majority: 153 (.34%) over Conservative 4-way;
Description: Formerly the base of the Cecils, its long tenure by Tories was previously broken when Labour's Guy Barnett captured the seat at the '62 by-election when the Conservatives fielded both a pro-European and an anti-European candidate; it has Weymouth, the former Portland naval base and the marbled Isle of Purbeck and some of the finest beaches, coves and cliffs in the country, including Lulworth Cove, Studland and the Purbeck Hills with their white horse;
Position: On the Defence Select Committee '01-; Frome Town Councillor (Mayor '98) '95-; Mendip District Councillor (Leader of its Labour Group '99-00) '97-; on the National Policy Forum '97-01 and Labour's Britain in the World Commission '97-01;
Outlook: Labour's 'Dorset Boy': the first Labour MP to be elected at a general election for South Dorset or any part of Dorset, having benefited from LibDem tactical voting; a pro-Euro liberal internationalist; despite his private school and Cambridge education, he was inspired by

Leftist Fenner Brockway;
History: He was educated at Eltham College, "a private school founded for the sons of Baptist missionaries"; "I never truly started to question my own privileged background until Fenner Brockway returned to the school to speak to us; as a 14-year-old I had appeared for nine months in the West End production of 'Oliver' and had enjoyed working with boys of my age from every background; that started to open my eyes to what a narrow group of friends I had then; but Fenner Brockway came to the school and spelled it out explicitly"; "I carried the inspiration of Fenner with me to university where I expressed my politics through theatre more than party political activity; this held true in a short career as an actor and arts administrator; but in my mid-twenties I was managing a local arts centre in the Westcountry when I came face to face with small town Toryism; I saw for myself how the local Tories ran everything; I was one of many carrying out their orders and taking the blame if it went wrong"; "I resigned from my job and stood against them in local elections as the Labour candidate"; he joined the Labour Party '90; he moved from the Tory bastion of Warminster to Frome '94; he was elected a Frome Town Councillor May '95; he was selected to contest Dorset South, where Labour had come third in '92, June '95; "the 1997 election was run on self-belief and enthusiasm but no phones, no computers and limited organisation"; he missed unseating Ian Bruce in South Dorset by only 77 votes May '97 but was elected a Mendip District Councillor; contested the European Parliament June '99; he was re-selected to contest South Dorset Mar '00; "the early support of the AEEU was followed by the MSF, GMB, UNISON, CWU, GPMU and others"; Millbank made this seat its top target nationally, apart from its being the only new winnable seat in the Westcountry, so he had priority backing; "we built up the computer records, the telephone skills and a strong organisation" Apr-May '01; he narrowly captured the seat from Ian Bruce by 153 votes, only a .25% swing to Labour from his missing winning the seat by 77 votes the previous time; there was an 8.7% drop in turnout and and a 6% drop in the LibDem vote by tactical voters who marginally favoured him June '01; in his Maiden speech he said "I look forward to campaigning for entry into the single European currency in the interests of farmers - just as soon as my right hon Friends tell me that it is in our national interest to do so"; local farming had been hard-hit; also "our education standard spending assessment is one of the worst in the country, our councils desperately need a fairer funding formula, and we need to go on trying to gain attention for those of our [local] industries that are struggling" June '01; was appointed to the Defence Select Committee July '01; he was feted at Labour's annual conference in Brighton for his "stunning victory" Oct '01; he worried about the World Bank prediction that the 11 September terrorist attack would push another 10m people into poverty in the 3rd World Nov '01;
Born: 6 March 1965, Bexley, Kent
Family: Son, of Philip Knight, accountant, and Hilary (Harper); m '89 Anna (Wheatley); 1s, 1d;
Education: Eltham College (private school for the sons of Baptist missionaries); Fitzwilliam College, Cambridge University (BA Hons in Geography and Social and Political Science);
Occupation: Manager of Dentone Directories (publishing company) '91-01; Director, West Wiltshire Arts Centre Ltd '90-91; Manager of an arts centres, Central Studio, Basingstoke '89-90; worked for a touring theatre company '87-89; Actor (in the cast of 'Oliver') '79;
Traits: Trim beard; balding; specs; enjoys football, tennis, cooking and cycling;
Address: House of Commons, Westminster, London SW1A 0AA; 28 Southview Road, Weymouth DT4 0JD (constituency); 25 Selwood Road, Frome, Somerset BA11 3BP;
Telephone: 0207 219 3000 (H of C); 01305 786181/712018 Fax (constituency); 01305 853408; 01373 303446 and Fax (home); 1373 822224 (work); 07970 833119 (mobile); jimknight@arsenalfc.net;

Norman (Peter) LAMB   **Liberal Democrat**   **NORTH NORFOLK '01-**

Majority: 483 (.9%) over Conservative 5-way;
Description: An unaltered agricultural seat, including coastal resorts such as Cromer and Sherringham and part of the Broads; it contains the villages of Little Snoring and smaller Great Snoring as well as the famous 18,000-acre estate at Holkham, "Britain's last remaining feudal estate" (DAILY TELEGRAPH); its once numerous and unionised farm workers underpinned Labour MPs from '45 to '70 when the farmer Sir Ralph Howell took it for the Conservatives, handing it narrowly to Lord Prior's son David in '97;
Position: Norwich City Councillor (LibDem Group Leader '89-91) '87-91; Chairman: Norwich South Liberals '85-87, Tottenham Liberals '80-81; Chairman/Secretary, Employment Lawyers Association;
Outlook: A third-time-lucky LibDem solicitor who finally ousted Tory Deputy Chairman David Prior, as the result of Labour voters delivering their tactical anti-Tory votes to him; the first Liberal/LibDem MP elected in East Anglia since '51, the first in Norfolk since '29, the first in North Norfolk since '18; he sees the need for "radical reform on Europe, decentralising power, defining limits of centralised power and increasing openness and democracy" (NL); in Association of LibDem Lawyers, Liberty;
History: He joined the Liberal Party '76; he became Chairman of the Tottenham Liberals '80, of the Norwich South Liberals '85; he was elected to Norwich City Council May '87; he first fought North Norfolk, polling 27.3% in second place, with a 23% Labour vote in third place, and the Tory MP ahead by 12,545 votes Apr '92; fought the seat for the second time, slashing the new Tory MP David Prior's majority to 1,293 on a 9% pro-LibDem swing - but still with a big Labour vote May '97; reselected in '98, he targeted the Labour vote so that "the council estates in North Walsham and Fakenham were a sea of orange" (NEW STATESMAN); he thought one more heave would win the seat, provided "you can present an alternative and beat a Tory MP"; he denied rumours of any unofficial understanding of Labour backing for the LibDems in North Norfolk in exchange for a LibDem go-slow in neighbouring marginally Labour-held North West Norfolk, insisting "we simply targetted our resources where we could win"; in the event, the Labour vote share dropped from 25% to 13% while his vote share rose from 34% to 43%, enabling him to oust the Tory by 483 votes June '01; in his Maiden speech he attacked the decline in rural post offices and transport, increased NHS waiting lists, and low rates of voting among the young June '01; he complained about inadequate office space in Westminster July '01; he launched a debate to deplore the appallingly long waiting times for orthopaedic care in Norfolk July '01; he supported the demand for a public inquiry into the death of Lauren Wright of Gillian Shephard Oct '01; as a "specialist employment lawyer" he judged that Jo Moore's behaviour amounted to "gross misconduct" and the failure to dismiss her required "wider investigation" Oct '01; led a motion endorsing more widespread use of speed cameras, especially in Norfolk Oct '01; he led a motion urging more generous funding for efforts to combat coastal erosion Nov '01;
Born: 16 September 1957,
Family: Son, of Hubert Horace Lamb, Professor of Climatology, University of East Anglia, and Beatrice Moira (Milligan); m '84 Mary Elizabeth (Green); 2s Archie '88, Edward '91;

New MPs of '01   *Norman (Peter) LAMB*

Education: George Abbot School, Guildford; Wymondham College, Norfolk; Leicester University (LLB '80); City of London Poly;
Occupation: Solicitor specialising in employment law - "I am listed in Chambers Directory as a leader in employment law in East Anglia" (NL) - with Steele & Co '84-, Partner '87-01, Consultant '01-; Author: Remedies in the Employment Tribunal (1998);
Traits: Fresh-faced; youthful-looking; front-combed grey hair; he likes five-a-side football; Norwich City season ticket holder;
Address: House of Commons, Westminster, London SW1A 0AA; Beechview, Lime Tree Road, North Walsham;
Telephone: 0207 219 8480 (H of C); 01692 403752/400925 Fax (constituency);

David (Anthony) LAWS   **Liberal Democrat**   **YEOVIL '01-**

Majority: 3,928 (8.2%) over Conservative 6-way;
Description: Yeovil (Westland) plus Crewkerne, Chard and Ilminster, in a fold of the previously-Conservative south Somerset hills; its previous MP, the Liberal Democrat Leader Sir Paddy (now Lord) Ashdown, managed to end 73 years of Tory control on the retirement of John Peyton in '83; he increased his majority steadily as well as the local base for his party, climaxed by wins in the '97 council elections in Yeovil, Chard, Crewkerne and Ilminster;
Position: On the Treasury Select Committee '01-; ex: Director of Policy and Research, Liberal Democrats, '97-99;
Outlook: A brilliant youngish economist who made a fortune as a merchant banker with J P Morgan and BZW but failed to shine against Michael Howard in the '97 election; as the LibDems' former Director of Policy, "David made the bullets for me to fire" (Malcolm Bruce); as a star in Paddy Ashdown's inner circle, he inherited his Leader's seat; "highly able" (WESTERN DAILY PRESS);
History: He joined the SDP and Liberals '84; he won the OBSERVER Mace in the Schools Debating Competition '84; at 28 he became the youngest-ever Managing Director at Barclays de Zoete Wedd '93; he became Economic Adviser to the LibDems '94; was selected to contest Folkestone & Hythe for the LibDems '95; he managed to come 2nd to Michael Howard in Folkestone & Hythe, despite losing 8.5% of the LibDem vote to the resurgent Labour candidate May '97; he became the LibDems' Director of Policy and Research '97; he provided the information which enabled Malcolm Bruce, the LibDems' Treasury Spokesman to get under the skin of the new Chancellor, Gordon Brown, inluding the "£5.3b black hole" in his spending plans; Bruce "has been aided in finding the cracks in the Treasury figures by David Laws, a highly intelligent young millionaire who gave up the City to join the party as Policy Director" (SUNDAY BUSINESS); he prepared the first draft of the partnership agreement setting up the Labour-LibDem coalition in the Scottish Parliament May '99; he was selected to succeed retiring Paddy Ashdown as the candidate for Yeovil; it was then claimed that he had sent a second letter to some selectors, instead of the one allowed July '99; he retained Yeovil by a majority of 3,928, a 7,500 drop from Ashdown's majority, partly from losing 534 votes to a rebel Liberal and a 9.5% drop in turnout, producing a 6.5% pro-Conservative swing June '01; in his Maiden speech, he welcomed a very low (1.5%) unemployment level but criticised

Copyright (C)Parliamentary Profile Services Ltd

David (Anthony) LAWS   *New MPs of '01*

long waits for hip replacements and larger secondary school classes, and called for a "constitution for Europe that would both define and limit its powers"; "that will be necessary before the Government can win a referendum on the Euro" June '01; he accused the Treasury of having "clearly misled the House" after Chief Secretary Andrew Smith had invented a report by the National Audit Office claiming that the Private Finance Initiative had been a success; after the INDEPENDENT disclosed no such report had been made by the NAO, Andrew Smith apologised to him July '01; he welcomed Defence Secretary Geoff Hoon's announcement that Westland would be an important subcontractor converting helicopters to incorporate the Bowman communications system, providing 120 jobs locally July '01; he was named to the Treasury Select Committee July '01; he asked the cost of performance-related pay for teachers July '01; he asked that pensioners enjoy the country's increasing prosperity July '01; he asked what savings were being generated by PFI July '01; he complained about how few NHS dentists were available in south Somerset Oct '01; he pressed Minister Hodges to disclose which faults in student financing the Government's review was trying to correct Oct '01;
Born: 30 November 1965, Farnham, Surrey
Family: Son, David Laws, banker, and Maureen (Savidge);
Education: St George's (RC) College, Weybridge; King's College, Cambridge University (Double 1st Class Hons in Economics, Scholarship);
Occupation: Director of Policy and Research, Liberal Democrats '97-99; Economic Adviser, to Liberal Democrats '94-97; Managing Director, Barclays de Zoete Wedd '92-94; Vice President, J P Morgan & Company '87-92;
Traits: Parted reddish-brown hair; "highly intelligent" (SUNDAY BUSINESS); "quietly-spoken but talented" (FINANCIAL TIMES); able debater: at 19 won Mace in OBSERVER's Schools Debating Competition '84; Roman Catholic by education;
Address: House of Commons, Westminster, London SW1A 0AA; 94 Middle Street, Yeovil, Somerset BA20 1LT;
Telephone: 0207 219 3000 (H of C); 01935 425025/433652 Fax;

Mark (Marek Jerzy) LAZAROWICZ   **Labour & Co-operative   EDINBURGH NORTH & LEITH '01-**

Majority: 8,817 (26.5%) over LibDem 6-way;
Description: The reshaped former Edinburgh-Leith seat, renamed in '95 after taking three-quarters of the former seat and adding 9,000 from Edinburgh Central and 4,500 from Edinburgh East; despite some Conservative strength in New Town and Stockbridge, it is still a traditional Labour seat containing the 'Transpotting' council estates of Granston, Royston and West Pilton; some depressed industrial areas around Leith docks have been gentrified with modish wine bars and warehouses converted into flats;
Position: On the Scottish Affairs Select Committee '01-; Edinburgh City Councillor (Transport Convener '99-01) '99-, '80-96; ex: Edinburgh District Councillor (Leader of Council '86-93) '80-96; on Labour Party Scottish Executive (Chairman, '89-90) '80-90; Chairman of Scottish Labour Party '89-90; Chairman, Scottish War on Want;

Founder-Member of Centre for Scottish Public Policy;
Outlook: The belatedly-successful, previously-thwarted Left-of-Centre veteran of Edinburgh and Scottish politics who was twice the bridesmaid in Edinburgh-Pentlands in '87 and '92 only to have the bouquet fall into the hands of Lynda Clark in '97 after he had decided not to seek nomination; "bright and a potential high-flier" who "is likely to put his constituency before his party and stand up for what he believes in" (SCOTSMAN); a former voluntary sector leader turned barrister; founder of the Leftwing think-tank The Centre for Scottish Public Policy (previously The John Wheatley Centre); in SERA; former Chairman, Scottish War on Want; one of eight independent-school-educated Labour newcomers;
History: He joined the Labour Party at 18, '71; he was elected to Edinburgh District Council May '80; elected to the Labour Party's Scottish Executive '80; elected Leader of Edinburgh City Council '86; contested Edinburgh-Pentlands against Malcolm Rifkind, increasing the Labour vote by 6.1% but coming 2nd, 3,745 votes behind June '87; he became the Chairman of the Scottish Labour Party for the year from '89; contesting Pentlands again, he only increased Labour's vote by 1.1%, against the SNP's 8.2% increase, trailing Malcolm Rifkind by 4,290 votes Apr '92; squeezed out of safe Labour seats by Establishment-backed women - including Cumbernauld & Kilsyth which went to Rosemary McKenna - he decided not to contest Pentlands a third time, with a woman candidate - Lynda Clark - duly ousting Malcolm Rifkind May '97; he was elected for the Broughton ward to Edinburgh City Council May '99; barred from selection to the Scottish Parliament, he attacked the "vetting panels" as taking the "real power of candidate-selection away from local party committees to small central committees"; in the wake of the impending retirement from Westminster to Holyrood of Malcolm Chisholm he was selected to contest the Edinburgh North & Leith, in which he lived '00; he retained the seat by a majority of 8,817, a drop of over 2,000 on a 13% cut in turnout; his victory, in the 330th seat announced, sealed Labour's majority June '01; led a motion urging a wide public debate on simplifying rail structure "so that it is capable of delivering a level of service envisaged in the Government's 10-year transport plan" July '01; backed a pro-Kyoto motion warning of the "catastrophic effect" of its failure July '01; was named to the Scottish Affairs Select Committee July '01; he presented his private Employee Share Scheme Bill July '01; while "deeply shocked" by the actions of Jo Moore, he claimed the Tories were also trying to exploit Jo Moore's attempted cynical exploitation of the events of 11 September "for their own narrow political gain" Oct '01;
Born: 8 August 1953, London
Family: Son, of a Polish draughtsman; m '93 Caroline (Johnston); 3s Thomas '93, Andrew '97 and Peter '00; 1d Charlotte '98;
Education: St Benedict's (RC) School, Ealing, London; St Andrews University (Moral Philosophy and Medieval History '76); Edinburgh University (LLB '92); Diploma in Legal Practice '93;
Occupation: Advocate, with a civil practice in reparation and administrative law '96-; Co-Author (with Jean McFadden), The Scottish Parliament (1999 and 2000); ex: Leader of Edinburgh District Council '86-93; Organiser, Scottish Education and Action for Development '82-86; General Secretary, British Youth Council (Scotland) '80-82; Organiser, of Scottish Education and Action for Development '78-90;
Traits: Grey-white, parted hair, somewhat in retreat; long, lean visage; specs; head aloft; straight-backed; poker-faced; solitary; "an independent free-thinking approach"; "health-conscious"(SCOTSMAN); he lost a couple of stone before the '01 election; likes jogging;
Address: House of Commons, Westminster, London SW1A 0AA; 17 Bellevue Place, Edinburgh EH17 4BS; 274 Leith Walk, Edinburgh EH6 5EL (constituency);

Mark (Marek Jerzy) LAZAROWICZ *New MPs of '01*

Telephone: 0207 219 3000 (H of C); 0131 556 4438 and Fax;

Ian (Richard) LIDDELL-GRAINGER   Conservative   BRIDGWATER '01-

Majority: 4,987 (10.4%) over LibDem 4-way;
Description: A beautiful banana-shaped seat in West Somerset stretching along the Bristol Channel coast from the light industrial town of Bridgwater across the Quantock and Brendon Hills to the heart of Exmoor; it includes the resort of Minehead and the picturesque nearby village of Dunster where he spent childhood holidays with the local lords of the manor, the Luttrells; Dunkery Beacon, the highest point on Exmoor, is "the purple-headed mountain" in "All things bright and beautiful"; provisional Boundary Commission proposals will make it safer for the Conservatives by adding all of rural West Somerset from the Taunton seat; Tom King held the seat for 31 years until '01;
Position: Ex: Adviser to late MP Michael Colvin when Defence Select Committee Chairman '92-96; Tynedale District Councillor '89-95; Ward Chairman, Hexham Conservative Association '92-94; President, Tyne Bridge Conservative Association '93-96;
Outlook: An ambitious, wealthy North Tyneside businessman-farmer who finally did unexpectedly well in the southwest; a monarchist as Queen Victoria's great, great, great grandson who has reached the Commons after losing Tory-held Torridge & West Devon to the LibDems in '97, but managed to see them off at Bridgwater in place of Tom King in '01; a leg-of-lamb-brandishing former farmer who punned that "Labour hasn't got a leg to stand on" on agriculture policy; he was unrevealing about his Leadership preferences following his anti-Hague gaffe during the general election; former Devon Chairman of the Countryside Alliance, he says on fox-hunting, "you have to listen to both sides of the argument", but backs hunting to preserve wildlife through countryside management and to save local jobs; an uninspired orthodox super-loyal Unionist;
History: He was elected to Tynedale District Council May '85; claimed at the party conference that the Conservatives were the only party taking defence seriously Oct '90; claimed the Conservatives were the only party not blindly accepting all Europe says Oct '92; was selected as candidate for the hopeless Euro-constituency of Tyne and Wear Aug '93, losing it June '94; was shortlisted for Dumfries Dec '94; came within four votes of winning selection for North Shropshire in succession to John Biffen '95; missed selection for North Norfolk Sep '95; was defeated by Norman Lamont in selection contest for Harrogate Jan '96; was chosen as the Conservative candidate for Torridge & West Devon, in the wake of the desertion to the Liberal Democrats of the sitting Tory MP, Emma Nicholson Mar '96; wrote to WESTERN MORNING NEWS: "I find it almost imposssible to believe that the Scottish and the Welsh people would ever consider leaving the Union" Sep '96; opening the agriculture debate at the Tories' annual conference he pretended that the BSE-protesting farmers outside were all in favour of the Tory Government, which would "put the interests of the British farmer first, second and third"; he blamed the EU for the beef ban and CAP; "British beef is safe"; claimed Francis Drake as a constituent and a fellow Eurosceptic Oct '96; he declared against a single European currency Apr '97; he lost Torridge & West Devon, held by the

88 *Copyright (C)Parliamentary Profile Services Ltd*

Tories since '59, to the LibDems by 1,957 votes May '97; brandishing a leg of lamb at the Conservative Party conference to dramatise the plight of sheepfarmers, he said Labour's farming policy did not have a leg to stand on Oct '99; he was selected for Bridgwater in succession to retiring Tom King July '00; Tory MPs questionned Speaker Martin's competence in allowing Tony Blair to quote a leaflet written by candidate Liddell-Grainger saying "We have to explain to Conservatives who do not like William Hague that the only way to find a new Leader is to get the Conservatives into power under William Hague so that a new Leader can emerge from the more unknown Conservative members", which drew from the GUARDIAN's Simon Hoggart the quip, "Vote for Hague in order to get rid of him!" May '01; held off an expected LibDem challenge helped by a resilient Labour vote, and upped his inherited majority of 1,796 to 4,987 on a 3.6% swing from LibDem to Tory June '01; his leadership ballot votes were undisclosed July '01; in his Maiden speech he recalled that the last battle on British soil was fought in Bridgwater, "the last time, I am glad to say, that republicanism reared its ugly head", and warned that unless Somerset's sea defences and silted-up rivers were cared for to prevent flooding, he would have to have "an office in the yellow submarine" July '01; introduced his Patents Act 1977 (Amendment) Bill to enable a court to award exemplary infringement damages July '01; after serving on the standing committee of the Export Control Bill, he wondered whether applications could be processed adequately to keep up with the speed of technology and licensing to foreign countries Nov '01;
Born: 23 February 1959, Edinburgh
Family: Son, of David Liddell-Grainger, farmer, and Anne (Abel-Smith), great, great, granddaughter of Queen Victoria, great grand-daughter of Leopold, Duke of Albany, Queen Victoria's youngest son, grand-daughter of Princess Alice, Countess of Athlone;; m '85 Jill (Nesbitt); 1s Peter '88; 2d Sophie '89, May '92;
Education: Wellesley House Prep, Broadstairs, Kent; Millfield School, Street, Somerset; South of Scotland Agricultural College, Edinburgh (National Certificate of Agriculture);
Occupation: Consultant (on land management) to Army Land Command HQ, Salisbury, and MoD, London '99-01; Research Assistant, to Lord Vinson '98-00; Director: his own Newcastle-based property management investment company '85-99. a construction company '85-90, office furniture company '85-95, Okehampton OK (Somerset-based local radio company), local regeneration company; Farmer on a 250-acre arable family farm in Berwickshire '80-85;
Traits: Burly; parted, thin blond retreating hair; protruding upper lip; a toothy smile; thin eyes with bags; receding chin; puckish-looking; "wild-eyed" (GUARDIAN, on his party conference leg-of-lamb-waving); "short, fat and balding; just a rich bloke with a big mouth" (Northumberland Tory); "has a good sense of humour" (another Northern Tory); ex-TA Major; the next monarch but 282 - "approximately 283rd in line to the throne" (DAILY TELEGRAPH);
Address: House of Commons, Westminster, London SW1A 0AA; 16 Northgate, Bridgwater, Somerset TA6 3EU; Domons House, Bratton Clovelly, Okehampton, Devon EX20 4LD;
Telephone: 0207 219 3000 (H of C); 01278 243110/431034 Fax; 01837 871557/871573 Fax;

LORDS PROFILES
We also do profiles of Lords, based on forty years of observation and the best files in the country, bar none. Price: £40 each.

Ian (Colin) LUCAS   **Labour**   **WREXHAM '01-**

Majority: 9,188 (30.6%) over Conservative 5-way;
Description: An industrial town centred on the now-defunct northeast Wales coalfield which suffered the infamous Gresford colliery disaster costing hundreds of lives in '34; a mixed seat with affluent private estates as well as 30% in socially-owned housing stock; recent industrial diversification has reduced unemployment to 3.3%, below the Welsh average; in '95 it lost 12,000 voters to Clwyd South; John Marek, who narrowly retained the seat for Labour in '83 after its sitting Labour MP defected to the SDP and it traded urban areas for a farming region, held it until opting for the Welsh Assembly in '00;
Position: On Select Committees on Procedure '01- and Environmental Audit '01-; ex: Gresford Community Councillor '87-91; Chairman, Wrexham CLP '91-92; Vice Chairman, North Shropshire CLP '93-97;
Outlook: An Oxford-educated local solicitor proud of his working-class Tyneside council house origins and his Durham miner grandfather; "my politics are based upon the principles that everyone has the right to a fair chance in life and that we all owe obligations to support those who suffer disadvantage"; is in the Fabians, Society of Labour Lawyers;
History: He was a contemporary at Oxford of fellow new MPs Chris Bryant and Kevin Brennan; he joined the Labour Party at 26, '86; as Wrexham CLP's delegate to the Labour Party Conference, he spoke for their motion on criminal justice Sep '90; he was elected Chairman of Wrexham CLP '91-92; selected for Tory-held North Shropshire, he fought a campaign using bar charts to show "only Labour can win here" on the strength of Labour's capture of the Shropshire Euro seat in '94; he leapfrogged the second-place LibDems, and reduced the Tory majority from 13,181 to 2,195 on a notional 11.8% pro-Labour swing, its best-ever showing May '97; he was selected for Wrexham following the switch of its MP, John Marek, to the Welsh Assembly May '00; he held the seat comfortably by a 9,188 majority on a minimal 0.9% swing to the Conservatives June '01; in his Maiden speech he hailed the fall in local unemployment from 20% in '83 to 3.3% in '01, but also told of representing, as his solicitor, a "14-year-old who had committed 23 house burglaries to feed his heroine habit" June '01; he was named to the Select Committees on Procedure and Environmental Audit July '01; he pointed out to PM Tony Blair that "Wrexham Council has recently appointed a recycling officer" July '01; he pressed Environment Minister Michael Meacher to maximise recycling and minimise local incineration Oct '01;
Born: 18 September 1960, Gateshead
Family: Grandson of a Durham miner; son of Colin Lucas, process engineer, and Alice (Scott), who still live in the council house he was brought up in; m '86 Norah Anne (Sudd), music teacher in local comprehensives and Labour Party activist; 1s Patrick '93; 1d Ellen '91;
Education: Greenwell Comprehensive, Gateshead; Newcastle Royal Grammar School; New College, Oxford University (BA Jurisprudence '82); Chester College of Law;
Occupation: Solicitor '85-: Partner, Stevens Lucas '00-, Principal, Crawford Lucas '97-00; D R Crawford '92-97; Roberts Moore Nichols Jones '89-92; Lees Moore & Price '87-89; Percy Hughes Roberts '86-87; Articled Clerk, Russell Cooke Porter & Chapman '83-86; he acted for the crash-surviving Fayed-employed bodyguard of Princess Diana, Trevor Rees-Jones, and,

90   *Copyright (C)Parliamentary Profile Services Ltd*

"despite fierce opposition from Mohamed Fayed, advised and helped him tell the world of the events leading to the death of Princess Diana"(IL); MSF '96-;
Traits: Full-faced; high forehead; personable; self-described as "a High Street solicitor", "patient and polite", "determined, persistent and persuasive"; a supporter of Sunderland FC; enjoys films and painting;
Address: House of Commons, Westminster, London SW1A 0AA; 67 Regent Street, Wrexham, Clwyd LL11 1PG (office); Rhoslan Rhewesni Lane, Wrexham (home);
Telephone: 0207 219 5346 (H of C); 01978 355743/310051 Fax; (constituency); ian@ian-lucas.freeserve.co.uk;

Iain LUKE   Labour   DUNDEE EAST '01-

Majority: 4,475 (13.8%) over SNP 5-way;
Description: Scotland's little-known third city, on its East coast, once the base for 14 years of Winston Churchill when a Liberal MP, until "uniquely ousted by the only prohibitionist Christian Socialist Member of Parliament, Neddy Scrymgeor" (IL); boasting two Premier League football teams within a stone's throw of each other, it has moved on from being called "Juteopolis" and known for "jute, jam and journalism" to the base for Michelin, NCR and smaller research-based enterprises building on the technology of the city's two universities; although its most easterly suburb is affluent Broughty Ferry, its sprawling council housing estates make it a natural Labour seat; but through Labour's local factional infighting and corruption, the seat was held '74-87 by the SNP's Gordon Wilson, who was helped by tactical Tory votes; its previous Labour MP John McAllion '87-01 left to focus on the Scottish Parliament;
Position: On Broadcasting and Administration Select Committees '01-; ex: on Scottish Policy Forum '98-00; Dundee City Councillor (Convenor of Housing '96-01) '96-01; Dundee District Councillor (Leader '90-92) '84-96; Chairman, Dundee Partnership '94-95, '91-92;
Outlook: A through-and-through Dundonian son of OMOV and the GMB: born, bred, and employed in the city where he has been a modernising councillor for 17 years; less Whip-defying than his predecessor, John McAllion, but a pro-Arab like Dundee West's Ernie Ross; self-described as believing that "Britain's future lies within the European Union";
History: His father was active in the GMB and Labour Party; he joined the Labour Party at 27, Feb '79; he was elected to Dundee District Council May '84; he became Leader of the Council '90; he was elected to Dundee City Council May '96; he was selected for Dundee East to replace John McAllion who had been elected to the Scottish Parliament for the seat in '99 and decided to focus on it '00; at the Brighton Labour Party Conference he spoke loyally on crime, backing anti-social-behaviour orders Sep '00; he retained the seat with a halved majority of 4,475; a 12% drop in turnout yielding a pro-SNP swing of 5.4% June '01; his Maiden speech was an encomium for Dundee, "Scotland's friendliest city" and the possessor of "two Premier League football teams within a stone's throw of each other on the same road" June '01; he was named to the Select Committee on Broadcasting July '01; he baited SNP MP Angus Robertson with the claim that the SNP policy of "independence in Europe" had "been roundly rejected by the Scottish electorate on numerous occasions" Oct '01; he backed the Bill

Iain LUKE *New MPs of '01*

ratifying the Nice Agreement as part of a "continuing, constructive participation in the shaping of our joint European future and for the the enlargement of the European Union" Oct '01; he backed a policy of encouraging regional airports because "business location decisions are taken by executives who will not knowingly locate in regions that they perceive to be isolated" Oct '01; he urged the Trade and Industry Minister to heed the TUC's warning against the loss of pension and other rights when employees were transferred from public to private employment Nov '01; he complained that, despite Labour's progress, "areas such as mine still suffer from high levels of poverty and unemployment" Nov '01; he was added to the Administration Select Committee Nov '01;
Born: 8 October 1951, Dundee
Family: Son, of William Luke, school caretaker and GMB activist, "secretary of a public sector branch here in Dundee", and Charlotte (Campbell); married to Marie (Campbell); three children;
Education: Stobswell Boys' Junior; Harris Academy, Dundee; Dundee University (MA Hons in History and Politics '80); Edinburgh University (Diploma in Business Administration '81); Jordanhill Teacher Training College (TQFE '89);
Occupation: Ex: Lecturer/Senior Lecturer in Public Administration/European Studies, Dundee College of Further Education '83-01; Civil Servant: Assistant Collector of Taxes '69-74; (GMB)
Traits: Egg-shaped head; retreating hairline; receding chin; big ears; pursed mouth; dour expression; Dundee accent; GSOH; "I am a died-in-the-wool true blue Dundee [FC] supporter"; also an enthusiast for William Topaz McGonagall whose poetry "unfairly earned him the title of the world's worst poet"; proud to be Chairman of the McGonagall Centenary Celebration Committee and a Director of its Contemporary Arts Centre;
Address: House of Commons, Westminster, London SW1A 0AA; 18B Market Gait, Dundee DD1 1QR (constituency);
Telephone: 0207 219 3000 (H of C); 01382 224628 (constituency);

John LYONS   Labour   **STRATHKELVIN & BEARSDEN '01-**

Majority: 11,717 (28.2%) over LibDem 5-way;
Description: A seat centred on three suburbs north and northeast of Glasgow, which were forts on the ancient Antonine Wall to keep out northern barbarians: ultra middle-class Bearsden, Bishopbriggs, and pro-Labour Kirkintilloch; one of its most famous sons was ILP MP Tom Johnston, "born and educated in Kirkintilloch in the heart of the constituency, he was chairman of the first municipal bank, a gifted writer and went on to change the face of postwar Scotland" (JL); its last pit and its last foundry, Gartcosh, have closed; its main employer is the NHS with 11,000 on the local payroll; in '93 it lost part of Bearsden and gained a Labour-voting ward from former Monklands West, making it safer for Labour; its MP of 14 years, Sam Galbraith, quit initially to focus on being an MSP and a Minister in the Scottish Executive, but then quit entirely on health grounds '01;
Position: Ex: on Select Committee of Procedure July '01; on Forth Valley Health Board

New MPs of '01   *John LYONS*

'99-01;
Outlook: A mechanical engineer turned union official inheriting a safe seat; "said to have featured on a secret list of union-approved candidates" (RED PEPPER); is interested in "international development, employment rights, transport and...homelessness" (JL);
History: He joined the Labour Party '79; long UNISON's Scottish organiser, he was selected to replace the departing-for-Holyrood and ailing Sam Galbraith; he retained the seat comfortably with a majority of 11,717 over the LibDems, risen from fourth place; the majority dropped by 5,000. partly due to a 12% drop in turnout June '01; in his Maiden speech he boasted of his constituency's famous sons, Tom Johnston and Thomas Muir and how it had attracted Murdoch's HarperCollins publishing house July '01; he was named to the Procedure Committee and, within days, discharged from it July '01; he asked whether "the unsuccessful companies [would be] excluded from bidding for subcontract work under the Bowman [military communications] programme"; Defence Secretary Geoff Hoon said that "Thales and other unsuccessful companies may bid succcessfully" for subcontracting work July '01; he insisted that if Parliament valued caring, "we must put our money where our mouth is" Oct '01;
Born: 11 July 1949, Glasgow
Family: He does not disclose his family's names or jobs; Partner; 1s, 1d;
Education: Woodside Secondary School, Glasgow; Stirling University (MSc, Human Resource Management '00);
Occupation: Regional Officer, Scotland, for UNISON (previously NUPE) '88-00; Mechanical Engineer '70-88; (AEEU '65-88, UNISON '88-01);
Traits: Square face; parted dark hair; jowly; terse; Nicholas Parsons look-alike; enjoys hill-walking;
Address: House of Commons, Westminster, London SW1A 0AA; 2 Townhead, Kirkintilloch, nr Glasgow (constituency);
Telephone: 0207 219 3000 (H of C);

Khalid Mahmood   **Labour**   **BIRMINGHAM-PERRY BARR '01-**

Majority: 8,753 (23.4%) over Conservative 8-way;
Description: Northwest Birmingham's previously marginal seat made safe for Labour by boundary changes in '83 and '95; three-quarters outer suburbs, largely of skilled owner-occupying workers; one quarter inner-city, with high concentrations of non-white voters in its Perry Barr and Handsworth wards; with 38% non-white residents, on '91 Census figures, only ten constituencies had higher numbers of blacks and Asians; its CLP has been the scene of faction-fighting and legal actions over many years, aggravated by tension between rival ethnic minorities of Muslims, Hindus and Sikhs, with Kashmiri Muslims dominating the constituency organisation; Mahmood's predecessor, locally-born Jeff (now Lord) Rooker, represented the constituency for 27 years;
Position: Ex: Birmingham City Councillor (Chairman, Race Relations Committee) '90-93; South Birmingham Community Health Councillor;

Copyright (C)Parliamentary Profile Services Ltd   *93*

Outlook: A Birmingham-born Muslim thrust into the limelight in the wake of the World Trade Centre atrocity as the newer of the two-man group of Muslim Labour MPs; has spoken for integrated Muslims against those who "purport to be Muslims" but killed innocent thousands; is worried about the third generation of unemployed :Muslim; youths who can fall prey to Muslim fanatics; a controversially-selected Kashmiri Muslim whose female Sikh opponent for the selection alleged ballot-rigging; the outgoing Labour MP, Jeff Rooker, was opposed to his selection; he was one of two new Asian MPs elected in '01, and only the second Muslim, bringing the black and Asian total to 12; a former adviser to the President of the Olympic Council (Asia); in the Socialist Health Association, Socialist Environment Association;

History: "I came to this country when I was nine and my first language was not English"; having joined the Labour Party, he was elected to Birmingham City Council for Sparkbrook ward May '90; he disappeared from Birmingham for over a year, leaving the council after one term '93; the council-backed British-Kashmiri Association collapsed with huge debts '94; beating seven rivals, he won the nomination to succeed Jeff Rooker by 196 votes to 82 for Sukvinder Stubbs, a Sikh and former Chief Executive of The Runnymede Trust; her supporters alleged that Khalid Mahmood's supporters had obtained blank postal votes from members in Perry Barr ward and cast them for him, but an appeal to the High Court was rejected and Labour's NEC, after suspending his selection, endorsed him, possibly wanting to avoid a spat so close to the election Mar '01; Leon Cook, Chairman of the Perry Barr CLP, claimed most of his membership had been working for Mahmood's LibDem opponent June '01; Mahmood retained the seat for Labour with a halved majority of 8,753 and a vote share of 46%, much lower than Rooker's 63% in '97; turnout was down 12% June '01; he made his Maiden speech July '01; he spoke again on Urban Community Relations, emphasising the need for care in "how we build up the moral fabric of our societies"; he urged parental education, particularly of isolated immigrant mothers; children of immigrants should be encouraged to do projects after visiting their parents' lands of origin July '01; in the first special meeting of Parliament after the terrorist bombings of the World Trade Centre and Pentagon, he warned against targeting the overwhelming majority of loyal Muslims for the terrorist outrages of a few who "purport to be Muslims" Sep '01; at a conference fringe meeting he claimed the differences between Islam, Judaeism and Christianity were being exaggerated by leaders for their own purposes, giving religion a bad name; he feared fanatics would target the third generation of badly-educated Muslim youths, ignorant about their own religion Oct '01; he backed "ethical trade" with developing countries, partly because it protected minimum labour standards Oct '01; his OBSERVER article showed him wholly loyal to the Blair-Bush campaign against Afghan-based terrorism, later admitting it had been part-written by Denis MacShane of the FCO Nov '01;

Born: 13 July 1961, Kashmir

Family: His grandfather served as a seaman on British ships in World War II; his father "came from a rural area in Kashmir";

Education: Golden Hillock Comprehensive, Sparkbrook; Garrets Green College; Birmingham Polytechnic; in '01 he was studying for an MBA in Management Studies;

Occupation: Ex: Lecturer, in South Birmingham College; former engineer (AEEU);

Traits: Brown skin; parted dark hair; large eyes; droopy moustache; light Brummie accent; stocky; short legs; cumbersome walk; waddling gait; soft-spoken; mild-seeming;

Address: House of Commons, Westminster, London SW1A 0AA; 1 George Street, West Bromwich, West Midlands B70 6NT;

Telephone: 020 219 3000 (H of C); 0121 569 1937;

John MANN　　　　　　　　Labour　　　　　　　　BASSETLAW '01-

Majority: 9,748 (25.1%) over Conservative 4-way;
Description: A seat centred on the mining town of Worksop, which has two working pits feeding three power stations; in '83 it lost some Tory rural areas and marginal East Retford but gained the mining town of Warsop; these towns have a large rural hinterland including "the strawberry capital of Britain" (JM); its farms also feature sugar beet production; the seat previous knew only two MPs since '34; Fred Bellenger held it for half that span; Joe Ashton retired after 33 years in '01 in the wake of unflattering tabloid press attention to a raid on a 'massage parlour';
Position: Ex: Labour Party Liaison Officer based at Millbank '95-00; Lambeth Borough Councillor '86-90;
Outlook: "An ambitious apparatchik" (Michael White, GUARDIAN) with a long loyal record of fighting the Left; "a veteran opponent of Militant and other forces to their Left" (Heffernan and Marqusee); a former youthful anti-Marketeer who has become an avid Europhile and advocate of enlargement to exercise joint resistance to "the growth of multinational companies" and to simplify trading for his family export company; a very talkative former Millbank-based union fixer who stalked a safe Labour seat on Joe Ashton's retirement;
History: He was born into a Leeds family active in Labour politics since 1901; "at the age of 11 I made my first political speech" "on the reform of the Common Agricultural Policy and what I saw as the scandal of the European Community and the way in which it was bleeding this country dry" '71; he joined the Labour Party at 14, '74; in the National Association of Labour Students he was an "anti-Left machinator" (RED PEPPER); "I was in Poland in 1980 in the month when Solidarity was formed; in 1983 I was thrown out of Czechoslovakia"; "I was in Hungary, meeting autonomous trade union organisations and what were then described as dissident groups"; elected to Lambeth Council in '86, he again became an "anti-Left machinator" (RED PEPPER); in Millbank, as Liaison Officer for the trade unions, he was also responsible for ensuring more female Labour candidates from '95; contested Midlands East in European Parliament election May '99; he intensively canvassed Labour members in Bassetlaw, resisting his AEEU's pressure to switch his energies to succeeding Tony Benn at Chesterfield; he was selected, winning 191 votes in preference to 50 for Blairite adviser Andrew Hood, 11 for Asian barrister Yasmin Qureshi, and 14 for Joe Ashton's daughter Lucy Ashton, but was booed "by a small minority" (JM) after allegations about alleged postal vote irregularities, a third of the membership having voted by postal ballot May '00; he retained the seat with an almost-halved 9,748 majority; a 13% cut in turnout helped produce a 5.7% pro-Tory swing June '01; despite this, he claimed in his Maiden speech that local farmers had removed the blue Tory posters from their fields; he also mocked Lord Hattersley's threatened anti-Blair rebellion and urged building on the brownfield sites offered by closed collieries; he boasted of his constituency's strawberry fields and its American tourist potential as "the home of the Pilgrim fathers" June '01; in a letter to the GUARDIAN he complained that "I, with other new MPs, have neither offices nor computers as yet; I have, however, been given a place to hang my sword" June '01; in the debate on the European Communities (Finance) Bill he worried about his local sugar beet industry and urged that "we carefully monitor the role of the large sugar-cane barons so that they do not get hold of the industry world-wide and destroy

Copyright (C)Parliamentary Profile Services Ltd

John MANN *New MPs of '01*

British sugar production; in my constituency that would be a disaster"; he backed a strong push for EU enlargement July '01; he urged a much improved transport infrastructure for the East Midlands, including linking it with a national rail freight network, opening an airport, extending the A1M to Newark, getting rid of most road humps and freeing the A1 of cyclists ("I want to take cyclists off the A1 and put them somewhere safe for them and for motorists") July '01; he urged more sports coaches in schools throughout the country July '01; he insisted that none of his constituents were interested in Jo Moore and that the only reason the "grey mouse" now leading the Tories was interested in a "witch hunt" was to cover the collapse of Railtrack Oct '01; he again enthused about boosted status for local Finningley Airport which "can take both long-haul and freight away from London" Oct '01; as "part-owner of a family micro-business" he could not understand complaints about unnecessary burdens; the minimum wage was an overdue improvement and the linkage with the employer of the working families tax credit was "coherent and sensible" Nov '01;
Born: 10 January 1960, Leeds
Family: "My forefathers came from Epworth; they were saddlers and contemporaries of John Wesley" (JM); son, of James Mann, self-employed, and Brenda (Cleavin); m '85 Joanna (White), "a businesswoman, an occasional lorry driver, and an exporter to Europe" (JM); 1s Aidan; 2d: Rachel, Heather;
Education: Swinnow County Primary; Waterloo County Junior School, Leeds; Bradford Grammar School (on a county scholarship); Manchester University (BA Econ '82);
Occupation: "Small businessman"(JM) as Director of Abraxas Communications involved in translation and, with his wife, in European trade: "last year, our business sent a lorry to Hungary"; "one can overcome...obstacles and cope with the costs to reach the border of Hungary, where one has to spend 24 hours on the way in and another 24 hours on the way out waiting for the bureaucracy of a non-EU country to allow us to trade" '98-; ex: National Trade Union and Labour Party Officer '95-00, National Training Officer TUC ("I taught industrial relations and negotiating skills in this country and across Europe") '90-95; Head of Research and Education, AEEU '85-90 (GMB and AEEU '85-; Author, 'Labour Youth: The Missing Generation' (Fabian Society 1986);
Traits: Full-faced; specs; has a whimsical-bombastic speaking style; an "unpleasant Rightwing thug with no imagination and an extremely nasty temper" (an "old friend" quoted in RED PEPPER); in contrast to Joe Ashton's enthusiasm for Sheffield Wednesday, "my own preference is for the Tigers, Worksop Town";
Address: House of Commons, Westminster, London SW1A 0AA; 68a Carlton Road, Worksop S80 1PH (constituency);
Telephone: 0207 219 8130 (H of C); 01909 506200 (constituency);

LAW OF UNEVEN DEVELOPMENT

One cannot impose pure egalitarian standards on MPs' profiles. One MP's file will be anorexia-slim, another's as overstuffed as that of former MP Sir Cyril Smith. This is not merely a difference of talent or attainment. A rent-a-quote backbencher with a flow of vivid views can mop up more publicity than a squad of Parliamentary Secretaries answering boring questions with more boring answers. Some MPs retire from controversy into being chairmen of committees. Others go into the Whips' Office, where they tear off strips in private. These strain our effort at equal treatment.

Rob(ert Howard) MARRIS   Labour   WOLVERHAMPTON SOUTH WEST '01-

Majority: 3,487 (8.5%) over Conservative 5-way;
Description: Although "in the industrial heart of the West Midlands" (RM) this was seen until '97 as Wolverhamton's safe Conservative seat, because of its association with Enoch Powell '50-74 and his acolyte Nicholas Budgen '74-97; until then its midtown Labour-voting fifth of non-whites were counter-balanced by the Tory-leaning middle-class residential wards on its periphery; Jenny Jones, who ended 47 years of Tory control in '97, decided to pack it in after just four years;
Position: In Foundation for Conductive Education '90-;
Outlook: A "sympathetic idealist", "socially-concerned" (Lord Rees-Mogg, TIMES); an environmentally-motivated hometown solicitor who opposes the death penalty; one of eight public school products in Labour's '01 intake, he worked his way through university in Canada; he is unusual in coming up through neither the municipal nor union routes and without any previous campaign experience; coming from "the industrial heartland of the West Midlands", he acknowledges that most jobs in Wolverhampton depend on manufacturing directly or indirectly; his legal work has made him a "leading expert on the industrial disease of vibration white finger" (Lord Rees-Mogg, TIMES); one of his heroes is Alan Turing, the wartime codecracker who pioneered the computer;
History: He joined Canada's New Democratic Party '79, Greenpeace '81, the Labour Party '84, the TGWU '85; he was selected to replace disillusioned one-term Labour MP Jenny Jones Apr '00; retained the seat with a 3,487 majority on a 1% swing to the Conservatives after a 12% drop in turnout June '01; he voted against the Labour Government over the composition of Select Committees June '01; in his Maiden speech he attacked as "a major evil" "the indiscriminate peddling of weaponry around the world", urging "strict controls on the export of military equipment and know-how"; "there must be no export of items for repression"; he called for the tightening up of part of the Export Control Bill which the Government had finally introduced three years after the Scott Report which had underlined the inadequacies of the existing 1939 controls July '01; he supported moves to prevent the takeover of the Wolverhamptgon and Dudley Brewery because "the Park brewery is in my constituency" and produced ales approved of by the Campaign for Real Ale July '01;
Born: 8 April 1955, Wolverhampton
Family: Son, of Dr Charles Marris, consultant radiologist, and Margaret Chetwode (Crawley) JP; his Partner since '84 is Julia (Pursehouse);
Education: St Edward's School, Oxford; University of British Columbia, Canada (Sociology and History, Double First BA '76, MA in History '79); Birmingham Polytechnic (CPE '83, LSF '84);
Occupation: Solicitor '87-: Thompson's '88-; Articled Clerk, with Manby & Steward '87-88; ex: Bus Driver, in Canada '79-82; Trucker, in Canada '77-79; Labourer, for Walter Derkaz & Co '75; Firefighter, in British Columbia Forestry Service '74;
Traits: A mop of curly parted dark hair; specs; "serious-minded, likeable;" (Lord Rees-Mogg, TIMES); "I may not be as big a beer-drinker as...the Member for Wolverhampton South East (Dennis Turner) - few people are - but I do drink beer"; describes himself as "well-versed in matters Canadian" (RM);

Rob(ert Howard) MARRIS *New MPs of '01*

Address: House of Common, Westminster, London SW1A 0AA; 1 Meadow Street, Wolverhampton WV1 4NZ;
Telephone: 0207 219 3000 (H of C);

John (William) MacDOUGALL   Labour   **FIFE CENTRAL '01-**

Majority: 10,075 (31%) over SNP 5-way;
Description: A seat centred on the new town of Glenrothes, excluding the old Fife coalfield; it includes the industrial ports of Buckhaven and Methil; in '97 one in five families had no working member; until '87 it was the base of the Rightwing anti-monarchist Labour MP Willie Hamilton who was replaced by Henry McLeish, who withdrew in '01 to devote himself to the Scottish Parliament as its new First Secretary;
Position: Fife Councillor (Convenor of the Council '96-01) 96-01; Fife Regional Councillor (Leader '87-96) '82-96; Vice Chairman, St Andrews Links Trust '98-; ex: Leader of Controlling Group of CoSLA '91-92; Chairman, East of Scotland European Consortium '93-96; on Scottish Broadcasting Authority '93-96; in Scottish Constitutional Convention; Bureau Member, Assembly of the European Regions '92; Political Education Officer, Kirkcaldy CLP '82-84; Chairman, Burntisland Labour Party Branch '83-85; JP;
Outlook: A low-profiled big-wig local government leader with working class credentials who inherited a safe seat from the withdrawal-to-Holyrood of former Scottish First Secretary ('00-01) Henry McLeish; as a former boilermaker and GMB Convenor of shop stewards in the Methil oil rig yard, he has a long involvement in fighting to save jobs in the area's main industrial site at Rosyth dockyard; he also set up the Fife Race Equality Group and East of Scotland European Consortium;
History: He was born into "an ordinary working-class family" (JMacD); was elected to Fife Regional Council May '82; became Leader of the Council May '87; became Chairman of its Policy and Resources Committee '89; was elected to its successor, Fife Council, of which he was elected Convenor Apr '96; he beat former Scottish Labour Party Secretary Alex Rowley for selection for Fife Central on the departure of Henry McLeish to the Scottish Parliament May '00; he easily retained the seat with his 10,075 majority, 3,000 down on a 15% cut in turnout and a 1.3% swing to the SNP June '01;
Born: 8 December 1947, Dunfermline
Family: Grandson of a farmer; son of William MacDougall, process worker, and Barbara (Lyons); married; 2 grown-up children;
Education: Templehall Secondary Modern School, Kirkcaldy; Rosyth RN Dockyard College; Fife College (Certificate in Industrial Management); Glenrothes College (Diploma in Industrial Management);
Occupation: Director, Fife Enterprise Ltd; Alternate Director, East Neuk Ltd: Councillor (full-time) '87-01; ex: Boilermaker and fulltime Shop Steward; Convenor of Shop Stewards, Methil Oil Rig Yard, '78-80 (GMBU); on GMBU's Forth District Committee;
Traits: Parted dark hair; heart-shaped face; broad forehead;
Address: House of Commons, Westminster, London SW1A 0AA; 36 Croft Crescent,

Markinch, Fife KY7 6E (constituency); Fife Council, Fife House, North Street, Glenrothes, Fife KY7 5LT;
Telephone: 0207 219 3000 (H of C); 01592 712204 (constituency); 01592 416209/413413 Fax;

Ann McKECHIN   **Labour**   **GLASGOW-MARYHILL '01-**

Majority: 9,888 (44.5%) over SNP 5-way;
Description: The northern half of the abolished Kelvingrove seat plus the old Maryhill constituency in north Glasgow; it has many council estates; in '93 it acquired an extra 5,000 voters from Springburn; mostly working-class; it formerly had flourishing mining, glass, chemical and engineering industries; it is now the site of the West of Scotland Science Park; her predecessor, Maria Fyfe, served '87-01 as an independent Leftwing voice of working women;
Position: On Select Committee on Information '01-; Scottish Representative of World Development Movement '98-; ex: Women's Officer '00-01, Constituency Secretary '95-98, Kelvin CLP;
Outlook: Radical solicitor in Scotland's Muir Society of Leftwing lawyers and international development campaigner, anxious to reform world trade, particularly to curb the arms trade; on Board of Jubilee Scotland, campaigning for international debt relief; one of four incoming new women Labour MPs partly replacing nine women retired or defeated in '01;
History: From a standard West-of-Scotland Catholic Labour background she joined the party at 30 in '91; she was elected Constituency Secretary of Glasgow-Kelvin CLP '95; she was a candidate on the West of Scotland list for the Scottish Parliament election June '99; she was selected for Maryhill to succeed Maria Fyfe, who retired belatedly, from an NEC-imposed all-women short-list, following criticism of Labour's failure to select women in safe seats since the legally-imposed discontinuance in '96 of all-women short-lists; there were complaints that no local women had been short-listed Mar '01; she retained the seat for Labour with a 9,888 majority, 4,000 down from an almost 17% drop in turnout, producing a 1.8% swing to the SNP June '01; in her Maiden speech, which was better understood than her predecessor's local dialect, she loyally welcomed progress in cutting local employment but urged more social justice, particularly for the 3rd World June '01; she asked a prompted question about the quinquennial review of the Defence Intelligence and Security Centre Defence Agency July '01; she was named to the Information Select Committee July '01; she strongly supported the Government's International Development Bill because it was "poverty-focused" Nov '01;
Born: 22 April 1961, Renfrewshire
Family: Daughter of William McKechin, lecturer and Labour councillor '61-78, and Anne, school librarian and NALGO shop steward;
Education: Sacred Heart High School, Paisley '73-75; Paisley Grammar School '75-78; Strathclyde University (LLB in Scottish Law, Diploma in Legal Practice) '78-82;
Occupation: Solicitor '83-; in Pacitti Jones, Glasgow (Partner '90-00) '86-00;
Traits: Dark bobbed hair; pallid complexion; classic Glaswegian features; enjoys dancing, films, art history; she expected to attend her "first-ever football match" at the local grounds of "Glasgow's best-loved football team - Partick Thistle, of course - which [in '01] not only

celebrated its 125th anniversary but succeeded in winning promotion to the First Division";
Address: House of Commons, Westminster, London SW1A 0AA; John Smith House, West Regent Street, Glasgow G2 4RE (constituency); 5 Loudon Terrace, Downhill, Glasgow G12 9AQl
Telephone: 0207 219 3000 (H of C); 0141 572 6900; 0141 334 118; amcketchin@msn.com;

Colonel Patrick (John) MERCER OBE   Conservative   NEWARK '01-

Majority: 4,073 (9%) over Labour 5-way;
Description: A Nottinghamshire seat of twin market towns, Newark and Southwell, with its Minster, on the A1 trunk road; beseiged several times by Parliamentary forces in the Civil War, it was the first seat of the then-Tory William Gladstone; its passing into Conservative hands in '79 was further buttressed by its loss of mining communities in '83; in '97 it fell to Labour but its new MP, Fiona Jones, was soon troubled with allegations of over-spending on poll expenses and alienated many local activists;
Position: On the Defence Select Committee '01-;
Outlook: A Eurosceptic former professional Army officer who is a strong opponent of the European Rapid Reaction Force: "I do no not believe in it; I do not consider it feasible, and I do not think that it is needed"; for 25 years he served in the locally-recruited Nottinghamshire Regiment, the Sherwood Foresters, enabling him to meet old soldiers on the doorstep; the son of the former Bishop of Exeter, he captured a churchy seat, assisted by dissension within local Labour ranks and the rocky career of his precedecessor, Labour MP Fiona Jones; she was expelled from the House then reinstated when she won an appeal against a conviction for exceeding election spending limits; he reacts strongly against Army over-stretch as a result of its undermanning; he made "an important contribution to Army recruitment in his previous role in the Army Training and Recruiting Agency" (Defence Minister Adam Ingram);
History: He joined the Conservative Party in '77, but was not able to be active under Queen's Regulations until discharged from the Army in '99; he then made up for lost time while the BBC Defence Correspondent by trying for various seats; he was runner-up at Leominster Mar '99; was short-listed for a possible Newark by-election Apr '99; he assisted the Tories in the North Shropshire local election and Euro-election Apr, June '99; was short-listed for the Eddisbury by-election July '99; he was selected for Newark '99; the DAILY TELEGRAPH listed him as Eurosceptic Sept '00; he was elected for Newark - one of only eight Conservative seat gains in '01 - with a 4,073 majority on a 7.4% anti-Labour swing June '01; voted for the Eurosceptic Rightwinger Iain Duncan Smith in the Leadership ballots July '01; in his Maiden speech he attacked the Government's policy of taking on more responsibilities than its over-stretched and under-manned forces could handle; the Army's shortage of 5,000 men made it incapable of providing enough forces for Kosovo, Northern Ireland and the European Rapid Reaction Force; "we do not have enough combat pilots to pilot aircraft off the two proposed new aircraft carriers" June '01; insisted that "soldiers [previously] detached from regiments contribute disproportionately to the number of civilians who come forward for enlistment" July '01; emphasised that "the European Rapid Reaction Force will not add a single ounce to Europe's combat power; not a single extra gun, tank, bayonet, aircraft or ship

will be added to the strength; the proposals deal with headquarters, communications and sappers only, not with anything directly involved in fighting" July '01; he intervened in the speech of Northern Ireland hard-liner Jeff Donaldson to point out that "to my certain knowledge a policy has been in place in Ulster for the past 10 years for the British Army to step further and further back and for the RUC to move forward; if troops are deployed almost at the first sign of serious violence, it suggests that police numbers are woefully inadequate" July '01; he ridiculed the "safety culture" increasing in the Army over things like the health effects as the impact of barking dogs on soldiers' hearing July '01; he was named to the Defence Select Committee July '01; he was one of 14 new Tory MPs who together wrote to the DAILY TELEGRAPH endorsing Iain Duncan Smith as a Leader who "can unite the party on Europe" Aug '01; in the second recall of Parliament he made a mournful speech about the incapacity of the over-stretched Armed Forces to meet the terrorist threat Oct '01; in the debate on Afghanistan, he predicted the next stage would involve the use of helicopters from ground-troop-defended forward bases in the country Oct '01; he urged the anti-terrorist campaign be used to increase recruitment Oct '01; he urged photographic identity cards to avoid the electoral fraud at polling booths which he had patrolled in all his nine Ulster tours of duty Oct '01; he urged a UK commitment of a brigade in Afghanistan, instead of the 200 men - "a rifle company" - already promised Nov '01;
Born: 26 June 1956, Stockport, Cheshire
Family: Son, of Rt Rev Eric Mercer, former Bishop of Exeter, and Rosemary (Denby); m '90 Catriona Jane (Beaton), marketeer for HP Bulmer, Hereford; 1s Rupert John Holisey '91;
Education: King's School, Chester; Exeter College, Oxford University (MA, 2/1 in Modern History, Boxing Blue); Staff College (PSC '88);
Occupation: Co-Director, of specialist travel firm '99-; Journalist (free-lance) '99-; Author: Inkermann: The Soldier's Battle; Give Then A Volley And Charge; ex: Defence Correspondent of the BBC '99; Regular Army Officer in the Nottinghamshire Regiment's Sherwood Foresters '74-99: commanded the Sherwood Foresters in Bosnia and Canada '95-97; served nine tours of duty in Northern Ireland; OBE (Bosnia) '97, MBE (Northern Ireland) '93; Gallantry Commendation, Northern Ireland '90, Mentioned in Despatches, Northern Ireland '82; retired as a Colonel;
Traits: Dark parted greying thin hair; heavy eyebrows; pallid grey complexion; pursed mouth; dimpled chin; soldierly mien; small neat handwriting; enjoys painting and shooting;
Address: House of Commons, Westminster, London SW1A 0AA; Belvedere, 29a London Road, Newark, Notts NG24 1T<0E>N
Telephone: 0207 219 3000 (H of C); 01636 703269 also Fax (constituency); patrick@mercer95.fsnet.co.uk;

KEEPING PARLIAMENTARY SECRETS
A rueful MP claimed, with some truth, that the best way to keep something secret is to make a speech about it in the Palace of Westminster. He was commenting on the emptiness of the Press Gallery (except for HANSARD writers and the Press Association). Long gone are the days when serious newspapers carried a full or half-page summarising Parliamentary debate. Of late, Westminster has been used as a source of news stories. In our old-fashioned way, we read HANSARD daily and watch the Commons and Lords on the Parliamentary Channel. Parliamentary debaters are very self-revealing in debate. And we don't mean only Kerry Pollard MP, in whose Maiden he disclosed that until 12 he had to drop his trousers regularly to prove that Kerry was not a girl's name.

David (Wright) MILIBAND   **Labour**   **SOUTH SHIELDS '01-**

Majority: 14,090 (46.3%) over Tory 5-way;
Description: The shipbuilding town at the mouth of the Tyne, with a sideline as a North Sea seaside resort; safely Labour since 1935, its longest-sitting MP was Mr Attlee's Home Secretary, Chuter Ede, who also sat on Surrey County Council; its Labour loyalties were reinforced by 5,700 voters from Jarrow in '95; it was put on the map politically in '01 as the site of the shoe-horning out of previously-sacked Cabinet Minister David (now Lord) Clark and the parachuting-in of Downing Street's most senior policy adviser, David Miliband;
Position: On EU group on future of Europe chaired by the Prime Minister of Belgium '01; ex: Head of the Prime Minister's Policy Unit '98-01;
Outlook: Tony Blair's former righthand manifesto-writing man who has pledged himself to give his battered constituents "the full benefit of the policies in that manifesto"; the highest-flying of a clutch of policy insiders to emerge, mostly close to the election, from the inner portals of power to inherit safe seats; said to be close to both Tony Blair and - through his brother Ed - Gordon Brown; he is the modernising son of the late Marxist academic Ralph Miliband; is credited with conceiving the term 'stakeholding'; author/drafter of the '97 and '01 Labour manifestos; his deft inheritance of willing South Shields on the eve of the campaign, contrasted to the unpopular simultaneous painful insertion of the floor-crossing Shaun Woodward at St Helens South; reportedly enjoyed working for the Prime Minister, but after masterminding his second manifesto he felt "a sense of closure" (Valerie Grove, TIMES);
History: Reared in an academic Marxist setting, he joined the Labour Party '87; he became Secretary of the Commission on Social Justice '92; he was appointed Head of Policy in the office of the new Leader, Tony Blair '94; co-drafted the election manifesto Apr '97; transferred to No 10 Policy Unit May '97; drafted the manifesto '01; was selected for South Shields, from an NEC-imposed short-list, in place of its retiring-for-a-peerage incumbent David Clark, helped by self-cancelling rivalries of local aspirants, and by his own rapid three-day mugging-up on the constituency; he won selection by 184 votes to 35 for Andrew Howard, who had stood in the Romsey by-election May '01; was elected with a 14,090 majority, 8,000 down, on a 13% drop in turnout, producing a pro-Tory swing of 5.3% June '01; he was appointed to an EU panel preparing the next major EU treaty, a post allegedly destined for Peter Mandelson June '01; in his outstanding Maiden speech, he disclosed that a predecessor as MP for South Shields, Chuter Ede, had, when Clement Attlee's Home Secretary, initially refused his Jewish grandfather Samuel the right to continue to reside in Britain or to bring over his wife and daughter, who had survived in Nazi-occupied Belgium; his son, Ralph, David's own father, had been given leave to stay and had served in the Royal Navy; the main theme of his speech was his commitment to unemployment-battered South Shields to enable it to "receive the full benefit" of the opportunities promised in the manifesto he had written for the Prime MInister June '01; he backed a campaign to inquire into deep vein thrombosis on long-distance flights Aug '01; with the experience of having participated "in a group chaired by the Belgian Prime Minister...considering...the future of Europe" he judged the Bill to ratify the Nice Agreement as one that "sorts out some thorny questions that could block progress on the big issues if they are not dealt with" Oct '01;

New MPs of '01 *David (Wright) MILIBAND*

Born: 15 July 1965, London
Family: His Polish-born grandfather, Samuel Milliband, spent the war years in Britain, but was initially refused the right to stay or bring over his wife and daughter from Belgium by Chuter Ede, the MP for South Shields and Attlee's Home Secretary; son, of Marion (Kozak) and the late, Belgian-born Ralph Miliband, former Professor of Politics at Leeds University and Brandeis University, USA, and previously Lecturer at LSE and author of Parliamentary Socialism, a book berating Labour Governments for not being "socialist"; he says of his Marxist father: "We had different political views, but people are products of their time; he knew I was on the right side of the fence"; m '98 Louise (Shackleton), violinist; his brother Ed Miliband is an adviser to Gordon Brown at the Treasury;
Education: Haverstock Comprehensive, London (Oona King was a contemporary); Corpus Christi College, Oxford University (BA, 1st in PPE); Massachusetts Institute of Technology (Kennedy Scholar; MSc, in Political Science);
Occupation: Author: Re-inventing The Left (1994); Paying For Inequality: The Economic Cost Of Social Injustice (1994); ex: Head of Prime Minister's Policy Unit '98-01; Director of PM's Policy Unit '97-98; Head of Policy, Office of Leader of the Opposition '94-97; Secretary, Commission on Social Justice '92-94; Research Fellow, IPPR '89-94;
Traits: Tall; dark; short hair; specs; very boyish-looking; was once compared to Donny Osmond in appearance; "his fingers tend to do that spider-doing-press-ups-on-a-mirror thing clever people do" (Simon Carr, INDEPENDENT); South Shields Labour activists' descriptions include: "very, very tall"; "very young - doesn't shave yet - but very sharp, very bright"; "he's humble, lovely manners"; "very sincere"; first-class objective mind; "Brains" (his No 10 nickname); Polish Jewish family background, with his grandfather arriving in Britain via Belgium in '40; supports Arsenal but has become President of South Shields FC;
Address: House of Common, Westminster, London SW1A 0AAl
Telephone: 0207 219 3000 (H of C);

Andrew (John Bower) MITCHELL   Conservative   **999]|SUTTON COLDFIELD '01-**

Majority: 10,104 (23.3%) over Labour 5-way;
Description: Conservative since '45, this 'royal town' was the Tories' 3rd safest seat in '97, after Huntingdon and Surrey Heath; it is Birmingham's prosperous middle-class dormitory area - 84% owner-occupied - surrounding pleasant, leafy, 2,000-acre Sutton Park; it was previously the safe base for Sir Norman Fowler '74-01;
Former Seat: Gedling '87-97
Position: Ex: Under Secretary for Social Security '95-97; Lord Commissioner/Whip '94-95; Assistant Whip '92-94; Vice Chairman of the Conservative Party (Candidates) '92-93; PPS to John Wakeham '90-92, to William Waldegrave '88-90; Secretary, British-East African Parliamentary Group '87-97?; Chairman, Coningsby Club (Conservative graduates) '83-??; Secretary, One Nation Group '89-??; ex: Vice President and Chairman, Islington North Conservative Association '83-85; Chairman, Cambridge University Conservative Association '77; on Islington Health Authority '85-87;

Copyright (C)Parliamentary Profile Services Ltd

Andrew (John Bower) MITCHELL

Outlook: A pragmatic Eurosceptic who managed to vault from Eurosceptic David Davis's bandwagon to that of Ken Clarke in the '01 Leadsership stakes; he did this with two other relocated retreads from John Major's Whips' Office, Derek Conway and Greg Knight; it was Greg Knight, as Deputy Chief Whip, who assigned him as the first Whip on the Members' Interests Select Committee where Labour MPs claimed he tried to cover up Neil Hamilton's stay at al-Fayed's Ritz Hotel, Paris, a charge rejected by the Privileges Committee; "the most overtly ambitious man I know" (Cambridge contemporary); "almost crazy with ambition" (Giles Brandreth, Tory ex-Whip); his political ambitions are such that he risked five well-paid City jobs and the humiliations of six selection defeats to make his comeback; a happy retread who has moved from a lost marginal, Gedling, to the Tories' 28th safest seat; a smooth, bright, young, assiduous climber with all the right connections; although he promised to "follow that rocky path...between toadyism and revolt," has tended to the first; a superloyalist but not overly partisan; an able witty debater with an over-flattering style who seconded the Queen's Speech '92;; pro: hanging, competitive tendering (in the NHS), privatisation of coal and BR, "right to buy", rate-capping; as a doctor's husband "I am a passionate and devoted supporter of the Health Service" with an internal market;

History: He comes from a well-to-do Conservative political family: his father, Sir David Mitchell, was a Tory MP and Minister and he has two 18th century MP-ancestors; a Selsdon-type Tory at Rugby at 14, he was defeated by the Somerset Cider Drinkers Party '70; he joined the Conservatives at 16, '72; was an undergraduate Tory activist, becoming Chairman of Cambridge University Conservative Association '77; at annual conference urged Lords reform Oct '77; became President of the Cambridge Union '78; contested Islington Borough elections May '82; in his first Parliamentary candidacy made an unimpressive showing in Sunderland South, polling 34.6%, as against 37.6% for Tories in May '79, June '83; as Chairman of Islington Conservatives, argued for ratecapping and enforced disposal for non-productive local authority assets '83-85; as the only Tory on Islington Health Authority urged competitive tendering '85-87; was selected for then safe Gedling in succession to Sir Philip Holland July '85, was elected with a 16,539 majority June '87; in his Maiden complained there was too little job mobility because of lack of private rented accommodation and immobility within the council housing system July '87; enthused about fall in unemployment Nov '87; suggested merger of four NHS areas in London as a step toward needed efficiency through an internal market Nov '87; opposed David Alton's abortion-curbing Bill Jan '88; voted against televising the Commons Feb '88; visited Hartford, Connecticut, to study health insurance as guest of Crusader Insurance Feb '88; urged an "internal market" in NHS to funnel work to most efficient Mar '88; rejoiced in increased productivity of Gedling colliery Mar '88; enthused about usefulness of privately-sponsored Nottinghamshire Development Enterprise to energise and market the area Mar '88; criticised decision to display bust of Parnell as "sad and provocative" Apr '88; in Granada TV interview favoured restoration of hanging Apr '88; welcomed separate taxation of married women May '88; welcomed new British Library July '88; was named PPS to William Waldegrave Aug '88; backed privatisation of BR Nov '88; loyally enthused about Government's Security Service Bill Dec '88; co-sponsored Andrew MacKay's Sunday Sports Bill Dec '88; asked a stooge question on NHS reform Jan '89; was found to have been one of the most assiduous committee attenders of the '87-88 session Apr '89; with Alan Meale co-hosted a press conference calling for stronger badger-protection laws June '89; visited Hongkong as guest of Hongkong Government Sep '89; visited Italy as guest of Konrad Adenauer Foundation Sep '89; expressed disappointment that Environment Protection Bill did not hit harder at graffiti Nov '89; enthused about NHS reforms Bill, asking to serve on its standing committee Nov '89; voted against Associated British Ports (No 2) Bill, fearing coal imports threatened Gedling's last mine Nov '89; backed Government's Coal

Industry Bill as a carrot-and-stick that might keep alive his constituency's last, marginal coal mine, Gedling Colliery Dec '89; spoke up for public support for constituent receiving conductive education at Peto Institute in Budapest Dec '89; presented a Bill to amend the law governing public exhibition by performing animals Jan '90; backed trading fund status for Land Registry, Companies House, Driving and Vehicle Licensing Centre Jan '90; was named PPS to John Wakeham Jan '90; in filibuster complimented Government on its Social Security upratings, praising changes already debated Feb '90; secured amendment enabling Audit Commission to review Ministerial decisions Feb '90; supported Graham Bright's Bill to curb acid house parties Mar '90; fed Mrs Thatcher questions about Militant-led "disgraceful and dangerous scenes in our council chambers", urging her to "utterly condemn" Labour MPs who refused to pay their poll tax Mar '90; on the resignation of Margaret Thatcher, Mitchell's joining the bandwagon for Thatcher-backed John Major was seen as significant, since he was rated a "Centrist" (INDEPENDENT) as Secretary of the One Nation Group Nov '90; he enthused about the Audit Commission Jan '91; he urged restraint on the national tabloids in their handling of bereaved relatives of Gulf War casualties Jan '91; he cited the "horrific" happenings in local government in Lambeth as giving "some indication of what a Labour Government would be like" Jan '91; Conservative Party Chairman Chris Patten named him Chairman of the Conservative Collegiate Forum of Conservative students Feb '91; he launched a 10-minute-rule Bill to compel further and higher education establishments to make examination results available for publication Mar '91; he urged more competition in the telecommunications industry Mar '91; he enthused about PM John Major's 'Citizens' Charter' Mar '91; he urged persuading the US to bring pressure via China on the brutal impoverishing Burmese military regime June '91; he, Simon Burns, Jacques Arnold and James Paice were accosted in the Members' Lobby as "fucking Tories" by Labour's extrovert John Prescott Nov '91; he insisted its "deep and difficult recession" was not "made in Britain" but also affected Germany Feb '92; he was re-elected by a reduced majority of 10,637 over Vernon Coaker Apr '92; in wittily seconding the Loyal Address, he was reassured by a colleague that this task was normally done by "an oily young man on the make" May '92; he was named Vice Chairman of the Conservative Party in charge of unearthing plausible candidates June '92; he complained that he had lost his last pit because gas was priced too low Oct '92 he was promoted an Assistant Whip, saying he would be sorry to leave Central Office and end his consultancy with Lazards Dec '92; as a new Whip he erred in not objecting when Labour called for the House to be adjourned in the midst of turmoil on the Maastricht Bill, losing a day's debate Feb '93; he visited Estonia as a guest of the Konrad Adenauer Foundation Sep '93; he voted to restore capital punishment Feb '94; Deputy Chief Whip Greg Knight named him as the first-ever Whip to serve on the Members' Interests Select Committee June '94; he was promoted a full Government Whip, or Lord Commissioner July '94; on the Members' Interest Select Committee he argued against a full inquiry into Neil Hamilton's stay at al-Fayed's Ritz Hotel in Paris; with the support of its Tory Chairman - who had received an undisclosed dossier from al-Fayed; a full inquiry was blocked Oct '94; Mitchell sent a later-disclosed letter to his Chief Whip Richard Ryder about his investigations in the wake of an INDEPENDENT article about Neil Hamilton's failure to register in the MPs' Register of Interests his links with Strategy Network International, a front for South African intelligence, as well as his stay at al-Fayed's Paris Ritz Hotel; he reported that the Registrar told him that "in normal times" the supervising committee would take "a relaxed view", which Mitchell judged "not very helpful I'm afraid" Oct '94; Labour MPs threatened to boycott the Members' Interests committee if he continued as a member May '95; named Under Secretary for Social Security, he was released from the Members' Interests Select Committee July '95; his constituency party was accused of having accepted a £5,000 contribution from the local Home Brewery which was threatening to sack his constituents Sep '95; he announced that the Child Support Agency would begin paying interest on late payments to lone parents caring for children Mar '96; he welcomed "clear and significant" improvements in the workings of the Child Support Agency Apr '96; he voted against a Labour amendment to the Family Law Bill allowing equal rights for divorcing wives to their husbands' pension funds June '96; he said that, instead of emulating the Australian JET model of offering training, as the Labour Opposition suggested, it was better to draw on the "work first" experiments in California, both of which he had visited June '96; he voted loyally to cap MPs' pay rise at 3% July '96; Labour MP Dale Campbell-Savours used Mitchell's belatedly-discovered Ryder letter of Oct '94 to demonstrate that Mitchell was using his "privileged position" to try to manipulate a "quasi-judicial" Commons select committee to curb investigations of Neil Hamilton Nov '96; the SUNDAY EXPRESS accused him of using his Government chauffeur and car to drop off his two daughters at their £4,800-a-year Clerkenwell school Dec '96; in the wake of David Willetts' resignation as Paymaster General a month before for having "dissembled" about his Whips' activities on the Members' Interests Committee, Mitchell was called before the Standards and Privileges Committee, the first MP compelled to testify on oath; he insisted that he had behaved honourably and had "compartmentalised" his activities, sometimes acting as the MP for Gedling, sometimes as a Tory Whip trying to postpone a full inquiry into Neil Hamilton's acceptance of presents and money from al-Fayed; he said that perhaps it would have been better not to appoint Whips to a quasi-judicial select committee Jan '97; his assurances were accepted Feb '97; he predicted that the Tory Cabinet's backing for a Family Benefits Guarantee to rise with inflation was "likely to split the Labour Party" Mar '97; he lost his once-safe Gedling seat by a 3,802 majority for Labour's Vernon Coaker on a 13% pro-Labour swing May '97; he said losing Gedling was like "being dumped by your first girl-friend" but compensated for his loss by five new City jobs: based again at investment bank Lazards, he advised Boots, Anderson Consulting and Financial Dynamics Apr '98; he was excluded as "too moderate" by Rightwing Europhobes from the Thatcherite 'Conservative Way Forward' when the selectors of safe Cities of London & Westminster chose Peter Brooke's successor; he "was put on the list of 15 interviewees at the last minute and only with great reluctance" (James Landale, TIMES); selection went to Mark Field Nov '99; he was "unexpectedly defeated" (Michael White, GUARDIAN) for selection for Faversham by Hugh Robertson, a local candidate Mar '00; he was expected to try for ultrasafe Huntingdon, vacated by John Major, but it went to John Djanogly Apr '00; initially the favourite, he oversold himself as a Eurosceptic to the Tory selectors of Witney; instead David Cameron was chosen for this safe Tory seat abandoned by floor-crosser Shaun Woodward Apr '00; despite Virginia Bottomley's support for his opponent, Sharon Buckle, he was selected finally as the candidate for super-safe Sutton Coldfield in succession to Sir Norman Fowler May '01; he retained Sutton Coldfield by a majority of 10,104, over 4,000 down from Sir Norman's '97 majority, with a 12% cut in turnout June '01; in his "retread Maiden speech", he urged more effective policing and improved delivery by the local NHS June '01; he initially backed fellow-Eurosceptic David Davis in the Tory Leadership stakes but, on his elimination, switched his support to Europhile Ken Clarke, a former fellow Tory MP for Nottinghamshire July '01; he urged a monthly debate on the achievement of NHS targets Nov '01;

Born: 23 March 1956, London
Family: Son, of Sir David Mitchell, Tory MP for NW Hampshire '83-97, Basingstoke '64-83 and wine merchant, and Pamela Elaine (Haward), company director; m '85 Sharon Denise (Bennett), recently an NHS doctor; 2d: Hannah '87, Rosie '90;
Education: Ashdown House Prep, Sussex; Rugby (as Head of House was known as "Thrasher" for his stern discipline); Royal Military Academy, Sandhurst; Jesus College, Cambridge (MA Hons in History); President, Cambridge Union '78;

New MPs of '01   *Andrew (John Bower) MITCHELL*

Occupation: Director '97-, Adviser '87-92, Lazard Brothers (merchant bank; previously executive in international division and Director of a subsidiary '79-87); Director: Financial Dynamics '97-, Commer Group '98-; Senior Strategy Advisor, Anderson Consulting/Accenture '97-; on Supervisor Board, Foundation '99-; ex: Director, Miller Insurance Group '97-01, Senior Strategy Adviser, Boots '97-00; Shareholder: El Vino Company Ltd (family wine import business with Fleet Street wine bar of which he held a significant 9% shareholding) '82-01, LEP Plc (freight forwarders) '89-91, Scope Communications Management Ltd (communications advisers) '88-92, Sedgwick Group '91?-92, Cray Electronics '91-92, Ferrum Holdings '91-92; Adviser: UEI Plc (high tech electronics) '88-89; held short service (limited) commission in First Royal Tank Regiment '75;
Traits: Boyish; bespectacled; parted greying brown hair; "smoothie" with "floppy-haired good looks"; enthusiast with an ingratiating, Polyanna-like approach; "ever keen" (Matthew Parris, TIMES); super-polite in an old-fashioned way; "a somewhat sleek image" (Peter Riddell, FINANCIAL TIMES); "immaculately attired as always" (CrossBencher, SUNDAY EXPRESS); was voted the 'Best Pressed MP'; "an overbearing David Mellor look-alike" (PRIVATE EYE); thinks "people who go into politics do so from a mixture of altruism and egotism...I don't think there's anything wrong with ambition"; "whenever we went for a drink, he always seemed to have left his wallet behind" (Cambridge contemporary); "while he was in the Army his troops named him 'Cornflakes' because of his fondness for the breakfast cereal at all hours' (SUNDAY TELEGRAPH); replies to offensively cranky letters: "some loony crank has written to me impersonating you...I am sure you would like me to report this to the police...";
Address: House of Commons, Westminster, London SW1A 0AA; 36 High street, Sutton Coldfield B72 1UP (constituency); 30 Gibson Square, Islington, London N1 0RD; 8 Tudor Road, Sutton Coldfield; Bingham, Nottinghamshire NG13 8GT;
Telephone: 0207 219 3000 (H of C); 0207 226 5519/5419 Fax (London home); 0121 354 2229 (constituency);

Meg (Margaret Patricia) MUNN   **Labour-Co-operative**   **SHEFFIELD-HEELEY '01-**

Majority: 11,704 (34.3%) over LibDem 6-way;
Description: A safe Labour south Sheffield seat with nearby steel and engineering industries and "the beautiful Derbyshire hills...at [its] southern boundary" (MM); it has much social housing and suffers above-national-average unemployment following steelworks contraction; "we are not proud to live in an area that is among the poorest in Europe" (MM);
Position: On the Select Committees on Procedure '01, Education and Skills '01-; ex: Nottingham City Councillor '87-91; Chairman, Barnsley branch of Co-operative Retail Services '97-01;
Outlook: The experienced former social worker who landed a safe seat in her native heath, replacing hard-Leftist Bill Michie, in her first Parliamentary contest; she is veru much more sympathetic to "a Europe with a social conscience" and wants to end Britain's "half-heartedness" about the EU; an enthusiast for EU pump-priming and successful child adoptions; one of only four new

Copyright (C)Parliamentary Profile Services Ltd   *107*

Meg (Margaret Patricia) MUNN   *New MPs of '01*

women Labour MPs in '01; in the Co-operative Party, GMB, Christian Socialist Movement, Fabians, Amnesty International; on the Management Committee of Wortley Hall, South Yorkshire;

History: She was born into a politically-active family with her father and uncle both Sheffield Labour councillors; "the seat was first won for Labour in 1966, when my father was the election agent" with the slogan Frank "Hooley for Heeley"; in the next election, narrowly lost by Labour, she argued Labour's cause in school and was photographed with her 'Hooley for Heeley' sticker '70; she joined the Labour Party in Heeley at 15, '74; she joined the Co-operative Party '75; "in 1979 I was a student in Strasbourg for a year"; "my newly-elected MEP [Richard Caborn]...made sure that I had two good meals that day" when he arrived there; she contested Bracknell District Council May '83; she was elected to Nottingham City Council May '87; she was short-listed for the South Yorkshire Euro-Parliamentary by-election May '98; she was the first reserve for both the Northeast and Yorkshire & Humberside European lists June '99; she won selection for Heeley in place of retiring Bill Michie, a hard-Left rebel July '00; as one of the very few successful women aspirants to land safe seats she addressed a women-only fringe meeting for women candidates at the Labour Party Conference at Brighton Oct '00; she was elected for Heeley with 11,704 majority, down over 5,000 from Bill Michie's '97 result on a 10% cut in turnout, yielding a 2.6% swing to the LibDems June '01; in her Maiden speech, having had responsibility for making decisions on adoptions for five years, she backed the Adoption and Children Bill: "adoption cannot be viewed merely as substituting one set of parents for another for a child who needs a new family; adopting has lifelong implications for all three sides of the adoption triangle: the birth family, the child and the adoptive family" June '01; in the debate on the European Communities (Amendment) Bill she emerged as a strong pro-European: "for me, developing the European Union further promotes the security and stability that the people of my parents' generation saw as so important to the whole of Europe; enlargement is in our interests"; "it is time we stopped dithering" July '01; she was named to the Procedure and Education and Skills Select Committees July '01; she made a sharp attack on the anti-EU posture of the Tory Opposition, pointing out that they demanded a referencum on the Nice Treaty but resisted one on the Euro; she sneered that ten Tory MPs had signed two amendments to the Bill carrying it into effect but most were not even in the Chamber; "my constituents receive [from the EU] Objective 1 funding"; "we are not proud to live in an area that is among the poorest in Europe; we are extremely concerned about that; I hope that Objective 1 funding will do what it is intended to do - help to lift the people in my constituency and the surrounding area out of that situation" July '01; as a former social worker, she welcomed the advances in early-years education and recommended that local schools should be "regarded as the local family centre" to advise parents Oct '01; backing the Bill to ratify the Nice Agreement, she disclosed "my area of Sheffield in south Yorkshire currently receives [EU] Objective 1 help of £711m to help it recover from 18 years of Conservative Government" Oct '01; in adoption reforms she urged emphasis on the "adoption triangle"; while the adoptee's interests were paramount, those of the adoptive and original families should not be ignored Oct '01;

Born: 24 August 1959, Sheffield

Family: Daughter, of Reg Munn, representative and Sheffield Labour councillor '53-88, and Lillian (Steward), nurse tutor; m '89 Dennis Bates, researcher;

Education: Rowlinson Comprehensive, Sheffield; York University (BA, Languages '81); Nottingham University (MA, Social Work '86); Open University (Certificate and Diploma in Management Studies);

Occupation: Social Worker '86-00: Assistant Director, Children's Services, City of York '99-00; Child Services Manager, Wakefield Metropolitan Council '96-99; District Manager,

New MPs of '01 *Meg (Margaret Patricia) MUNN*

Barnsley Council '92-96; Senior Social Worker, Nottinghamshire County Council '90-92; Social Worker, Nottinghamshire County Council '86-90; Social Work Assistant, Berkshire County Council '81-86 (NALGO shop steward '82-84, UNISON '81-96, GMB '97-);
Traits: Big; curly-haired; pleasant; wholesome, Girl-Guide-mistress look; "strapping with a pleasant toothy smile" (DAILY TELEGRAPH); self-deprecating: "daunted at the prospect of becoming an MP" (MM); unusually, these days, she cites her Methodism in her cv; a linguist: fluent German and French, conversational Italian, some knowledge of Hindi and Urdu; in the Co-operative Group, Woodland Trust and the RSPB; enjoys tennis and swimming;
Address: House of Commons, Westminster, London SW1A 0AA; 2nd Floor, Barkers Pool House, Burgess Street, Sheffield S1 2HR;
Telephone: 0207 219 8316 (H of C); 0144 263 4004 (constituency);

Dr Andrew (William) MURRISON   Conservative   WESTBURY '01-

Majority: 5,294 (10.5%) over LibDem 5-way;
Description: "My constituency straddles much of the territory that lies between Bath and Salisbury" (AM): four towns in west Wiltshire, including Westbury itself, the county town of Trowbridge, with its Cow & Gate headquarters, Bradford on Avon and Warminster, with its Army presence, plus a rural hinterland; near Edington in the constituency "King Alfred finally defeated the Danes and... founded the kingdom of Wessex"; "nestling under the escarpment of Salisbury plain is the ancient settlement of Westbury with its famous chalk white horse" (AM); in '95 it lost its most Labour-inclined town, Melksham, to the Devizes constituency; more oddly, in '00 it lost Harold Macmillan's 39-year-old grandson, Old Etonian David Faber, who had served 9 years as its MP;
Position: Ex: Assistant to Lord Freeman, Conservative Central Office '99-00; Research Assistant, to Fareham's Sir Peter Lloyd '99-01;
Outlook: His relatively late arrival in politics after a career as a Royal Navy doctor, was eased by his post as assistant to Lord Freeman in the Candidates Department at Conservative Central Office, from which he landed a safeish Westcountry seat at his first electoral outing; he "strenuously opposes membership of a European super-state" (WILTSHIRE TIMES); he backed the less Eurosceptic Michael Portillo and not Iain Duncan Smith in the '01 Leadership ballots;
History: He joined the Conservative Party at 16, '77; he was politically inactive while serving fulltime in the Navy until '97; he served as Agent for Hampshire County Council and Fareham Borough elections '97-98; worked at Conservative Central Office with Lord Freeman '99; was selected to defend Westbury after the departure of David Faber Sep '00; he campaigned for fair state funding and, on behalf of local hospitals, improved health facilities; he retained the seat with a 5,294 majority, only 800 down on David Faber's '97 vote on a much-reduced poll yielding a tiny (.1%) swing to the LibDems June '01; he led his Maiden speech with an attack on PM Blair's "autonomous European military capability" as a "threat...to one of the most succesful postwar organisations, NATO, and to our symbiotic relationship with the United States"; he wound up by deploring the "parlous state" of the undermanned medical branch of

Dr Andrew (William) MURRISON *New MPs of '01*

the Royal Navy which he had just left, like "a rat leaving a sinking ship" according to one of his more acerbic colleagues July '01; he urged "increased recruitment into academic medicine" July '01; he urged the tightening of rules about locating mobile phone masts July '01; he voted for Portillo in the Leadership ballots; as he went to vote, a colleague told Frank Johnson of the DAILY TELEGRAPH, "He was a ship's surgeon; now he's a sinking ship's surgeon!" July '01; he complained that extra funds for neighbouring counties might enable them to buy up places and deprive the elderly of Wiltshire of places in their county's homes for the ailing elderly Oct '01; in the debate on Breast Cancer Strategy, he cast doubt on all Labour's initiatives in the field, concluding that "generally, the position is improving but we continue to lag behind our European counterparts, and the United States simply leaves us standing" Oct '01; in the debate on Genetics and Insurance, he insisted "our first concern must be to protect people from explicit and implicit compunction in genetic testing" Oct '01;

Born: 24 April 1961, Colchester

Family: Son, of W G Murrison VRD, marine engineer, and Marion (Horn); m '94 Jennifer (Munden), physiotherapist; 5d: Sophia '94, Arabella '96, Henrietta '00, and twins Sarah and Philippa '97;

Education: Harwich High School; Harwich School; Bristol University (MB, ChB, on a RN Scholarship); Hughes Hall, Cambridge University (MD, DPh); RNC Dartmouth; RNC Greenwich;

Occupation: Examiner, Faculty of Occupational Medicine, Royal College of Physicians '96-; ex: Locum Consultant Occupational Physician, Gloucestershire Royal Hospital '00; Locum GP, Wiltshire '00; Staff Officer, Commander-in-Chief, Fleet Headquarters, Northwood '99-00; Surgeon Commander, Royal Navy '99: Principal Medical Officer, Portsmouth Naval Base '96-99; Service Fellow, Hughes Hall, Cambridge '95-96; GP in Navy and NHS practice, Northwood, Middlesex '94-95; Hospital Doctor '92-94; Research Registrar '89-92; Hospital Doctor, Portsmouth and Plymouth '87-89; Ship's Doctor on HMS Bristol '85-87; House Surgeon and Physician, Bristol and Plymouth '84-85; Author: Investors in Communities;

Traits: Parted dark hair; slim triangular face; awarded Gilbert Blane Médal for Research into diving-related illness;

Address: House of Commons, Westminster, London SW1A 0AA; Lovemead House, Roundstone Street, Trowbridge, Wilts BA14 8DG; Castle Cottage, 219 Castle Street, Portchester, Fareham, Hants PO16 9QW (home);

Telephone: 0207 219 8337 (H of C); 01225 752141/776942 Fax (constituency); 023 923 26244/391 Fax; murrisona@parliament.uk;

WADING IN FILES:

Apart from the boiled-down versions which appear in these books and on our computers, we have shelves and shelves full of information built up over our over forty years of existence. Since we are not run by accountants, we are not compelled to purge the best bits by having junior assistant librarians culling our files. If you want to write the biography of ex-MP Sir John Stokes, it will only cost you £30 to see his file. There you will find that he was so pro-Franco during the Spanish civil war, that Balliol put up its own anti-Franco candidate against him for President of the Oxford University Conservative Association. This win was the springboard for Ted Heath's political career. Postwar, having held this position helped him overcome the deep prejudice among Conservative selectors who resisted choosing as the candidate for a winnable seat the son of a carpenter and a housemaid.

George (Gideon Oliver) OSBORNE   Conservative   TATTON '01-

Majority: 8,611 (20.9%) over Labour 8-way;
Description: The fifth safest Conservative seat before its dramatic loss to Independent Martin Bell in '97, despite the '95 addition of the upmarket Cheshire commuting town of Alderley Edge, to add to equally upmarket Knutsford (Canute's Ford) and Wilmslow; Bell's decision not to contest it again - and the extinction of Neil Hamilton - put it back into the Conservative camp;
Position: On the Public Accounts Committee '01-; ex: Political Secretary and speech-writer to former Conservative Leader William Hague and Secretary to the Shadow Cabinet '97-01; Special Adviser to Douglas Hogg at MAFF '95-97;
Outlook: "A Eurosceptic from the socially liberal wing of the [Tory] party" (David Ward, GUARDIAN) who supports ballistic missile defence; "one of the brightest and best" (Ken Clarke); has been used by Iain Duncan Smith as well as William Hague as a 'phoney Tony' to second-guess PM Blair in Tory rehearsals before Wednesday's PM's questions; Independent Martin Bell's young, elegant, articulate Tory successor who has retrieved the safe Conservative seat lost by sleaze-tainted Neil Hamilton in '97; William Hague's former chief speech-writer and briefer before Prime Minister's Questions; "his political acumen has long been the subject of criticism within Conservative circles; after all he had been adviser to Douglas Hogg at the time of the BSE crisis" (Andrew Pierce, TIMES); a part-Hungarian future 18th baronet who is the heir to a wallpaper fortune;
History: He joined the Conservative Party '92; backed John Major's Leadership and worked on his campaign June '95; backed William Hague's Leadership bid May-June '97; he was selected for Tatton, defeating among others Chris Grayling, later MP for Epsom & Ewell, and Mark Field, MP for Cities of London and Westminster Mar '99; he was partly blamed for attacking Deputy Leader Peter Lilley's attempt to modernise the Tories' outlook Apr '99; backed the building of Alderly Edge by-pass May '99; backed call for CCTV in Knutsford and Wilmslow; said Neil Hamilton's libel action verdict "speaks for itself; there can be no place for corruption in British politics" Dec '99; participated in International Democrat Union (IDU) 'Young Leaders' Forum Jan '00; attended the the Republican National Convention as a Conservative Party observer Aug '00; backed building of Manchester Airport's Eastern Link Road Jan '01; claimed Tory grass roots' morale was high and many ex-Tories were returning to the fold, in GUARDIAN article May '01; he recaptured Tatton with a 8,611 majority June '01; in his elegant Maiden speech he highly praised his Independent predecessor and seat-sanitiser, Martin Bell, and claimed his constituents had "a Danish view of the Government's plan to join the single [European] currency"; although he opposed unsolicited Euro-integration, "no one is more passionate about enlargement than I am; no one is more anxious than I am to see the countries of central and eastern Europe brought in from the cold and welcomed fully into the concert of democratic European nations; let me declare an interest: I am part-Hungarian" July '01; in his first adjournment debate, he lengthily urged control of the aircraft noise pollution making his constituents' lives miserable July '01; campaigning in Tatton, Ken Clarke said of him, "he has a reputation of being one of the brightest and best but I don't think you should get into a Shadow Cabinet after six months in Parliament" July '01; in the 3rd recall of Parliament he wondered whether the terrorist attack

George (Gideon Oliver) OSBORNE   *New MPs of '01*

had not increased the value of President Bush's NMD scheme Oct '01; in a Westminster Hall debate he aired the complaints of his constituents "who suffer the tyranny of sleepless nights caused by unnecessary commercial night flights" Oct '01; aligning himself with PM Tony Blair in favour, he urged a debate on ballistic missile defence, Oct '01; he backed Eric Pickles' Food Labelling Bill as a weapon for improving sales of British farm produce Nov '01;
Born: 23 May 1971, London
Family: "My [maternal] grandmother's family fled to Britain from Budapest just after the war because they had lived through the devastation of the Nazi tyranny and wanted to escape the tyranny of Soviet rule"; "his uncle was the gambler, John Aspinall" (Rachel Sylvester, DAILY TELEGRAPH); son, of Sir Peter Osborne 17th Baronet, Chairman and Founder, Osborne & Little (Wallpaper) Plc, and Felicity (Loxton-Peacock), food shop owner; m '98 Frances (Howell), financial journalist, former Barrister and daughter of Lord (David) Howell, former Secretary of State for Energy and MP for Guildford '66-97; 1s Luke Benedict '01;
Education: Fox Primary, Notting Hill; Colet Court Prep; St Paul's School, Barnes; Davidson College, North Carolina, Dean Rusk Scholarship '90; Magdalen College, Oxford University; Scholarship (MA, Modern History 2:1 '93);
Occupation: Political Secretary, William Hague, Leader of the Conservative Opposition, and Secretary to the Shadow Cabinet '97-01; in Political Office, Downing Street '97; Special Adviser MAFF '95-97; Head of Political Section, Conservative Research Department '94-95; Freelance Journalist (DAILY TELEGRAPH, SUNDAY TELEGRAPH, TIMES) '93-94;
Traits: Full face; dark wavy hair; patrician air; mistaken for an Etonian; a long-distance traveller: he crossed the Sahara in a 4-man expedition in '90 and travelled down the Amazon in '91; big-name collector: met Texas Governor Bush '99, President Bush '01; "an ambitious young Turk" (DAILY TELEGRAPH); has compared himself with his namesake in 'Vanity Fair' who "died at Waterloo defying a madman (Napoleon) trying to build a single European state" (GO); was known as 'Gideon' at St Paul's School; "Boy George"; "vain, supercilious, arrogant, disgustingly smug" (MAIL ON SUNDAY); the Editor of ISIS and on the clay pigeon shooting team at Oxford; wallpaper heir; heir to a baronetcy; enjoys cinema, theatre, football; Church of England;
Address: House of Commons, Westminster, London SW1A 0AA;
Telephone: 0207 219 3000 (H of C); 0207 221 4184 (home);

Albert OWEN   **Labour**   **YNYS MON '01-**

Majority: 800 (2.4%) over Plaid Cymru 6-way;
Description: The scenic island of Anglesey renamed in Welsh in '83 to please its 62% Welsh-speakers, despite increasing immigration by retired English and emigration by unemployed young Welshmen and women; an economy reliant on tourism, agriculture, a ferry port to Ireland and a nuclear power plant; its reputation for multi-coloured serial political monogamy - from Liberal (Megan Lloyd George) to Labour (Cledwyn Hughes) to Conservative (Keith Best) to Plaid Cymru (Ieuan Wyn Jones) - between 1951 and 1987 was enhanced by its reversion to Labour in '01;
Position: On the Welsh Affairs Select Committee

'01- and the Commons' Accommodation and Works Committee '01-; Chairman, Anglesey Regeneration Project '00-; on WEA's North Wales Management Committee '99-; on Coleg Harlech Shadow Governing Body '00-; Director, Homeless Project '98-; ex: Anglesey CLP Press Officer '99-01; Holyhead Town Councillor '97-99

Outlook: One of Labour's least-expected newcomers in one of the party's two seat gains in the '01 election, compensating for Plaid Cymru's capture of Labour's seat at Carmarthen East & Dinefwr; his victory was seen as "a massive blow to Plaid Cymru" (Rhodri Hornung, WESTERN MAIL); he won by concentrating on Plaid's failures to do anything significant about local economic issues: high unemployment and de-population; he was helped by dissension in the Plaid over the choice of its candidate to replace the Plaid Leader Ieuan Wyn Jones, its MP for 14 years, departing for the Welsh Assembly;

History: He joined the Labour Party '80; he became chairman of his local branch '87, Treasurer of the CLP '91, Vice Chairman '92; he contested the seat at the Welsh Assembly election, trailing badly behind Ieuan Wyn Jones May '99; selected to fight the seat again at the general election, he started over six months before the general election with a traditional local campaign including leaflets, newspaper advertisements, door-knocking, and public meetings; this was climaxed by eye-catching meetings featuring high-profile Anglesey-born Glenys Kinnock and Anglesey-born Lady Cledwyn, widow of the seat's last Labour MP Cledwyn Hughes, later Lord Cledwyn; with Plaid resources spread too thinly, trying to take the neighbouring Conwy seat from Labour, Owen overturned the Plaid's '97 majority of 2,481 with a Labour majority of 800, on a 4.3% swing June '01; with 123 other Labour MPs he voted against the Labour Government on the composition of Select Committees June '01; in his Maiden he paid tribute to his predecessors, especially Cledwyn Hughes, and highlighted local unemployment and depopulation - the highest in Wales - urging better road links June '01; he was named to the Welsh Affairs Select Committee and the Accommodation and Works Committee July '01;

Born: 10 August 1959, Bangor

Family: Son, of William Owen, labourer, and Doreen (Woods); 'm '83 Angela Margaret (Magee); 2d: Rachel '85, Fiona '86;

Education: Holyhead County Comprehensive School; Coleg Harlech (Diploma in Industrial Relations); York University (BA, Politics, '97);

Occupation: Manager of Holyhead's Advice, Information and Training Centre for Anglesey County Council (UNISON) '97-01; Welfare Rights and Employment Adviser '95-97; Welfare Officer '92-94; Merchant Seaman (RMT) '75-92;

Traits: Balding; oval face; Welsh-speaking; he enjoys cycling and cooking;

Address: House of Commons, Westminster, London SW1A 0AA; 18/181 Thomas Street, Holyhead, Anglesey LL65 1RR; 4 Trefonnen Estate, Llaingoch, Holyhead, Isle of Anglesey LL65 1AJ;

Telephone: 0207 219 8415 (H of C); 01407 769777; 01407 760194/769871 Fax; 0777 5670837 (mobile);

CHECKING DRAFTS

We submit drafts of our profiles to MPs to minimise errors and reduce the threat of libel actions. It sometimes produces amusing insights. One MP, whose daughter was reported as having been arrested for prostitution, set us straight. She had gone to Bristol to procure drugs. When arrested, she claimed she was offering sexual favours, knowing it would incur a much lighter sentence.

Ann (Moffat) PICKING **Labour** **EAST LOTHIAN '01-**

Majority: 10,830 (29.4%) over Tory 6-way;
Description: A "stunningly beautiful" (AP), moderately-safe Labour seat east of Edinburgh made less so by the loss of Musselburgh in '95; it comprises the defunct mining areas around Tranent and Prestonpans, the seaside commuter towns of North Berwick and Dunbar, the Torness (nuclear) and Cockenzie (coal-fired) power stations, and livestock farming in the Lammermuir Hills; '01 saw the departure for Holyrood of Labour's sole farmer, John Home Robertson;
Position: On the Select Committee on Transport, Local Government and the Regions '01-; on the Commons' Accommodation and Works Committee '01-; ex: on Labour's National Executive, representing UNISON in its trade union section '97-00, Chairman of its Organisation Subcommittee '99-00; on UNISON's National Executive, its President '99-00; Ashford Borough Councillor '95-98; Chairman, Ashford CLP '94-98
Outlook: A self-confessed "pro-European" former nurse who comes from a local Scottish dynasty of miners' trade unionists; is loyal both to the party leadership and the largest union, UNISON, of whom she was elected national President in '99; she is clear on her union's policy of opposing privatising the NHS; her approach: "let's modernise the NHS, not privatise it"; one of Labour's small clutch of four new women MPs in '01, owing everything to her union and party status plus paternal family history as a Moffat and an inter-union pact not to compete for the nomination in the same seats;
History: "I was born Anne Moffat of the famous dynasty of Moffats who are steeped in the history of the Scottish miners' trade union movement and who hailed from Fife and East Lothian"; after becoming a nurse, "I became a member of COHSE in '75 and soon became active"; joining the Labour Party, she was elected to Ashford Borough Council, Kent May '95; she was elected national President of UNISON '99; she was selected to succeed departing-for-Holyrood John Home Robertson in East Lothian May '00; she successfully defended the seat with a 10,830 majority, almost 4,000 lower than Home Robertson's majority on a 13% drop in turnout June '01; she hailed her election as its first-ever woman MP: "women in East Lothian have come a long way since they worked in the mines" there; her strongest message was on the NHS: "I was a nurse in the NHS and was privileged to be elected national President of the UK's largest trade union, UNISON; the NHS is a unique and wonderful British institution; it is also at a crossroads; to hear the contenders for the Tory crown of thorns is to listen and marvel; they criticise the state of the Health Service, but how do they think it got to that position? I worked in the unfashionable mental health services as successsive Tory governments ripped the heart out of the service by deep cuts in spending and pernicious neglect; there is no doubt that this Government's prescription of massive extra funding is the way forward; the NHS plan agreed last year was the right path for investment and reform. I have seen the Government's proposal for the next 10 years and I utterly refute the suggestion that they represent a privatisation agenda; everything now being proposed was in that plan and the service bought into it; I have to be honest and say that I do not believe that in an ideal world the PFI would be the way to build hospitals; it is a fact, however, that the investment programme is based on harnessing private capital for public good; the question is whether the price is too high" July '01; she was made a member of the Select Committee on

New MPs of '01   Ann *(Moffat)* PICKING

Transport, Local Government and the Regions July '01; she was named to the Commons' Accommodation and Works Committee July '01; at Labour's Brighton annual conference she introduced the NEC statement against international terrorism Oct '01;
Born: 30 March 1958, Dunfermline
Family: "I was born Anne Moffat of the famous [mineworkers'] dynasty of Moffats"; Scots miners' leader Abe Moffat was her grandfather's cousin; m '84 David Adair Harold Picking; 1s Scott;
Education: Woodmill High School, Dunfermline (leaving with 3 'O' levels);
Occupation: National President of UNISON '99-00; Nurse '75-99: Nursing Assistant '75-77, Pupil Nurse '77-78, Student Nurse '80-81, Staff Nurse '82-83 (COHSE/UNISON '75-) worked with people with learning difficulties and in general medical and surgical fields; "I moved to Northern Ireland and did my psychiatric training and then specialised in drug and alcohol abuse" (AP); in the mid '80s she organised a development course in Ashford Hospital, threatened with closure and transferring of patients to the community; she reconciled hospital staffs to job cuts and community care, and saw this as "an excellent example of management and unions working in partnership" (AP);
Traits: Parted blonde hair (with darker roots) in pageboy bob; attractive; mild Scottish accent; brisk; tough; "I appear to be well known for my ability to get straight to the point in a brief, sharp and concise way"; "I have become a very confident public speaker; I have addressed 10,000 people in Hyde Park" (AP);
Address: House of Commons, Westminster, London SW1A 0AA; 65 High Street, Tranent, East Lothian EH33 1LN; 2 Wilson Close, Ashford, Kent TN24 0HX;
Telephone: 0207 219 3000 (H of C); 01875 610320 also Fax; 01233 643140 (home); 07711 677751 (mobile);

Adam PRICE   Plaid Cymru   **CARMARTHEN EAST & DINEFWR '01-**

Majority: 2,590 (6.8%) over Labour 5-way;
Description: The UK's 4th most agricultural seat; its 500,000 acres cover the rich farmland in the Towy Valley with big landlords such as the Earl of Cawdor and Lord Dynevor, and smaller hill sheep farmers; it also has Britain's only anthracite coalfield; the old mining towns of Ammanford and Brynammam harbour the Labour vote but the seat's 66% Welsh-speaking population make it a closely-fought Labour-Plaid Cymru marginal, with Welsh-speaking Labour MP Alan Williams '87-01 having opposed Plaid's demand for Welsh-medium primary education; the seat was captured by the Plaid's Gwynfor Evans in '66 and in the '99 Welsh Assembly election, and again in '01, when Labour suffered here its only Welsh setback and one of its eight seat losses nationally;
Position: Ex: Plaid Cymru Director of Policy, Director of Political Education;
Outlook: The Plaid's new eager-beaver, "non-sectarian by nature" enabling him to "attack the Labour Party while at the same time supporting it" (AP); a "reluctant Eurosceptic" who almost turned Plaid Cymru into another Eurosceptic party; a self-described "democratic socialist" and miner's son whose capture of this seat made him Wales' youngest MP; an economist who

helped Welsh Secretary Ron Davies promote the case for EU Objective 1 funding for West Wales and the Valleys with his co-authored report 'The Other Wales: The Case For Objective 1 Funding post-1999'; he assisted Davies "in the teeth of Treasury and DTI opposition, to convince Brussels of the case for a West-East division of the aid map, the crucial first step in winning Objective 1 status" (AP); he dubs the Western Valleys of the South Wales coalfield, "the Forgotten Valleys";

History: Untypically for a Plaid politician, he comes from a mining background and was politicised by the "injustice and hardship" of the miners' strike '84; as a founder member of the Federation of Plaid Cymru Students he became a student representative on Plaid Cymru's National Executive; at 23 he contested Gower for Plaid, coming 4th with 3.5% of the vote Apr '92; he became Plaid's Director of Political Education then its Director of Policy; he was selected as candidate for Carmarthen East & Dinefwr; he campaigned in the mining villages, pointing out that his ex-miner father suffered from vibration white finger and "was still awaiting payment"; with the backing of miners' leader Bleddyn Hancock and Plaid elder statesman and former MP for Carmarthen, Gwynfor Evans, he ousted Labour's Dr Alan Williams with a majority of 2,590 on a 7.5% swing to the Plaid, the only seat lost by Labour in Wales June '01; this win balanced Plaid Cymru's loss to Labour of the Ynys Mon seat and its failure to repeat its Welsh Assembly successes in the other mining valley seats; he called to the attention of the new Culture Secretary Tessa Jowell a "recent University of Newcastle study which showed that in rural and disadvantaged areas, the Community Fund was responsible for providing up to 50% of the funding for voluntary and community groups; in the light of that, will the Minister explain why the Wales Committee of the Community Fund is projecting a cut in expenditure of 43% over a three-year period compared to a reduction in the UK of 17%?" July '01; in his Maiden speech he insisted, "as a miner's son and the youngest Member representing a Wales constituency", Labour had lost the support of Welsh youth and promised a gloves-off battle to abolish tuition fees July '01; he urged a free banking system for rural areas July '01; he asked for more biomedical scientists in the NHS July '01; he pressed for more money for renewable energy in Wales July '01; he urged a referendum on stronger taxing powers for the Welsh Assembly Aug '01; describing himself as a "reluctant Eurosceptic", at Plaid Cymru's annual conference he chalked up 36 votes to 38 for his motion calling for a 'no' vote in a referendum on whether Britain should join the Euro; he justified his new opposition on the risk of sinking into a 1930s-style depression because the Euro's Stability and Growth Pact restricted the size of budget deficits that member-states were allowed, on pain of massive fines Sep '01; deplored hundreds of Welsh job losses in US-owned plants Oct '01; he deplored the doubling of debts among less well-off students, backing maintenance grants for Welsh FE students Oct '01; he claimed mines' surface workers were being denied justified claims Nov '01; with three other nationalists, voted against the war Nov '01; he insisted that in its insistence on real comprehensives and better proposals for student financing, the education policies of Welsh Labour were superior to those of the Scots and English Labour parties Nov '01; he worried about job losses due to the "persistent overvaluation of the pound" Nov '01;

Born: 23 September 1968, Carmarthen

Family: His grandfather, a farmer, became a miner; son of Rufus Price, miner and "a former Welsh middleweight champion" (AP);

Education: Amman Valley Comprehensive; Saarland University; University of Wales, Cardiff (BA in European Community Studies '99); North East Wales Institute, Wrexham;

Occupation: Author: Quiet Revolution (1994), The Diversity Dividend (1996), Rebuilding our Communities (1993), The Case for Objective 1 Funding Post 1999 (Jointly 1998); The Welsh Renaissance: Innovation and Inward Investment in Wales (Jointly 1992); Managing Director, Newidem, his Cardiff-based economic development consultancy '98-; ex: Project

New MPs of '01　　　　　　　　　　　　　　　　　　　　　　　　　　　　*Adam PRICE*

Manager and Executive Director, Menter a Busns '93-98; Research Associate, Department of City and Regional Planning, University of Wales, Cardiff '91-93;
Traits: Oval-faced, short, dark-blond hair; boyish-looking; Welsh-speaker; German-speaker;
Address: House of Commons, Westminster, Loondon SW!A 0AA;17 Wind Street, Ammanford SA18 3DN;
Telephone: 0207 219 3000 (H of C); 01259 597677/501344

Mark (Michael) PRISK　　　**Conservative**　　　**HERTFORD & STORTFORD '01-**

Majority: 5,603 (11.9%) over Labour 4-way;
Description: A Conservative seat on Hertfordshire's border with Essex, comprising the expanded market towns of Bishop's Stortford, Hertford, Ware and Sawbridgeworth, made safer by the removal of Labour-leaning Stevenage in '83; "in many ways the epitome of shire England...a combination of attractive market towns, historic villages and that soft, gentle rolling countryside that could only be England" (MP);
Position: Joint National Co-ordinator, Conservative Countryside Campaign '99-; ex: Chairman, Bushey Heath Conservatives '98-00; Founding Chairman of Youth For Peace Through NATO '83-85; National Campaigns Vice Chairman, Federation of Conservative Students '82-83; on Conservative National Union Executive '81-82;
Outlook: A mainstream surveyor and former FCS activist finally inheriting a safe seat after two earlier failed Parliamentary attempts; despite his FCS past he was listed by the DAILY TELEGRAPH's Julie Kirkbride as among One Nation Tory candidates in '97; a campaigner for small businesses, the countryside and the re-empowerment of the Commons; he voted for Portillo in all the ballots of the Leadership election in July '01;
History: He joined the Conservative Party aged 17, '78; became Chairman of Cornwall YCs '79; he founded Youth For Peace Through NATO, leading many campaigns against CND '83; he was selected for hopeless Newham NW '91; he drew up a Charter For Small Businesses with the Newham Chamber of Commerce urging swift payment of bills, flexible rules on VAT payment and curbs on illegal traders Sep '91; he co-signed an anti-Euro-federalist letter to the DAILY TELEGRAPH Oct '91; he fought Tony Banks at Newham NW, coming 2nd with 25.9% of the vote Apr '92; he was pipped at the post by Francis Maude for Horsham Nov '95; adopted for Tory-held Wansdyke (majority 10,000 under changed boundaries)) Dec '95, he fought the seat as an opponent of the Euro, and lost to Labour's Dan Norris by 4,799 votes May '97; he was selected for safe Hertford & Stortford, in succession to the retiring Bowen Wells May '00; he retained the seat with a 5,603 majority on a miniscule .4% swing to Labour June '01; in his Maiden speech he promised to "fight and fight again to ensure that we breathe life back into our towns and that we defend our green belt from excessive development" and also to fight to maintain the status of Parliament against encroachment by the EU and Government agencies July '01; he echoed Tory calls for increased police manpower for his constituency July '01; he asked Home Secretary Blunkett what safeguards there would be to protect "law-abiding citizens" from anti-terrorist measures Oct '01; he urged the Minister responsible not to "allow housing intended for affordable homes to be replaced with more expensive market housing" Oct '01; he asked what the Government planned to do about

Copyright (C)Parliamentary Profile Services Ltd　　　　　　　　　　　　　　　　　　　　*117*

Mark (Michael) PRISK   *New MPs of '01*

flooding in his constituency Oct '01; launching his Small Business (Regulatory Burden) debate, he urged a reduction of bureaucratic burdens and financial hurdles Nov '01; he complained to Chancellor Brown about "the administrative costs of measures such as the Working Families Tax Credit" Nov '01;
Born: 12 June 1962, Redruth, Cornwall
Family: Son, of Michael Prisk FSA, Chartered Surveyor, Valuer, Auctioneer and Irene June (Pearce); m '89 Lesley (Titcomb), Chartered Accountant with Financial Services Authority;
Education: Truro School '73-80; Reading University (Hons BSc in Land Management) '80-83;
Occupation: Chartered Surveyor (ARICS) '85-; Principal, The Mark Prisk Connection, his own strategic business and communications consultancy serving property, construction and environmental markets '91-97; Joint Founder Director, Freelance Business Forum '98-00; Director, Derrick, Wade & Waters (surveyors, architects & engineers) '89-91;
Traits: Rugged face with ski-slope nose; front-combed hair; "as Hon Members can probably guess from my shape...at school I played Rugby in the front row...where we do not take a genteel subtle approach; indeed some would say we take no prisoners"; also likes cricket, classical and choral music; in Stanmore Choral Society; played King Herod in 'Jesus Christ Superstar' '00;
Address: House of Commons, Westminster, London SW1A 0AA; Unit 4 Swains Mill, Crane Mead, Ware, Herts SG12 9PY; "I live in Much Hadham, in the heart of the constituency";
Telephone: 0207 219 3000 (H of C); 01920 462182/485805 Fax;

Dr John (David) PUGH   **Liberal Democrat**   **SOUTHPORT '01-**

Majority: 3,007 (7.3%) over Conservative 5-way;
Description: Attractive, genteel, upmarket Merseyside seaside resort from which the sea has retreated; it retains its shrimp industry, but has become mainly a commuting base and retirement area for affluent Merseysiders; a perennial Conservative-LibDem marginal won by the Liberal Democrat Ronnie Fearn twice, in '87 and '97; after his seven runs at the seat, he finally stood down in '01 and saw it pass successfully to his replacement, John Pugh;
Position: On the Transport, Local Government and the Regions Select Committee '01-; Sefton Borough Councillor (Leader '00-) '87-; ex: Chairman, Southport Liberal Democrats '87-89;
Outlook: The more intellectual replacement for veteran MP Ronnie Fearn, adding Southport to the six other seats successfully passed on by retiring LibDem incumbents in '01; a public schoolmaster and local councillor strongly committed to the NHS;
History: He joined the Liberals in '77; he was elected for Birkdale Ward to Sefton Borough Council May '87 and became Leader of the Council '01; he was selected to fight Southport on the retirement of Ronnie Fearn Oct '00; he successfully defended the seat, seeing off a Conservative challenge from the Wirral-based undertaker and George Formby Society member Laurence Jones, with a halved majority of 3,007 on a 2.4% swing to the Tories June '01; in his Maiden speech he deplored the fall in police manpower and democratic accountability June

New MPs of '01   *Dr John (David) PUGH*

'01; he was named to the Select Committee on Transport, Local Government and the Regions July '01; at the Bournemouth LibDem conference he made an impassioned speech deploring the depiction of the NHS as a battleground between doctor-nurse "producers" and patients as "consumers"; an accident victim or woman giving birth was no "consumer"; the medical staff were committed public servants; for "parasitical" private medicine, which trained no medical staff, the balance sheet was crucial Sep '01; he asked Secretary of State Stephen Byers whether he could explain to Labour MPs complaining about the BR's fragmentation how this would be avoided on London Underground Oct '01; he deplored the behaviour of the Merseyside waste disposal authority which penalised those councils with the best recycling records Oct '01; in the Student Finance debate he insisted the Government should have admitted its policy was "an acknowledged disaster" and the Scottish system was better Oct '01; he asked for reassurance that his seat's SSSI for wild fowl would not bar wind farms Oct '01;
Born: 28 June 1948, Liverpool
Family: Son, of James Pugh, Managing Director, British Plastics Federation, and Patricia (Caig); m '71 Annette (Sangar); 1s 3d; "I have three children at university" "and I am very familiar with the telephone rquests for extra money and the constant need to reach for the cheque book";
Education: Prescott Grammar School; Maidstone Grammar School; Durham University (BA in Philosophy) '68-71; Manchester University (MA, MEd, MPhil, PhD in Logic);
Occupation: Author: Christian Understanding of God (1990); ex: Schoolteacher '71-01; Head of Philosophy, Merchant Taylors' School, Crosby, '83-01; (ATL)
Traits: Thin-faced; gaunt; spare; his large and high forehead contrasts with his very slight chin; interested in "fiddling with computers and lifting weights" (JP);
Address: House of Commons, Westminster, London SW1A 0AA; 27 The Walk, Southport, Lancashire PR8 4BG (constituency);
Telephone: 0207 219 8318 (H of C); 01704 5690215;

James (Mark Dakin) PURNELL   Labour   **STALYBRIDGE & HYDE '01-**

Majority: 8,859 (27.6%) over Conservative 4-way;
Description: A white working class constituency with a strong Catholic component, comprising Stalybridge, Hyde and Mossley, in the southern half of the Tameside borough in the Manchester conurbation; it has rebuilt its local economy after losing many of its traditional factories; Labour-held since '45, its veteran MP of 30 years, Tom (recently Lord) Pendry, stood down early in '01 and was replaced by a Downing Street insider;
Position: Ex: Special Adviser, Downing Street Policy Unit '97-01; Islington Borough Councillor;
Outlook: A clear-minded young French-educated pro-European who identifies with the anti-Left factionalism of Hugh Gaitskell; a loyalist ("I do not plan to incur the wrath of the Whips regularly"); former policy adviser who worked for Tony Blair when Employment Spokesman, helped his '94 Leadership campaign and followed him into Downing Street in '97 as an adviser on Culture, Media, Sport, Telecommunications and the Internet; a friend of Derek Draper and

Copyright (C)Parliamentary Profile Services Ltd   119

James (Mark Dakin) PURNELL *New MPs of '01*

co-conspirator with Stephen Twigg against Islington Council's hard-Left councillors, especially Liz Davies;
History: "When I was two, I moved with my parents to France, where I went to school"; afterwards "I grew up in Guildford" where his Labour-voting grandparents long lived; "as a child I could not understand why Guildford kept on returning Tory MPs"; he became a Researcher for Tony Blair from '89; he joined the Labour Party '90; he was elected to Islington Borough Council; in the run-up to the '97 general election he was involved with fellow councillor Stephen Twigg in blocking the candidacy for Leeds NE of fellow-councillor Liz Davies, including allegations that she had incited a crowd; he described the subsequent libel action and the joint withdrawal of charges as a "classic score draw settlement to give both sides a satisfactory way out of a libel case that was based on a misunderstanding"; "we did not pay her costs" and described his payment to the 'Jeremy Corbyn Election Fund' as something "which each of us had alway done" and "not an admission of guilt" '96-97; he joined the Downing Street Policy Unit May '97; one of a number of insiders rumoured to be lined-up for dropping into safe seats, he was duly selected for Stalybridge & Hyde from an NEC-devised short-list Feb '01; he held the seat with a 8,859 majority on an adverse 3.4% swing June '01; in his Maiden speech he recalled Hugh Gaitskell's making Purnell's new constituency the site of his angry attack on the Bevanites, the Leftwing rebels of their time, assailing up to a sixth of them as Communist fellow-travellers; aligning himself with Gaitskell, he insisted that "there should be no place in our party for talk of counter-insurrections or coups" as suggested by Roy Hattersley July '01; he described Labour's defeat in '92 under Neil Kinnock as a "good thing" July 01; in PROSPECT he explained the LibDems' great achievement in capturing Guildford, his grandparents' home, by their targeting the middle-class vote in affluent areas July '01; he asked about a constituent who had lost her partner in a car crash but could not obtain a pension from the Teachers Pensions Agency which discriminated against partners Oct '01; in the Education and Lifelong Learning debate he concentrated on egalitarianism and avoiding divisiveness: "we must have a spectrum of ability in state schools" Nov '01;
Born: 2 March 1970, London
Family: Son, of John Purnell, accountant, and Janet (Ireland);
Education: Lycee International, St Germain en Laye; Guildford Royal Grammar School (independent); Balliol College, Oxford University (BA in PPE);
Occupation: Ex: Special Adviser, on Culture, Media and Sport, Downing Street Policy Unit '97-01; Head of Corporate Planning, BBC '95-97; Research Fellow in Media and Telecommunications, IPPR '94-95; Strategy Consultant, Hydra Associates '92-94; Researcher to Tony Blair, Labour's Spokesman on Employment '89-92;
Traits: Young-looking; short hair; an Andy Rosindell look-alike; Captain, 'Demon Eyes', Labour Party researchers' football team; "arrogant young pup" (RED PEPPER); secretive (about his own education at an independent grammar school and time on Islington Council);
Address: House of Common, Westminster, London SW1A 0AA; St James Court, Wilderpool Causeway, Warrington WA4 6PS; 114 Vesage Court, Leather Lane, London EC1N 7RE;
Telephone: 0207 219 3000 (H of C); 01925 574913; 0207 2428465;

WEEKLY UPDATES
The weekly shifts in Parliamentary conflicts are analyzed by us in WESTMINSTER CONFIDENTIAL (£50 for 40 issues). A sample issue is available to you on request.

Alan REID   **Liberal Democrat**   **ARGYLL & BUTE '01-**

Majority: 1,653 (5.3%) over Labour 5-way;
Description: Nearly 2m square acres of rough Highland terrain, making it Britain's 4th largest and 9th most agricultural seat, "one of the most feudal corners of Scotland" (Glasgow HERALD); apart from a score of inhabited islands, including Bute, Mull, Jura and Islay, it has Argyll's vast moorland on the mainland, divided by deep sea lochs; its farmers raise beef and sheep; 7% speak Gaelic; it includes the resorts of Oban, Rothesay and Dunoon, former base for Holy Loch's US nuclear submarines;
Position: Ex: Renfrewshire District Councillor '88-96; Vice Convenor, Scottish Liberal Democrats '94-98;
Outlook: A top class chess-playing computer programmer who promises to follow Ray Michie as a defender of Gaelic culture; he was his party's second choice as her successor, replacing the anti-Section-28 campaigner Paul Coleshill who withdrew early in '01;
History: He joined the Liberal Party in '81; he was elected to Renfrewshire Council May '88; contested Paisley South by-election '90; contested Paisley South, coming 4th with 9.1%, Apr '92; he became Vice Convenor of the Scottish Liberal Democrats '94; he contested Dumbarton against John McFall, coming 4th with 7.6% May '97; he was Election Agent to George Lyon in the Scottish Parliament election May '99; following the withdrawal for personal reasons of LibDem candidate Paul Coleshill he was selected to fight Argyll and Bute, Mar '01; he retained the seat, but on a minimal 29.9% share of the vote, with the three runners-up all on similar shares of the vote, but with the supposedly challenging SNP in fourth place; his meagre 1,653 majority compared poorly with Ray Michie's '97 majority of 6,081, and his 29.9% vote share badly with her 40%, June '01; in his Maiden speech he said "Europe has been a tremendous help, both for the markets that it has provided and the great financial assistance brought about by Objective 1 status; Europe appreciates the difficulties of running a business and delivering services in remote islands; indeed, it has done so to a much greater extent than many British Governments; not joining the Euro at the outset has been a financial disaster for many businesses in Argyll & Bute; our farmers, fishermen and tourism industry must sell to other Europeans and they are finding it difficult to compete at the present exchange rate" July '01; he wanted the 110 Gigha islanders to have the opportunity to buy their island Sep '01;
Born: 7 August 1954,
Family: He does not disclose his parents' names or jobs;
Education: Prestwick Academy; Ayr Academy; Strathclyde University (BSc in Maths '75; Jordanhill College (teacher-training qualification '76); Bell College (computer studies '79);
Occupation: Computer Project Manager, Glasgow University (AUT) '85-01; Computer Programmer, Strathclyde Regional Council (NALGO) '77-85; Maths Teacher (EIS) '76-77;
Traits: Round face; bald with a dark fringe; pudgy cheeks; an international chess player: "the strongest player in either Chamber for some time, and the only one to have represented his country at full international level" (Malcolm Pein, DAILY TELEGRAPH);
Address: House of Commons, Westminster, London SW1A 0AA; 8 Cederwood Court, Cardross, Argyll and Bute G82 5B;
Telephone: 0207 219 3000 (H of C); 01389 841 862;

Copyright (C)Parliamentary Profile Services Ltd

Angus ROBERTSON   **SNP**   **MORAY '01-**

Majority: 1,744 (5.3%) over Labour 7-way;
Description: A combination of the old county of Moray and the western side of former Banffshire in northeast Scotland; this is lovely fishing, farming, tourism and distilling territory; it has over half of Scotland's distilleries; it has also been Ewing country, with both Winnie and her daughter-in-law Margaret having held the seat for the SNP until '01;
Position: The SNP's Shadow Minister for Foreign Affairs '01-; in the SNP Shadow Cabinet '01-; SNP Spokesman on Europe '01-, on Defence '01; Vice Chairman, all-party Whisky Industry Group '01-; ex: SNP Deputy Spokesman on Constitutional and External Affairs '98-99; European Policy Adviser, SNP Group in Scottish Parliament '99-01 National Organiser, Federation of Nationalist Students '88;
Outlook: A hyper-active half-German Scottish nationalist carrying on the fight for separate statehood within the EU; "one of the SNP's new young breed of talented rising stars...expected to be one of the party's leading lights at Westminster" (SCOTSMAN); a journalist-turned-consultant-turned-party-apparatchik who won a safe seat as "the first non-Ewing to represent Moray for the SNP in the fourth decade of SNP victories in the constituency" (AR);
History: He joined the SNP aged 16, '85, becoming active in its student and youth wings; he contested the Scottish Parliament election in Midlothian in May '99; he was selected for Moray on Margaret Ewing's withdrawal from Westminster politics to concentrate on the Scottish Parliament Apr '00; he lost most of Ewing's majority of 5,566 in an 8.3% swing to Labour, who replaced the Tories in a much more challenging second place only 1,744 votes behind the SNP June '01; in his Maiden speech he welcomed ratification of the Nice Treaty but wanted Scotland also to "have a direct seat at the top table of the EU" along with the central European states like Germany from which his mother came; he also urged a reduction of the voting age July '01; he welcomed warship orders coming to the Clyde July '01; he asked how the impending cut in the number of UK MEPs would affect Scotland, Wales and Northern Ireland July '01; he found it "mind-boggling" that the Conservatives could not find truly compatible friends in the European Parliament July '01; he asked Defence Secretary Geoff Hoon to specify which units he would commit to the European Rapid Reaction Force and whether it would include RAF units based in Moray July '01; he asked about the impact of duties on whisky sales July '01; he asked about compensation for former trawlermen in Icelandic waters July '01; in backing the Bill to ratify the Nice Agreement he repeated the SNP demand that Scotland and Wales he granted equality of status in the EU "with other member states; we seek a seat at the top table and do not wish to hang on the coat-tails of Westminster Ministers" Oct '01; he backed a motion demanding more Treasury money for Scottish care for the elderly Oct '01; he was rebuffed by Armed Forces Minister Adam Ingram when he asked only about the Scottish servicemen going into Afghanistan Oct '01; with three other nationalists voted against the Afghan war Nov '01; he complained that sustainable development was not included as a target for the Export Control Bill Nov '01;
Born: 28 September 1969, London
Family: Son of Struan Robertson, retired from Royal Navy and Edinburgh University, and

German-born Anna (Haenlein), retired Health Visitor: "my mother and grandmother came from the Continent in the wake of the second world war" (AR);
Education: Flora Stevenson Primary, Edinburgh; Broughton Highj School, Edinburgh '81-88; Aberdeen University (MA in Politics and International Relations '87-91);
Occupation: Communications Consultant, with Communications Skills International '94-01; ex: Journalist: News Editor, Austrian Broadcasting Corporation; BBC Reporter, Vienna; Contributor to US, Irish and German radio (NUJ) '91-94;
Traits: Big; curly, light-brown hair; full-faced; jowly; personable; "ebullient" (NORTHERN SCOT); linguist: German broadcaster, has conversational French;
Address: House of Commons, Westminster, London SW1A 0AA; 17 South Street, Elgin, Moray IV30 1JZ; 3/3 Chessels Court, 240 Canongate, Edinburgh EH8 8AB;
Telephone: 0207 219 2000 (H of C); 01343 542058 also Fax; 0131 5570694; angus.robertson@snp.org;

Hugh ROBERTSON   Conservative   **FAVERSHAM & MID KENT '01-**

Majority: 4,183 (10.2%) over Labour 6-way;
Description: A seat created in '95 from parts of Maidstone, Faversham, Mid Kent and Canterbury constituencies; it contains much rural commuter country and was previously solidly Conservative, but Labour's strength in newly-acquired Maidstone council estates -some of them very deprived - made it a Tory marginal in '97;
Position: Ex: in Shadow Defence Secretary John Maple's Defence Policy Group '99; Special Adviser on Security to Andrew Mackay, Shadow Northern Ireland Secretary '98;
Outlook: A thoughtful, widely-experienced Army officer-turned-investment-banker who inherited a safeish seat from ailing Andrew Rowe; one of a clutch of former military officers landing safe Tory seats, he wants to see defence rethinking in the wake of the terrorist attacks on New York and Washington; a Portillo supporter during the '01 Leadership contest;
History: He was a Conservative party worker in the Kent County Council elections May '80 and the '83 general election before joining the Army; he participated in the Gulf War '91; he joined the Conservative Party on leaving the Army in '95, having been previously barred under Queen's Regulations; contested the Greater London Council elections in Coningham Ward, Hammersmith & Fulham May '98; he was selected for Faversham & Mid Kent, unexpectedly pipping ex-Minister Andrew Mitchell Mar '00; retained the seat with a majority almost identical to that inherited from Andrew Rowe on a minimal swing June '01; after being interviewed by all candidates, he voted for Michael Portillo in the Leadership ballots July '01; in his Maiden speech he spoke up for the fruit farmers in his constituency and their problems with imports, labelling and attracting enough migrant labour July '01; as a veteran of the Gulf War, he urged the maintenance of a broad coalition of support, the speedy creation of a plan to rebuild Afghanistan and increased momentum to settle the Arab-Israeli conflict; in Britain, having been "personally involved in the last large-scale [Conservative] defence review, 'Options for Change'...I know that much of the thinking that went into that was based on 'cold war' calculations"; he felt the Government would have to "think carefully about the

configuration of the armed forces"; intelligence services had to be expanded and ambulance services had to be enabled to work with the Territorials Oct '01; he believed a NATO force, including Turks, should be committed to Afghanistan to hothouse a post-Taliban regime "representing all the different tribes" Nov '01;
Born: 9 October 1962, Canterbury
Family: Son, of George Robertson, headmaster, and June (McBryde);
Education: King's School, Canterbury; Reading University (Land Management) '82-85; RMA Sandhurst '85-86;
Occupation: Assistant Director, Schroder Investment Management 99-; ex: Army Officer, in The Life Guards, retiring as a Major; he saw active service in Northern Ireland (Londonderry), the Gulf War (as Adjutant of a main battle tank regiment), in Bosnia and Cyprus '85-95;
Traits: Spruce; parted dark hair; commanded Household Cavalry at Trooping the Colour and State Opening of Parliament '93; enjoys cricket (playing member, MCC), hockey, skiing; Fellow of Royal Geographic Society;
Address: House of Commons, Westminster, London SW1A 0AA; 8 Faversham Road, Lenham, Kent ME17 3PN; 37 Halford Road, Fulham, London SW6 1JZ;
Telephone: 0207 219 3000 (H of C); 01622 850574/850294 Fax: 0207 381 3567 (home); 0207 658 3020 (work);

Mrs Iris ROBINSON   **DUP**   **STRANGFORD '01-**

Majority: 1,110 (2.6%) over UUP 6-way;
Description: A heavily Protestant constituency, created in '83, based on the Ards peninsula and Strangford Lough; it has substantial agriculture, some fishing, tourism, industry and commuters; the fight here is mainly between rival strands of Unionism; in '01, on the departure of the UUP's veteran Deputy Leader John Taylor, the seat fell to Iris Robinson, wife of the Deputy Leader of Ian Paisley's DUP;
Position: Northern Ireland Assemblyman (Whip and Spokesman on Health, Social Services and Public Safety) '98-; Castlereagh Borough Councillor (Mayor: '92, '95, '98 and '00) '89-; ex: in Northern Ireland Forum '96-98;
Outlook: A pretty but hard face of Unionist resistance to the power-sharing Good Friday Agreement; her success gives the Commons its first husband-and-wife pair from Ulster; along with her husband she sees Unionism as "weakened by the policies and actions of Mr Trimble" (IR); she abhors feminism but supports equal pay and creches for working women;
History: She was elected to Castlereagh Council May '89, and to the Northern Ireland Forum '96; she fought Strangford against UUP incumbent John Taylor, giving him his closest-ever run but still trailing by almost 6,000 votes May '97; in the contest for the Assembly the DUP trailed the UUP totals by just 200 votes, with Mrs Robinson beating John Taylor in first-preference votes June '98; on his retirement she evened the score by beating his would-be UUP successor David McNarry by 1,110 votes, insisting her victory was a vindication of her party's stand against the Good Friday Agreement June '01; she repeated this in her Maiden speech, saying her win was based on the fact that enough of her constituents "felt that they had been betrayed and let down, not just by the Ulster Unionist Party but by this [Labour]

New MPs of '01 *Mrs Iris ROBINSON*

Government", particularly over the changes in the RUC, "the real heroes of the Ulster troubles" June '01;
Born: 6 September 1949, Cregagh, Belfast
Family: Daughter, of Marie and Joseph Collins, a Londoner in the British Army who died of his war wounds when she was 7; she often acted as the head of the family; m '70 Peter Robinson, Deputy Leader of DUP and MP for Belfast East '79-; 2s Jonathan '73, Gareth '80, 1d Rebekah; 2 grandchildren: Michael, Olivia;
Education: Gregagh Primary School; Knockbreda Intermediate School; Castlereagh Technical College (where she met Peter Robinson);
Occupation: Fulltime politician;
Traits: Short brown hair; steely good looks matching the intensity of her husband's; "I am not a polished or professional politician"; "I was an uncomplicated working-class girl who was driven by circumstances and lifted up by the people in spite of my limitations; I can only hope that down-to-earth loyalty, compassion, honesty and effort can substitute for all else that I lack" (IR); "if Peter is the party's intellectual heavyweight and pragmatist, Iris is the passion and the heart" (Kevin Hurley, BELFAST TELEGRAPH); an Evangelical Christian, not a Free Presbyterian; "recovered fully" from recent illness; she enjoys interior design;
Address: House of Commons, Westminster, London SW1A 0Aa; Room 345, Parliament Buildings, Stormont BT4 3XX; 2B James Street Newtownwards BT23 4DY;
Telephone: 0207 219 3000 (House of Commons); 02891 829701/827703 Fax; iris.robinson@ukgateway.net;

Andrew ROSINDELL   **Conservative**   **ROMFORD '01-**

Majority: 5,977 (16.7%) over Labour 5-way;
Description: The Conservatives' 94th safest seat until '97, when it was lost to Labour, for whom it became London's most marginal seat; "a major office and retail centre for Essex and northeast London and boasts one of the largest and best open-air markets in the country" (AR); four-fifths owner-occupied, a mixture of skilled working-class and lower middle-class; made safer for the Tories by the exclusion in '74 of the gigantic GLC Harold Hill housing estate and including, in '95, Conservative-leaning Ardleigh Green from Upminster; all this was buried in a massive pro-Labour swing of 17% in '97, but reversed by a pro-Tory swing of 9.1% in '01;
Position: On the Deregulation and Regulatory Reform Select Committee '01-; Secretary: Falkland Islands Group '01-, Gibraltar Group '01-, Australia and New Zealand Group '01-; Havering Borough Councillor '90-; Chairman: International Young Democratic Union '98-, Romford Conservative Association '98-; International Director '99-, Director '97-99, European Foundation; ex: Chairman, European Young Conservatives '93-97, National YCs '93-94; on Conservative National Union Executive '86-88, '92-94;
Outlook: A hyperactive hard-line Thatcherite Tory Boy who has had second thoughts since being elected; "Essex man incarnate" (Robert Shrimsley, DAILY TELEGRAPH); "a formidable campaigner" (David Hencke, GUARDIAN); the young ultra Rightwinger who has

long favoured hanging, flogging, blocking persistent rapists, keeping Sunday special; "an archetype in the grand tradition of Tory Boy Thatcherites whose high jinks used to be reliable embarrassment generators while the Tories were in power" (Alex Renton, EVENING STANDARD); he opposes abortion, a single currency and a federal Europe; he has fought "on a consistent platform of Conservative and Christian values" (AR); he thinks Margaret Thatcher was "so successful in making government less important in people's lives that now they are less interested in influencing government" (AR); in Conservative Way Forward, Monday Club, Conservative Christian Fellowship until October 2001, when he was ordered by Iain Duncan Smith to quit;

History: "My family were Conservative but not that political"; he joined the Salvation Army at 7, '74; "even at junior school I loved the Queen, the royal family and the Union Jack"; he joined the Conservative Party at 14, Feb '81; he became Chairman of Romford Young Conservatives '83; he became Chairman of the Greater London YCs '87; having visited South Africa twice, he attacked a document supporting sanctions against South Africa being prepared for the Lambeth Conference as furthering "the Leftist trend in the Church" of England Sep '89; he captured Chase Cross ward on Havering Council from the LibDems on a swing of 25%, becoming its youngest councillor at 24, May '90; he co-signed DAILY TELEGRAPH letter opposing a single European currency Nov '91; he fought Glasgow-Provan, coming 3rd with 7.8% of the vote: "I secured the lowest share of the vote of any Conservative candidate in Great Britain" (AR) Apr '92; as an unopposed candidate, he became National Chairman of the Young Conservatives Feb '93, and Chairman of European YCs '93-97; at the YC's National Advisory Committee meeting in Grantham, it was agreed to junk all race relations legislation '93; he ended the Macmillan Memorial Lecture Aug '93 replacing it with the Ian Gow Memorial Lecture; he urged a referendum on Maastricht Sept '93; at the Tories' annual conference he proclaimed: "it's time to birch violent young thugs!" Oct '93; he supported moderating the Dangerous Dogs Act Jan '94; he was selected to fight Thurrock Dec '94; he invited Baroness Thatcher to a dinner of the European Young Conservatives; the Monday Club bought a few dozen seats of the 600+ who attended Sep '96; he rejected PM John Major's official 'wait and see' party line on the Euro Apr '97; again with his Union-Jack-coated Staffordshire bull terrier Spike, he fought Thurrock against Labour's Andrew Mackinlay and was buried under a 17% swing: "a Labour majority there of 1,000 turned into one of 17,000" (AR) May '97; retained his Havering Borough Council seat with a London-wide record vote-share of 88% May '98; his campaign to have Havering Council fly the Union Jack every day hit the national press Apr '00; he fought the extension of dangerous dog legislation to include Staffordshire bull terriers like his Spike Oct '00; with other Thatcherite candidates he indicated he would use her picture in his election literature Mar '01; Baroness Thatcher visited his constituency two days before the election, as did Lord Tebbit; he recaptured Romford from Labour on the biggest pro-Tory swing of 9.1%, replacing a Labour majority of 649 with a Tory one of 5,977: "the largest swing back to the Conservatives and it was achieved with the party's 11th highest share of the vote" (AR) June '01; as International Director of Bill Cash's European Foundation, in his Maiden speech he insisted that "the task of redefining Britain's relationship with Europe and thereby re-establishing self-government for our nation is the most fundamental question of our time" July '01; he asked about the "impact of third generation licensing costs on growth and employment in the UK telecoms sector" July '01; he asked about employment tribunal claims July '01; he asked about the cost to the private sector of employment regulations since '97, July '01; when the Leadership contest began, he invited contenders to come to his office; the only one who refused was Ken Clarke July '01; he was one of 14 new Tory MPs who together wrote to the DAILY TELEGRAPH endorsing Iain Duncan Smith as a Leader who "can unite the party on

Europe" Aug '01; he "chaired a meeting on the 197th floor of the World Trade Centre" Aug '01; having been instructed by his new Leader Iain Duncan Smith to leave the Monday Club, he quit the Monday Club and Conservative Way Forward, complaining: "I don't think we should single out one group or another group and say, 'we don't want you' or 'we want you'" Oct '01; at the third recall of Parliament, he urged more solid support for Pakistan's President Oct '01; he insisted "the taking of cannabis can lead to the taking of other drugs, which can devastate people's lives" Oct '01; he urged tougher action against Ulster electoral fraud Oct '01; "the most urgent and the most humanitarian action we can take is to continue the military action until the Taliban are disabled and removed from power in Afghanistan" Nov '01; he worried that Clare Short's International Development Bill did not acknowledge the problem of corruption or define poverty Nov '01;

Born: 17 March 1966, Romford
Family: Son, of Frederick William Rosindell, tailor, and Eileen Rosina (Clark), pianist and a dinner-lady at his primary school;
Education: Rise Park Junior and Infant School '71-77; Marshalls Park Secondary, Romford (6 O-levels, 1 A-level) '77-83;
Occupation: International Director '99-, Director '97-99, European Foundation; Freelance Journalist '86-97; Researcher, for Tory MP Vivian Bendall '86-97; Britannia Press Features '86-97; Central Press Features '84-86; Lambert Smith & Partners '83-84;
Traits: Light brown hair; wire-rimmed specs, broad nose; "a Jeffrey Archer look-alike" (PRIVATE EYE); when he sent a photo of himself and his Staffordshire bull terrier Spike for a Tory conference pass, officials cut out his face and sent a pass for Spike; "the only thing he loves more than the Union Flag is Margaret Thatcher" (Alex Renton, EVENING STANDARD); "he's got this presentable manner, but what he says about immigration, you can see the real man" (defeated Labour opponent Eileen Gordon); "a nasty buffoon" (PRIVATE EYE);
Address: House of Commons, Westminster, London SW1A 0AA; 1 Pettits Close, Romford Essex RM1 4EB (home); 85 Western Road, Romford, Essex RM1 3LS (constituency;
Telephone: 0207 219 8475 (H of C); 01708 766700/707163 Fax; andrew@rosindell.com;

Andrew (Edmund Armstrong) SELOUS   Conservative   SOUTH WEST BEDFORDSHIRE '01-

Majority: 776 (1.8%) over Labour 4-way;
Description: The southwestern strip of Bedfordshire along the Buckinghamshire border; its biggest town is Dunstable, former home of Bedford Trucks, with many skilled white workers from Vauxhall in nearby Luton and other vehicle manufacturers; it also contains Leighton Buzzard, 17 villages and Whipsnade; voting changed remarkably in the constituency between '92 when Sir David Madel had a Tory majority of 21,273 which shriveled to only 132 in '97, a 15% swing;
Position: Director, of the Conservative Christian Fellowship '90-; ex: Deputy Chairman, Battersea Conservative Association;
Outlook: As a world-travelling insurer and great-great nephew of Australia's Lord Casey, he

has strong views about foreign affairs; a churchy, socially-caring Eurosceptic international insurer who favours world trade: "I see the importance of the UK being internationally competitive worldwide as well as within Europe"; he voted for Iain Duncan Smith in the Leadership stakes; a strong supporter of NATO, he favours an increased role for Britain's reserve forces commanded by top-ranking officers; he also favours "strong families as the bedrock of our society and a country that is tolerant but not indifferent on social matters"; he has favoured offering accommodation in surplus MoD property to homeless ex-Servicemen; "my motivation for aspiring to become a Member of this House is my Christian faith"; active in the Conservative Christian Fellowship, he has called for more clergy, serving and retired, to become active in taking school assemblies;

History: Having first joined the Federation of Conservative Students, he joined the Conservative Party '87; he twice contested council seats in Lambeth, once with his wife; he fought Sunderland North, where his Tory vote dropped by 11% to 16.7% of the total May '97; he was in the final selection rounds for Sutton & Cheam and Hemel Hempstead; he was selected for SW Bedfordshire in succession to retiring Sir David Madel; he retained the seat with a majority over 600 votes up on Madel's previous 132, but still only 776 June '01; in his Maiden speech he urged improvements for his constituency's transport and health infrastructure and demanded to know why British Ministers and police did not use only home-produced vehicles, like the French and Germans; he disclosed that "my motivation for aspiring to become a Member of this House is my Christian faith; it is my wish to see the Conservative Party become the party for the poor and disadvantaged" July '01; he voted for Iain Duncan Smith in the Leadership ballots July '01; he was one of 14 new Tory MPs who together wrote to the DAILY TELEGRAPH endorsing Iain Duncan Smith as a Leader who "can unite the party on Europe" Aug '01; at the second recall of Parliament, he said it was very very important to urge on the US an even-handed policy to avoid deepening the hatred felt for it by Muslim people over America's policy toward Israel and the Palestinian Arabs; the financing of terrorist organisations in the US and UK should also be blocked and the Terriitorials be more extensively used Oct '01; he complained that "although the provision of child care has a zero rating for VAT, the erection of nursery buildings does not" Oct '01; in the debate on Jo Moore and spin, he spoke on local traffic congestion Oct '01; he was sure Eric Pickles' Food Labelling Bill would help despairing farmers Nov '01;

Born: 27 April 1962, London

Family: His great-great uncle, Lord Casey, was Foreign Minister and then Governor General of Australia; son, of Gerald Selous and Miranda (Casey); m '93 Harriet Victoria (Marston), a fellow Tory candidate for Lambeth Council; 3d: Camilla '95, Laetitia '97, Maria '00;

Education: Flexlands School; LSE (BSc Econ); ACII;

Occupation: Chartered Insurer: Reinsurance Underwriter with Great Lakes Reinsurance (UK) Plc '91-; previously with Price Waterhouse; Director, CNS Electronics (family electronics business) '84-94;

Traits: "Tall and dark with a strangely elongated face like a Modigliani" (Matthew Parris, TIMES); long thin triangular face; prominent chin and forehead; hooked sharp nose; neat dark parted hair; toothy smile; clean-limbed look; TA officer in Honourable Artillery Company who commanded troops in Cyprus, Netherlands and Germany '81-94; "I enjoy all sports " (AS);

Address: House of Commons, Westminster, London SW1A 0AA; 6c Princes Street, Dunstable, Beds LU6 3AX (constituency); 52 Kyrle Road, London SW11 6BA (home)

Telephone: 0207 219 3000 (H of C); 01582 662821/476619 Fax; 0207 228 7176 also Fax (home); andrew@seloous.freeserve.co.uk;

'Jim' (James) SHERIDAN   **Labour**   **RENFREWSHIRE WEST '01-**

Majority: 8,575 (25.6%) over SNP 5-way;
Description: A socially-mixed seat containing the tough working-class shipbuilding town of Port Glasgow and very affluent Kilmacolm; it was previously a three-way marginal as Renfrew West and Inverclyde until, in '95, the Inverclyde area around Gourock was removed and replaced by Port Glasgow;
Position: Renfrewshire Councillor '99-; ex: Chairman, TGWU's National Power and Engineering Committee; Chairman West Renfrewshire CLP;
Outlook: A more serious and low-profiled trade unionist replacing the equally-proletarian but boisterous previous incumbent, Labour MP Tommy Graham, who was expelled from the Labour Party in '98 for "bringing the party into disrepute";
History: He has "a long family history of involvement in the trade union and Labour movement" (JS): he joined the TGWU and the Labour Party in '84; he became Chairman of the West Renfrewshire CLP ; he became Chairman of the TGWU's National Power and Engineering Committee; he was elected for Erskine Central to Renfrewshire Council May '99; he set up a bus-users' forum; following the expulsion of incumbent Tommy Graham for infighting, he was selected to fight Renfrewshire West; he retained the seat with an increased 8,575 majority despite a 13% drop in turnout, yielding a 2.8% swing to Labour from the SNP June '01; in the wake of 11 September, he tried to persuade Defence Secretary Hoon to reconsider the closure of the local factory making the only "tested and safe propellants" for the armed forces Oct '01; he again sought to end the exclusion of airlines from the Disability Discrimination Act 1998, as referred to in his Early Day Motion 127, Nov '01; he again asked for assistance to Scotland's much-needed transport infrastructure Nov '01;
Born: 24 November 1952;
Family: He does not disclose his parents' names or jobs; m '77 Jean; 1s, 1d;
Education: St Pius Secondary School, Glasgow;
Occupation: Fulltime Councillor, Renfrewshire Council '99-01; Material Handler, Pilkington Optronics '84-99; Semi-skilled Painter, Yarrow Shipbuilders '82-84; Machine Operator, Bowater Containers '74-79; Semi-skilled Painter, Barclay Curle '70-74; Printroom Assistant, Beaverbrook Newspapers '67-70; TGWU '84-, TGWU Convenor '84-99, TGWU Standdown Officer '98-99; Chairman, TGWU National Power and Engineering Committee;
Traits: Triangular face with dark, front-combed parted hair and moustache; Catholic-educated; a keep-fit addict, he enjoys golf and football;
Address: House of Commons, Westminster, London SW1A 0AA; 31 Mainshill, Erskine, Renfrewshire PA8 7JA; 11 Park Glade, Park Mains, Erskine, Renfrewshire PA8 7 HH;
Telephone: 0207 219 3000 (H of C); 0141 840 3366; 0141 3579/5366 Fax;

According to its Librarian our volumes are "the most scurrilous in the DTI Library." Why not in yours?

Mark (Jonathan Mortlock) SIMMONDS Conservative **BOSTON & SKEGNESS '01-**

Majority: 515 (1.3%) over Labour 5-way;
Description: A new, largely-agricultural seat, apart from the fishing and resort town of Skegness; it was created in '95 out of two-thirds of the former Holland with Boston constituency, one-third from former East Lindsey; 15 miles wide and 30 miles long, "one boundary hugs the Wash and contains some of the best agricultural land in the United Kingdom" (MS);
Position: Ex: Wandsworth Borough Councillor (Chairman, Housing '92-94, Council Property Committee '91-92) '90-94; Vice Chairman, Putney Conservative Association '95-98;
Outlook: Sir Richard Body's replacement: a new Eurosceptic who denies he is Rightwing; another surveyor-MP, this time from the Conservatives' flagship borough of Wandsworth, where he was the first to introduce CCTV into housing; he also privatised the Borough Valuers Department;
History: He joined the Conservative Party '86; he was elected to Wandsworth Council for Southfields ward May '90, becoming Chairman of its Property Committee '91 and Chairman of its Housing Committee '92; he was selected for Ashfield Jan '96; in the election, fighting incumbent Geoff Hoon, he suffered an adverse swing of 11.3% May '97; he was selected to replace craggy, controversial Euro-rebel Sir Richard Body, retiring from Boston & Skegness after 39 years in Parliament, he retained the highly-marginal seat with a majority even slimmer - 515 votes - than Sir Richard's 647 in '97 June '01; in his Maiden speech, he emphasised the crisis among local farmers, pledging to fight for a level playing field for them; he spoke strongly against any EU enlargement threatening "cheap imports of agricultural produce, with associated concern about quality control and standards"; he opposed ratifying the Nice Agreement July '01; he voted for Iain Duncan Smith in the Leadership ballots July '01; he was one of 14 new Tory MPs who together wrote to the DAILY TELEGRAPH endorsing Iain Duncan Smith as a Leader who "can unite the party on Europe" Aug '01; he generally supported the Labour Government's Homelessness Bill but wanted it amended that those attracted to qualify in Skegness should need to establish the right by having lived there previously for a year Oct '01; while agreeing with some Labour educational improvements, he urged "coastal strip weighting" to lure needed teachers to Skegness Nov '01;
Born: 12 April 1964, Worksop, Notts;
Family: Son, of Neil Simmonds, teacher, and Mary (Griffith) teacher; m '94 Lizbeth Josefina (Hanomancin-Garcia); 2d Oriana and Isabella;
Education: Worksop College, Nottinghamshire; Trent Polytechnic (Hons BSc in Urban Estate Surveying '86); ARICS;
Occupation: Chartered Surveyor: Managing Director, Mortlock Simmonds 99-; Director: Hillier Parker 97-99; Partner, Strutt & Parker '88-96; Surveyor, with Savills '86-88;
Traits: Full-faced; dark, parted hair; he enjoys tennis, Rugby;
Address: House of Commons, Westminster, London SW1A 0AA; Main Ridge West, Boston, Lincolnshire PE21 6QQ;
Telephone: 0207 219 8143 (House of Commons); 01205 751414 (constituency); mordock.simmonds@virgin.net;

Sion (Llewelyn) SIMON   Labour   BIRMINGHAM-ERDINGTON '01-

Majority: 9,962 (32.6%) over Conservative 7-way;
Description: A slice of north Birmingham from the fumes of Spaghetti Junction to the blossoms of middle-class Sutton Coldfield; it has Fort Dunlop, Jaguar's Castle Bromwich complex and many motor component producers; in '95 the large Kingstanding council house ward was added, reinforcing Labour's hold; it is 91% white with unemployment standing at 7%;
Outlook: The Tory journals' favourite Blairite columnist who described his role in his recently-terminated DAILY TELEGRAPH column as "a notoriously craven and complicit mouthpiece of the Blairist conspiracy"; he credits SPECTATOR Editor Boris Johnson with urging him into politics: "He kept saying, 'Go on, you must!'"; selective in his encouraged ambition, he has emphasised his middle name, Llewellyn, when seeking Rhondda; he has emphasised his Birmingham roots in acquiring Erdington; if he ever wants to become an MEP, he may remember again his "short, swarthy Corsican" grandfather; "Mr Simon made his name as the DAILY TELEGRAPH's token Blairite; he quickly developed an appreciative following for his mixture of highbrow learning and low political barbs, extending his reach to take in a column on the NEWS OF THE WORLD and regular broadcasting slots" (Helen Rumbelow, TIMES); a mildly iconoclastic but on-message New Labour apparatchik-turned-columnist; "formerly part of Derek Draper's PROGRESS network" (RED PEPPER), which he denies; a realist who sees the problem of "a society with high welfare and service expectations, [but] which doesn't want to pay tax", and who sees Blair's "real task is to pull down the rusting superstructure of 20th century collectivism and replace it with something more modern"(SS);
History: He joined the Labour Party at 17 in West Bromwich East '86; he became Research Assistant to European Spokesman George Robertson '90; he was Europe Desk Officer at Walworth Road during the general election Mar-Apr '92; he was International Desk Officer at Millbank during the May '97 election; he described Ken Livingstone as "a man whose politics flow exclusively from two basic desires, to do mischief and to appear on TV" Feb '00; when it seemed as though Simon was interested in a safe Welsh seat, WALES WATCH did a hatchet job on him, quoting from his over-the-palate reviews of upmarket restaurants in SPECTATOR and pointing out that he had been associated with the Clear Communications consultants which had been accused of over-spending before the District Auditor inquiring into the accounts of the Vale of Glamorgan Council Feb '00; he rejected Gordon Brown's "bizarre onslaught" on Oxford's admission system as "not based on any facts", claiming that Magdalen, his old college, "is not a drag on progress; it is a transforming launch pad for able but unprivileged children"; "it is our government-run schools, not Oxford, which fail bright working-class children" May '00; he defended Labour candidate selections against Harriet Harman's call for more women, claiming the best candidates were being chosen June '00; he dismissed the foot-and-mouth outbreak as "just a crisis in one small industry" Feb '01; he attacked the Barnett Formula as "institutionalising the expenditure discrepancy between England and Scotland" Apr '01; he fiercely attacked Robin Cook's unwanted excursion into the Tories' racism row by raising chicken tikka massala ("a filthy concoction, reflectling almost equally little credit on either the Anglo- or the Indian part of the deal") Apr '01; he won

Copyright (C)Parliamentary Profile Services Ltd

Sion (Llewelyn) SIMON

selection for Erdington because "he made the best impression" of the four candidates short-listed by the NEC (excluding all locals), according to suddenly-retired Robin (recently Lord) Corbett; he defeated Andrew Hood, a Special Adviser to Robin Cook and Karen Livingstone, the Director of Communications for the TGWU Apr '01; he retained the seat with a majority of 9,962, down 3,000 from Corbett's in '97, with turnout cut by 14% June '01; he was initially barred from the Commons Terrace by attendants thinking he was still 'only' a journalist June '01; he dismissed Lord Hatterley's attack on Blair's 'New Labour' Party as misconceived and "out of date" June '01; he blamed Trotskyists for stirring up the Bradford race riots July '01; he accurately predicted that for the Tories, Portillo "might be more than they can bear" July '01; he fiercely attacked the siting of a future Olympics in brutally despotic Communist China July '01; he over-emphasised his roots as a "Brummie" in his Maiden speech; ignoring his Corsican grandfather or birth in Doncaster, saying: "I grew up in the adjoining constituencies of Perry Barr and West Bromwich East, the northern parts of which melt into Erdington"; "as it happens, I love Spaghetti Junction, which is lucky, because I live almost directly under it; but that is okay - I am a Brummie; I was raised among the concrete and the canals, so I feel the same about the contraflows and flyovers as did Priestley about his Pennines and Ted Hughes about the corncrakes, the kittiwakes and all that country malarkey that I am not au fait with"; "in Erdington we make the S-type Jaguar, which is a beautiful British car that is keeping alive a great British brand" July '01; he again predicted: "Ken Clarke will be the next Conservative Leader" July '01; he complained that the BBC was "bent on an expensive and ill-conceived digital adventure, the effect of which will be to undercut and destoy the private sector providers" Aug '01; he belated dug up his "short, swarthy Corsican grandfather" who had fought with the Free French Sep '01; accepting that he had found the "now notorious" Jo Moore "a most unusually single-minded and unsentimental woman" who should have resigned over her e-mail, as a former "humble junior spin doctor" he judged the Tories were complaining because "the tables have been turned": "twenty years ago we were hopeless at spin and not very clever at substance; those were the glory days of spin for the Tories, with the Saatchi boys, Tim Bell and 'Labour isn't working'; those people invented the modern theory and practice of spin"; Labour had learned to spin and deliver on substance Oct '01;

Born: 23 December 1968, Doncaster

Family: His grandfather, who fought for de Gaulle's Free French, was a "short, swarthy Corsican" seaman; son, of Jeff Simon, teacher, and Anne (Jones), teacher, who divorced; m '92 Elizabeth Jane (Middleton), solicitor, 2d: Carys '92, Nia '95, 1s Griff Llewelyn '01;

Education: Hamstead Infants and Junior Schools, Birmingham; Handsworth Grammar School, Birmingham; Magdalen College, Oxford University (President Junior Common Room '86);

Occupation: Columnist '97-, with DAILY TELEGRAPH '97-01, NEWS OF THE WORLD '00-, SPECTATOR (Associate Editor) '97-, DAILY EXPRESS '98, DECANTER '01- (NUJ); ex: Free-lance Speechwriter '95-97; Senior Manager, Guinness Plc '93-95; Research Assistant to George Robertson MP (TGWU) '90-93;

Traits: Dark hair; modishly narrow specs; slight (having slimmed-down from "grossly fat" [SS]); "taciturn" (his wife Elizabeth); "garrulous turncoat" (Matthew Norman, GUARDIAN); "Brion Bunter, the New Labour Punter" (RED PEPPER); writes letters in green ink;

Address: House of Commons, Westminster, London SW1A 0AA; 50a Reservoir Road, Erdington, Birmingham B23 6DG;

Telephone: 0207 219 3000 (H of C); 0207 916 5144/5175 Fax (home); 0121 373 1147 (constituency); 07788 457524 (mobile); sion.l.simon@dial.pipipex.com;;

Dr 'Bob' (Robert Michael) SPINK   Conservative   **999]]CASTLE POINT '01-, '92-97**

Majority: 985 (2.5%) over Labour 6-way;
Description: Canvey Island and Benfleet, lacking only Rayleigh, now in Rochford, to make up the late Sir Bernard (later Lord) Braine's old seat of SE Essex; largest proportion of owner-occupiers in UK; with the detested oil, chemical and liquefied gas storage facilities on Canvey Island;
Position: On Education and Skills Select Committee '01-; ex: PPS, to Ann Widdecombe '94-97; on Education Select Committee '92-94; Chairman, all-party Parliamentary Group on Prisoners Abroad '95-97; on Board of Parliamentary Office of Science and Technology (POST) '94-97; Vice Chairman, Conservative MPs' Employment Committee '93-84; Dorset County Councillor (Chairman, Educational Policy Committee '89-90, Deputy Leader Conservative Group '89-90) '85-93; on Dorset Police Authority '85-93; Deputy Chairman, Poole Conservative Association '84-92;
Outlook: Highly-educated but sometimes-primitive Yorkshireman, glad to be back as Castle Point's MP; seeks consensus except when angry; thinks capital punishment should be available for "the murder of children, the murder of uniformed officers such as the police or ambulance drivers"; not prepared to vote for any Conservative who backs unconstitutional abortion; "I do not wish to institutionalise gay relationships; I don't think the State should encourage them"; he want parents' approval of sex education in schools; he also opposes drug de-criminalisation but accepts "there is room to use some drugs therapeutically"; he thinks single mothers and their children should be considered a family; is even more caring about foxes and badgers; is also less bloodthirsty about Northern Ireland, where he supports the peace process; an assiduous voter; was pro-European because he saw it as a guarantee against losing his sons in another war there, but is Eurosceptic, saying in Nov '99: "on my selection as PPC for Castle Point in '91 and on every occasion since, I have made it clear that I seek only a trading relationship with Europe and nothing else; we should not enter EMU even if it was economically beneficial"; a super-loyalist anxious to win the approval of his Whips; "the swivel-eyed Rightwinger obsessed with sexual deviancy in schools, among social workers and on videos" (Stephen Bates, GUARDIAN); he began to worry about his once-safe seat when he saw the first-ever Labour capture of the local council in May '95; the selfmade, prolier-than-thou, former Keighley mill boy and belatedly educated 11-plus failure who became a pillar of the Dorset Tories; a management consultant and the former Director of Bournemouth Airport who became Bernard Braine's annointed successor; an enormously qualified engineer with the common touch but unpredictable ideas; for example, "we are a Christian society and we should teach the Christian faith; we should teach an awareness and understanding of other major religions but only in an academic manner"; "we should re-establish in all schools regular acts of communal worship with real hymns such as those which...I remember singing when we went to school" (RS); uses big words to support primitive old-fashioned morality; "he always expresses an interesting collection of ideas in an entertaining fashion" (Piers Merchant); does not sign early day motions; has a very high rate of participation; initially had a Yorkshireman's insensitivity to atmosphere and tried speaking more than his quota until stomped on by Yorkshirewoman Betty Boothroyd, then Speaker;

Copyright (C)Parliamentary Profile Services Ltd

Dr 'Bob' (Robert Michael) SPINK

New MPs of '01

History: He joined the Conservative Party '69; he became Vice Chairman of the Poole Conservative Association '84; was elected to Dorset County Council May '85; was elected Deputy Leader of the Conservative Group on Dorset County Council '89; was selected for Castle Point after the announced impending retirement of Sir Bernard Braine - 'Father of the House' - with Sir Bernard's enthusiastic support Mar '91; retained the seat with a majority of 16,830, down from Sir Bernard's 19,248, a swing to Labour of 4.67% Apr '92; failed in his effort to take over the Commons office of Michael Jopling, former Tory Chief Whip Apr '92; in his belligerent Maiden, said "I come from Keighley in West Yorkshire, a place where the weak die young and the strong envy them their fate"; warned: "I will take no lessons about the working class" from Labour MPs, "some of whom have never held down a real job in their lives"; deplored the absence of new trains on the "misery line", the Fenchurch Street Line serving his constituency May '92; had adjournment debate on the imprisonment of a constituent, allegedly for murdering a child June '92; complained of problems of Castle Point fishermen June '92; complained that his constituents had to travel to Basildon for their further education July '92; was named to Education Select Committee July '92; visited the USA as guest of British-American Parliamentary Group and USIA Sep '92; after a 1% cut in interest rates, loyally hailed its impact on mortgage rates and maintaining low inflation Oct '92; urged prompt action to ban cigarette advertising in sport Oct '92; presented a petition signed by 350,000 people in Mrs Whitehouse's National Viewers and Listeners Association; introducing his Obscene Publications (Amendment) Bill - which was later dropped - he urged strengthening of laws against obscenity and pornography; he deplored the activities of Madonna, "a confused and perverted woman, making millions by linking sex with violence in a way which normalises that link and puts decent women at risk"; presented a petition opposing the building of an industrial jetty on Canvey Island which would increase pollution Oct '92; urged closer trading relations with Europe because of likely growth of protectionism in the USA Nov '92; urged the importance of more academic research on engineering and technology with more "near-market research" Dec '92; criticised the Prince of Wales for defending the spiritual values encapsulated in France's small-scale rural life: "the Prince of Wales should be defending the people of this country who have to pay £16 a week per family extra on average to suport the French farmers and their food mountains" Dec '92; on the Education Bill, said "I also believe that parents generally know best which school is right for their child " - although his had not Nov '92; was loyal to the Tory Whips rather than his Tory Chairman on the Education Select Committee when the latter urged Education Secretary John Patten to back down from his confrontation with the teachers' unions over tests Apr '93; again urged a ban on "degrading material" from a book called 'Juliet' May '93; urged better funding for primary education: "that is where skill starts and where enthusiasm for education begins" May '93; asked for exclusion of poem on gang rape used in London's GCSE syllabus May '93; endorsed the Government's White Paper 'Science, Engineering and Technology', insisting that more financing was not needed so much as a cultural change "to improve the status of engineers, technologists and scientists, to attract the best brains to those disciplnes" June '93; backed Government's capping of Castle Point Borough Council, which had had to increase council taxes because of "budgeting and accounting irregularities" July '93; backed Britain's re-entry into UNESCO July '93; visited Japan as a guest of its government Nov '93; was rated the third most assiduous Commons voter Dec '93; deplored badger-baiting Jan '94; opposed reduction of age of homosexual consent to 16, Feb '94; backed restoration of capital punishment, especially for killing policemen Feb '94; urged more nuclear power generation to reduce carbon dioxide emissions from gas or coal generation Feb '94; declared his "consternation" about the distribution in schools by the Health Education Authority of sex education pamphlets Feb '94; after "21 homosexual men had been arrested committing acts of gross indecency" in "a public toilet that my chldren pass on their way to school every day", he insisted "there can be no equality between natural sexual intercourse and buggery, which is wrong because it is medically dangerous, socially destructive and unnatural"; "we must protect immature teenage boys from exploitation by homosexual men who tend to be more promiscuous than their heterosexual counterparts and live within a corrosive subculture"; "the law as it now stands does not in any way criminalise homosexuality itself or discriminate against homsexuals; it simply prevents the sodomy of teenage boys, all women, small chldren and animals; the proposed reduction in the age at which buggery would be legal would increase discriminatiion, on the basis of gender by making buggery legal with a teenage boy but keep it illegal with a woman of any age in or out of marriage; that would indeed be discriminatory"; he opposed any relaxation of prosecution of law-breakiing homosexuals Mar '94; urged the publication of the names and addresses of those appearing on court lists in respect of sex offences and convicted of those sex offences Mar '94; backed the PM's peace attempts in Northern Ireland, urged re-entry into UNESCO before the Americans and urged closer trading links with the EU: "I would sacrifice almost everything in life before I would sacrifice my three boys on the battlefields of Europe"; blamed the Turks and Turkish Cypriots for impeding unity and the entry of Cyprus into the EU Nov '94; was named PPS to Ann Widdecombe Dec '94; attacked the damage done to the people of Essex by the Liberal-Labour takeover of Essex County Council Jan '95; was replaced on the Education Select Committee by Nirj Deva Feb '95; was one of 28 Tory MPs who voted with Labour to ban fox-hunting Mar '95; urged more constituents to ring in to protest the sacking of a policeman who punched a teenager who threatened his baby's life Mar '95; was shocked when Castle Point lost 30 of its 35 Tory councillors in the worst setback ever in local council elections; Labour councillors, who had numbered four, the highest representation in the council's 20-year history, came out with 34; Spink blamed in on the media: "it's simply not fashionable to vote Tory any more" May '95; in a speech to Felixtowe Young Conservatives, urged Michael Howard to restore capital punishment, admitting: "I do not expect we would never have to hang an innocent person"; "the key question is whether innocent lives would be saved"; "seventy-five convicted murderers released after serving their sentences have gone on to kill a second time; therefore hanging would be a specific deterrent"; "I honestly believe we wouldn't hang innocent people; capital punishment would only be used for the most vicious, inhumane, premeditated murders" when the EAST ANGLIA DAILY TIMES reported this speech, he used the threat of libel lawyer Peter Carter-Ruck to force the paper to retract Oct '95; he introduced his Confiscation of Alcohol (Young Persons) Bill giving the police the right to confiscate the liquor drunk by youngsters in public Feb '97; he lost the seat to Labour's Christine Butler by 1,116 votes May '97; he reaffirmed his opposition to anything but a "trading relationship" with Europe and his opposition to a single European currency Nov '99; he was re-selected to win back the seat Nov '99; the SOUTHEND OBSERVER reported that 50 members of the Castle Point Conservative Association signed a motion calling for his de-selection as candidate Mar '01; he regained the seat by a majority of 985, ousting his Labour successor, Christine Butler, one of only two ex-Tory MPs to win back his old seat June '01; he urged "we work together to review the funding mechanisms for all hospices so that we can get the balance right between voluntary sector funding and Government funding" July '01; he asked about the contradiction between what the PM told President Bush and the EU planning staff's claims; he was told twice by Defence Secretary Geoff Hoon that "operational planning will be a matter for NATO" July '01; he was named to the Select Committee on Education and Skills July '01; in his retread Maiden, he paid tribute to educational advances on Canvey Island but waxed indignant about delays in prescribing beta interferon for a constituent afflicted with multiple sclerosis, the delays in ceasing the dumping of "poisonous ash" at the Pitsea landfill site and

Dr 'Bob' (Robert Michael) SPINK *New MPs of '01*

the need for a third road for Canvey Island July '01; he protested the seizure of cars for illegal imports when the owner was unaware of that use July '01; in 3rd recall of Parliament he urged avoidance of unnecessary casualties among Afghan civilians but wondered whether the war should be extended to Iraq Oct '01; while backing early-years education, he warned against limiting parents' duty or ability to care for their children "in their own way" Oct '01; he opposed a Canvey Island southern bypass road Oct '01; in backing the Marine Wildlife Conservation Bill, he worried about the impact of wind farms and, even more, P&O's plan to dredge millions of cubic metres from the Thames estuary Oct '01;
Born: 1 August 1948, Keighley
Family: Son, Brenda and George Spink; m '68 Janet Mary (Barham); 3s: Paul, barrister, George, neuro-surgeon, Robert, computer games designer; 1d Charlotte, bank clerk;
Education: Holycroft Secondary Modern School, Keighley; left school at 14, barely able to read and write; the only job he could get was sweeping up dross in a Yorkshire mill; "I wasn't just at the bottom of the pile; I was somewhere underneath the pile itself, a hopeless case"; "it all began when I got injured and was laid up; I picked up a book and discovered that I could actually read; then I discovered logarithms, slide rules and things like that"; at night school he took his ONC in Electrical and Mechanical Engineering and became an EMI apprentice; then "I decided I wanted to go to university and everybody fell about laughing"; "I believe I was the least qualified undergraduate in college history, but Manchester University took me in and the Dean himself, a famous nuclear physicist, decided to become my Tutor as a sort of experiment; I ended up majoring in nuclear physics and came out with a First Class Honours degree and with academic prizes for science and research"; Manchester University (BSc 1st Class Hons, Engineering); MSC; PhD in Management Economics; CEng; MIProdE; MIIM; MBIM; MIMC; C Dip AF;
Occupation: Director, Harold Whitewood and Partner (management consultants) '97-; Management Consultant '77-; ex: Director, Bournemouth International Airport '89-93; Director and Co-Owner, Seafarer Navigation International Ltd '80-84; Engineer, with EMI Electronics, including Apprenticeship '66-77; in RAF as Cosford Boy Entrant (invalided out) '64-66; Mill Boy '62-64;
Traits: Selfmade Yorkshireman; retreating brown hair; brown eyes; 5'10"; 11 stone; boxing-bent nose; Keighley accent; assiduous eager-beaver; was learning golf; plays squash; runs Marathons; registered as disabled (invalided out of RAF '66);
Address: House of Commons, Westminster London SW1A 0AA; 8 Green Road, Benfleet, Essex SS7 5JT (constituency); 75 Downer Road, Benfleet, Essex SS7 1BQ;
Telephone: 0207 219 3000 (H of C); 01268 792992 (constituency office); 01268 474466/474455 Fax;

EXPLOSIONS
Sometimes an explosion unveils those who rely on our volumes. After the 1994 explosion damaged the Israeli Embassy in London, an eagle-eyed Welsh fan of ours scanned one of the pictures of its damaged interior and spotted a set of these volumes. A similar photograph of the interiors of other embassies would often show the same - foreign diplomats have been among the most enthusiastic about our interest in the positions of MPs on crises abroad, such as the deep split in the Commons over former Yugoslavia.

Hugo (George William) SWIRE   Conservative   EAST DEVON '01-

Majority: 8,195 (17.1%) over LibDem 4-way;
Description: The Devon 'Costa Geriatrica' of Sidmouth, Seaton, and Budleigh Salterton, with Axminster inland; over a third of its residents are pensioners; one of them - Sir Peter Emery - retired as the area's MP in '01 after 41 years in the Commons;
Outlook: A clear-thinking locally-resident cut-glass old-style Tory from the famously rich family of Hongkong Taipans with a near-classical pedigree of Eton, Sandhurst, the Guards and Sotheby's; only Oxbridge is missing, replaced by St Andrews; one of five Etonians in the 33-strong Conservative intake of '01, contributing to a total of only 14 Old Etonian Tory MPs - the lowest ever; a Eurosceptic supporter of EU enlargement; in the Countryside Alliance; a charity fundraiser (including Macmillan Nurses, St John Ambulance, Save the Children, Arthritis and Rheumatism Council, St Vincent's Hospital); "he is touted by his supporters as being without political baggage" (KNOWLE WESTERN ECHO);
History: He joined the Conservative Party '82; he fought and lost Colville ward in Kensington & Chelsea May '86; he was 'blooded' for Westminster as candidate in hopeless Greenock & Inverclyde, sinking to the bottom of the poll with 11.5% of the vote May '97; he was selected to succeed retiring veteran Sir Peter Emery at East Devon Mar '00; despite LibDem attempts to undermine Tory MPs with ageing electorates with promises of free geriatric care, he retained the seat with ease, increasing the Tory vote share from 43.4% to 47.4% and adding 500 votes to his inherited majority on a pro-Conservative swing of 1.4%; he said, "I'm glad I am coming in as one of the new boys to reconnect with the voters" June '01; he was flattered and amused by the attention he received from the Leadership contestants: "If we had been in government most of us would not have been spoken to by these people for at least the first year," but his votes were not disclosed July '01; in his Maiden speech he pushed the claims of his region to World Heritage Site status and to more generous funding to revive its battered tourist industry in the wake of foot-and-mouth July '01; he asked about the relocation of the Whitehall statue of Sir Walter Raleigh July '01; he was one of 14 new Tory MPs who together wrote to the DAILY TELEPRAPH endorsing Iain Duncan Smith as a Leader who "can unite the party on Europe" Aug '01; he urged as much attention to Afghan refugees in Pakistan, living in "woeful" conditions, as to those suffering within their country Oct '01; although "one who passionately believes in enlargement", having "a Slovenian mother-in-law desperate to be enlarged", he opposed the Bill ratifying the Nice Agreement, insisting it had "virtually nothing to do with enlargement"; "the only thing that can pave the way for a successful enlargement is the reform of the Common Agricultural Policy" Oct '01; urged "clarification" of aims in the long struggle against Afghanistan-based terrorism before committing British ground troops Nov '01; said, "there can be no one left in the country who believes the Government care about farmers" Nov '01;
Born: 30 November 1959, London
Family: Son, of Humphrey Swire, company director, and Philippa (Montgomerie); m '96 Sasha Alexandra Mina Petrushka (Nott), d of Sir John Nott, former Tory MP and Defence Secretary and his Slovenian wife; 2d: Saffron '97, Siena Rose '01;
Education: St Aubyns Prep, Rottingdean; Eton College (Secretary, Eton Political Society)

Hugo (George William) SWIRE   *New MPs of '01*

'72-77; St Andrews University '78-79; RMA Sandhurst;
Occupation: Director, Sotheby's '96-; ex: Assistant Director (UK Business Development) Sotheby's '92-96; Head of Development, National Gallery '88-92; Financial Consultant, Streets Financial Strategy '85-87; Co-Founder and Managing Director, International News Services and Prospect Films '83-85; Lieutenant, 1st Bn Grenadier Guards '79-83;
Traits: High forehead/receding hairline; patrician good looks; "an Alan B'stard sound- and look-alike" (his Labour opponent '01); aesthete; he collected apologies and libel damages from the DAILY EXPRESS for claiming he had mistaken Gillian Clarke, wife of Ken, for a cloakroom attendant; FRSA;
Address: House of Commons, Westminster, London SW1A 0AA; 45 Imperial Road, Exmouth, Devon EX8 1DQ (constituency); Lincombe Farm, Sidbury, Sidmouth, Devon EX10 0QE; 56 Kilmaine Road, London SW6 7JX;
Telephone: 0207 219 3000 (H of C); 01395 264251/272205 Fax; 07831 716367 (mobile); swireh@parliament.uk;

Mark (Richard) TAMI   **Labour**   **ALYN & DEESIDE '01-**

Majority: 9,222 (26.0%) over Conservative 8-way;
Description: A compact, largely-industrial seat, previously called East Flint, at the head of the Dee estuary in Anglicised northest Wales; it includes Connah's Quay, British Aerospace at Broughton, the new Toyota engine plant and the remains of the once-giant Shotton steelworks;
Position: On the Northern Ireland Select Committee '01-,. on the Labour Party National Policy Forum '97-; ex: on the TUC General Council '99-01;
Outlook: Senior AEEU apparatchnik who inherited a safe seat after the last-minute retirement to the Lords of veteran MP Barry Jones; he was helped by his union's role in negotiations to secure the Super Airbus contract and £550m in investment for the local Broughton works and in opposing Corus's planned jobs cuts at Shotton steel works; like his union, favours First-Past-the-Post; is in the Fabians;
History: He joined the Labour Party at 18, '80; he joined the Welsh Young Socialists at Swansea's University College '81; for the AEEU he campaigned for the Fairness at Work legislation restoring union rights '97; with Tom Watson, he wrote the fiercely anti-PR pamphlet 'Votes for All' reflecting the strong First-Past-the-Post line of the AEEU's Rightwing union leadership '00; following the last-minute retirement of Barry Jones, his fellow Labour MP for Wrexham, John Marek, alleged it was due to Millbank's desire to parachute in "Blairite poodles" as candidates on an NEC-imposed short-list: "I think it is quite wrong that any Prime Minister of the day should ask sitting members of Parliament to delay an announcement of their resignations because that can only be for one reason, that there's a fix in the air" Feb '01; Tami beat off challenges from Margaret Hanson, wife of nearby MP David Hanson, and Nick Smith, Frank Dobson's aide, to win the nomination; "it's an absolute union stitch-up," said one party member leaving the selection; "this is the death of the Alyn & Deeside Labour Party" Mar '01; his union boss Sir Ken Jackson denied that AEEU officials were being shoe-horned into safe Labour seats Mar '01; Tami retained the seat with a majority almost halved from

New MPs of '01 Mark (Richard) TAMI

16,403 to 9,222 on a 14% drop in turnout, yielding a pro-Tory swing of 6.5% June '01; in his Maiden speech he spoke about the continuing decline of the Shotton steelworks and the rise of the Toyota engine-building plant and the building of wings for Airbus's new large aircraft, the A380 July '01; he led a motion protesting the collapse of Houseworks, a furniture and household products retail chain, leaving many creditors July '01; he was named to the Northern Ireland Select Committee July '01;
Born: 3 October 1962, Enfield
Family: Son, Michael Tami, Electricity Board worker, and Patricia (Barnard); m '94 Sally Ann (Daniels); 2 children;
Education: Enfield Grammar School; University College, Swansea (BA in History '95);
Occupation: Head of Policy, for AEEU '98-01; Head of Research, for AEEU '92-98; Clerical Officer, NALGO '86-87; Co-Author (with Tom Watson): Votes For All (Fabian Society, 2000);
Traits: Chubby-faced; parted dark hair; Art-Deco enthusiast; Norwich City supporter; in Glamorgan County Cricket Club;
Address: House of Commons, Westminster, London SW1A 0AA; Baines House, Glynne Street, Queensferry, Flintshire CH5 1TU; 122 College Road, Bromley, Kent BR1 3BF;
Telephone: 0207 219 3000 (H of C); 01244 823547; 0208 464 8561 (home); 0385 727023 (mobile);

Dr Richard TAYLOR Independent (KHHC) **WYRE FOREST '01-**

Majority: 17,630 (35.9%) over Labour 4-way;
Description: The northwestern corner of Worcestershire with the carpet towns of Kidderminster and Stourport as well as older riverside and recently flood-prone Bewdley, once Stanley Baldwin's base; an almost all-white owner-occupier constituency in the outer orbit of the West Midlands, safely Tory except in '45 and '97; as 'Kidderminster' it was associated with the names of Sir Gerald Nabarro, and scions of the Brinton carpet and Bulmer cider dynasties; in '01 it was sensationally lost by one-term Labour MP David Lock to Independent Dr Richard Taylor;
Position: On the Health Select Committee '01-; Founder-Chairman, of Kidderminster Hospital and Health Concern (KHHC) '00-; ex: Chairman, Save Kidderminster Hospital Campaign '97-00;
Outlook: "The oldest new boy" (RT) whose electoral upset produced a Government U-turn within four months; a retired hospital consultant-turned-one-issue-politician who won the seat on the back of local rage at the downgrading of Kidderminster Hospital and the closure of its local Accident and Emergency department; within four months a report commissioned by Health Secretary Alan Milburn recommended a big U-turn, the expansion of a new £14m unit to include up to 20 more beds; an Independent who entered the Commons as the other Independent, Martin Bell, exited; in resisting the shrinkage of Kidderminster Hospital he swept away Labour's David Lock against Conservative, but not LibDem, opposition, making him more of an Independent than Martin Bell, who was given a clear run against the sitting Tory MP, Neil Hamilton, by all other Tatton parties in '97; he also has more of a local base than

Copyright (C)Parliamentary Profile Services Ltd *139*

Dr Richard TAYLOR

Bell, with his 'Health Concern' (KHHC) holding 19 local council seats; was under-estimated by Labour's David Lock as a single-issue meddler; said he was "flattered to be carrying the flame of independence; it has a proud tradition; next time anyone angry at a school closing, the axeing of another hospital, a lack of bobbies on the beat, in fact any failure in any public service, they may be able to follow the example of Wyre Forest; perhaps we will create a whole band of Independents who will really break the mould of British politics" (RT); his KHHC has been described as "well-financed, with excellent PR and a clear message; running the district council in an inclusive way and addressing issues which concern ordinary people' (Charles Townley, local Labour Party member); Eurosceptic; pro: keeping the pound, fox-hunting, private schools; anti: 'spin'; "I'm a political mess; I've voted for all parties" (RT); only the fifth postwar Independent MP;

History: He voted for Labour's David Lock May '97; he created 'Health Concern' to campaign against the rundown of Kidderminster Hospital Mar-Apr '99; Health Concern elected 7 councillors to Wyre Forest District Council; holding the balance of power it formed an anti-Labour Rainbow Alliance with Conservative and Liberal Democrats to run the council; May '99; Health Concern won 19 of Wyre Forest's 42 council seats May '00; he claimed his local Kidderminster Hospital had facilities "like a London hotel", but that "all this will go; the bulldozers will move in; they'll sell the land for housing and squeeze the outpatient facility into a corner while the rest will have to travel to Worcester, 18 miles away, half an hour by car; what's the sense?"; with the continued rundown of Kidderminster Hospital it was decided to register Health Concern as a political party -Independent Kidderminster Hospital and Health Concern (KHHC) -with him as Parliamentary candidate Feb '01; LibDems' Lord Razzall announced his party would not oppose him, saying "Dr Richard Taylor is a very respected local doctor who is fighting a campaign for the hospital which has attracted widespread local support" May '01; he won the seat from on-message junior Minister David Lock, polling 28,487 votes (58.1%), burying Labour under a majority of 17,630 (35.9%) on a 68% turnout June '01; in his Maiden speech he claimed "an overwhelming mandate from the people with whom I have lived and worked for nearly 30 years", dubbing himself an 'Intentional MP' - in contrast to Martin Bell's self-description as an 'Accidental MP' - because of his "all-consuming passion born out of an intense anger about the arrogant, dismissive and unfair treatment that my friends at home have had to suffer at the hands of unelected quangos and civil servants", and announced he had appointed himself his party's Health Spokesman "against little competition" June '01; in the Private Finance Initiative debate, he pointed out "the devastating fact that the first call on a [hospital] trust's money, before anything goes into patient care, is paying off the PFI debt"; "the cost to a trust of capital charges, which were the previous way of paying for one's premises and equipment, is approximately 8% of a trust's income; the cost under PFI is approximately 13% of income; while the 8% is recycled within the NHS, the 13% goes into the private pocket" July '01; he asked about the performance-related pay of executive directors of the Worcestershire Health Authority July '01; he welcomed as "the biggest U-turn" the report of Professor Ara Darzi into Kidderminster Hospital proposing the expansion of a new £14m unit at the hospital to include up to 20 more beds; "it recognises that there aren't enough beds in Worcestershire," he said, adding "It's far, far less than we want but it's very welcome"; he and his supporters would still be pushing for full accident and emergency services to be restored to the town Sep '01; on the Health Select Committee he complained to Health Secretary Alan Milburn that, in Worcestershire, prostate surgeons had been unable to operate for 18 months because of the shortage of theatre nurses Oct '01; in an adjournment debate he again complained that the decision to reorganise Worcestershire hospitals had been based on "inaccurate and incorrect information" by managers resorting to "unscrupulous methods" Nov '01;

New MPs of '01   *Dr Richard TAYLOR*

Born: 7 July 1934, Manchester
Family: Son, of Tom Taylor, cotton spinner, and Mabel (Hickley); m 1st '62 Ann (Brett), 1s Stephen, 2d: Sally, Caroline; divorced '86; m 2nd '90 Christine (Miller), 1d Georgina '93, being privately educated; 4 grandchildren;
Education: The Leys School, Cambridge '47-53; Clare College, Cambridge University '53-56; Westminster Hospital Medical School '56-59; MRCP '65; FRCP '79;
Occupation: Retired Consultant in General Medicine (with special interest in rheumatology); formerly Consultant, Kidderminster General Hospital and the Droitwich Centre for Rheumatic Diseases '72-95; Senior Medical Registrar, Westminster Hospital '67-72; Medical Registrar, Westminster Hospital '66-67, St Stephen's Hospital, Westminster '65-66; Senior House Physician, St Stephen's Hospital '64-65; Medical Officer, RAF Hospital, Halton '63-64; Senior Medical Officer, RAF Christmas Island '63; General Duties Medical Officer, RAF '61-63; House Physician, London Chest Hospital '60-61; House Surgeon, Kingston Hospital '60, Westminster Hospital '59; BMA;
Traits: Tall, balding with grey sidepatches; sallow-skinned; specs; "softly-spoken" (Nicole Martin, DAILY TELEGRAPH); "benign" (Simon Trump, SUNDAY TIMES); "stooping" (Maurice Weaver, DAILY TELEGRAPH); archetypal consultant's manner; "quite, quite charming"; "he has that head trick, where he tilts his face forward at his patients/voters and looks from round about the top of his glasses; it makes him seem both kindly and patronising" (David Aaronovitch, INDEPENDENT); "a tall, stooping figure in a Cambridge Union tie"; "he is not quite the woolly old soul he likes to play; twice-married, he has a daughter of eight, and drives a Lotus" (Maurice Weaver, DAILY TELEGRAPH); the 17th oldest MP; likes wildlife - birds and butterflies - trees for small gardens, 1950s and 1960s cars, Victorian watercolours; is a member: of National Trust, Royal Horticultural Society, Severn Valley Railway, RSPB, Institute of Advanced Motorists and Club Lotus;
Address: House of Common, Westminster, London SW1A 0AA; 11 Church Walk, Kidderminster, Worcs DY11 6XY;
Telephone: 0207 219 3000 (H of C); 01562 60010/748371 Fax:

Viscount John (Archibald Sinclair) THURSO   Liberal Democrat   **CAITHNESS, SUTHERLAND & EASTER ROSS '01-**

Majority: 2,744 (11%) over Labour 6-way;
Description: A vast Highland seat comprising farmers, crofters and fishermen as well as the nuclear plant at Dounreay, the area's biggest employer; in '95 10,000 Easter Ross voters came in from Charles Kennedy's Ross & Cromarty seat; previously held by Robert Maclennan '66-01 for three parties: Labour, SDP and LibDem;
Position: On the Select Committee on Culture, Media and Sport '01-; as Viscount Thurso he sat in the House of Lords as a LibDem Spokesman on Tourism and Food '95-00; Chairman, Caithness, Sutherland & Easter Ross LibDems '98-01;
Outlook: A "fairly radical" (Nick Bibby, SCOTSMAN) aristocrat, successful hotelier and Managing Director of Champney's, the health farm for the rich and famous, which he turned around; "I have no difficulty in dealing with and

Copyright (C)Parliamentary Profile Services Ltd   *141*

Viscount John (Archibald Sinclair) THURSO

producing luxury goods and services for people and redistributing their wealth to others by creating jobs" (JT); the Old Etonian grandson of former Liberal Party Leader and local Caithness & Sutherland MP, Sir Archibald Sinclair, 1st Viscount Thurso, and the fourth generation of his family to represent the area; self-dubbed "a hereditary Liberal and a Liberal hereditary", who willingly voted to remove hereditaries from the Lords, and then became the first hereditary peer to win election to the Commons, styling himself 'John Thurso', though he is actually 'John Sinclair, Viscount Thurso'; an Old Etonian whose arrival in the Commons doubles the number of Old Etonian LibDem MPs; as a castle-dwelling 3rd Viscount and 6th Baronet he also ups the LibDems' otherwise suburban profile,

History: He was born into Liberal politics as the grandson of Sir Archibald Sinclair; he inherited the Thurso Viscountcy '95; from then he sat in the House of Lords, becoming LibDem Spokesman on Tourism '96-99, Food '98-99; he was on the Lords' Refreshment Committee '97-99; in a debate on Countryside Policy, he said "the most destructive force ever let loose to wreak havoc on the countryside was Thatcherism" which lost it its shops, post offices, its pubs and cottage hospitals; " I have never hunted...but it is a match that could well inflame the countryside" Feb '98; he led for the LibDems in the Lords' debate on the Scotland Bill Oct '98; he backed the reforms in the House of Lords Bill because every time it got into an argument with the Commons, its hereditary component was flung in its face Mar'99; the local constituency chairman, he was selected to succeed MP Robert Maclennan retiring after 35 years Oct '00; he successfully exceeded Maclennan's majority of 2,259, winning by 2,744 votes June '01; in his Maiden speech he apologised in advance if he lapsed into Lords style; he urged a speedy second-stage reform of the Lords so that it would be "either fully-elected or in large part elected", with the two Houses of Parliament then "complementary" but "fundamentally equal" June '01; he asked whether the AEA Technology Batteries factory in Thurso could provide batteries for the Bowman military radio contract July '01; he asked about assessing wave energy July '01; he backed his neighbouring MPs in urging a "public service obligation for the Inverness to Gatwick [air] link" Oct '01; he warned against damaging the committee system of the Scottish Parliament by reducing its numbers below 129, Nov '01; criticised the Blair-Irvine proposal for Lords reform as "a small step for democracy and a giant leap for complacency" while commending it for accepting his proposal for easing retirement Nov '01;

Born: 10 Sept '53, Thurso

Family: His great-great-great grandfather, Sir George Sinclair, 2nd Baronet, was Liberal MP for Caithnessshire 1811-18, 1831-41; his great-great grandfather, Sir John Sinclair, 3rd Baronet represented Caithnessshire 1869-85; grandson, of Sir Archibald Sinclair, 1st Viscount Thurso, 4th Baronet of Ulbster, Liberal MP Caithness & Sutherland '22-45, Leader of the Liberal Party '35-45, Secretary of State for Scotland '31-32, Secretary of State for Air in wartime coalition '40-45; son, of Sir Robin Macdonald Sinclair, 2nd Viscount Thurso, 5th Baronet of Ulbster ("a very competent Greek scholar" - JT), and Margaret Beaumont (Robertson); succeeded as 3rd Viscount Thurso and 6th Baronet of Ulbster '95; m '76 Marion Ticknor (Sage) d of Louis Sage of Connecticut, and Mrs Constance Ward of Kinnaird, Perthshire; 2s James Alexander Robin '84, George Henry Macdonald '89; 1d Louisa Ticknor Beaumont '80;

Education: Eton College; Westminster Technical College (day-release for hotel courses);

Occupation: Director: Fitness and Leisure Holdings (Champney's) '95-; Thurso Fisheries Ltd '95-; Walker Green Bank Plc '97-; Scrabster Harbour Trust '96; Profile Recruitment and Management Ltd '96-; Anton Mosiman Ltd '97; ex: Director, Lancaster Hotel '81-85; Cliveden House Ltd '87-93; Savoy Hotel Plc '93-98; Chairman, Bucks Game Conservancy '90-92; BHA Clubs Panel '92-; Management Trainee, Savoy Grooup '72-77; Master, Innholders Association '95-97; President, Licensed Victuallers Schools '96-97; President, Academy of Food & Wine

New MPs of '01 *Viscount John (Archibald Sinclair) THURSO*

Service '98-; Patron: Hotel Catering & International Management Association '97-, Institutre of Management Services '98 ; FHCIMA '91; FInstD '97; Author, Tourism Tomorrow '98;
Traits: Victorian-melodrama-style waxed moustache; thick dark parted hair; Lord Lucan lookalike; has a "Winchester drawl and a fondness for tweed capes" (Sarah Gracie, SUNDAY TIMES); at Champney's he scaled down from 16 stone to 13; 'Lord Torso'; his "most notable media exposure...was in a documentary devoted to his health farm; his lordship was seen leaping naked into a steaming plunge pool by an estimated 3.5m viewers" (EVENING STANDARD); listed his interests in Debrett's in '91 as "food, wine, fishing, and something else", but later admitted it was "not the sort of thing a budding politician should admit to; I should probably have said philately or something"; "a Highlander through-and-through, although admittedly this appears to bypass his voicebox" (Nick Bibby, SCOTSMAN); "no snob" (Nick Bibby, SCOTSMAN); he enjoys chopping up trees - "shades of Gladstone, except I use a chainsaw" (JT); member of Brooks;
Address: House of Commons, Westminster, London SW1A 0AA; Thurso Castle, Caithness KW14 8HW;
Telephone: 0207 219 1752 (H of C); 01442 291303;

Andrew (John) TURNER   **Conservative**   **ISLE OF WIGHT '01-**

Majority: 2,826 (4.5%) over LibDem 8-way;
Description: A Con-LibDem marginal seat since the '70s, enjoying Liberal Stephen Ross '74-87; Tory Barry Field '87-97, and LibDem Dr Peter Brand '97-01, who was one of only two LibDem MPs to lose their seats in '01; a quiet south coast holiday and retirement island with 100,000 electors and sixty miles of coastline; reachable only by ferry, whose delays impede further development of its industry, now including aeroplanes (Westland), and electronics (Plessey); Parkhurst and two other prisons also provide jobs; it is a considerable garlic-grower but has the lowest average GDP of any county;
Position: On Select Committee on Education and Skills '01-; ex: Oxford City Councillor '79-96; Sheriff of Oxford '94-95; Chairman, Oxford East Conservative Association;
Outlook: A hyperactive intervener and veteran Rightwing Eurosceptic education consultant; opposes a rail tunnel to overcome the island's ferry delays; "I am not the sort of Conservative who is known for wearing his compassion on his sleeve but I am passionate about public service"; was second-time-lucky on the Isle of Wight, despite being a mainlander, providing one of only eight Tory seat gains in '01; a former teacher and Tory apparatchik, recently an education consultant and campaigner for privatised education, including opted-out schools, vouchers and private funding;
History: He joined the Conservative Party '72; was elected to Oxford City Council May '79; selected for Hackney South & Shoreditch Feb '90, he suffered a 2.6% swing to Labour's Brian Sedgemore Apr '92; fought Birmingham East in the European Parliament election as an open Eurosceptic May '94; was selected to defend a 1,827 Conservative majority on Isle of Wight Feb '97; he lost the seat to LibDem local GP Dr Peter Brand by 6,402 votes May '97; remained on the Island to help fight local elections in which Tories made 9 gains and ended 17 years of

LibDem control of its county council May '98; he was listed as a Eurosceptic by the DAILY TELEGRAPH Sept '00; the incumbent LibDem MP Dr Peter Brand did not help his survival chances by speaking frankly as a doctor about euthanasia in a seat with an ageing population and also failed to dent the big Labour vote; Turner won the Isle of Wight from Dr Peter Brand by a 2,826 majority on a 6.6% pro-Tory swing after a 12% drop in turnout June '01; in his Maiden speech on the Homelessness Bill, he wanted it to be "fair to those who already live in a particular area", insisting that those claiming help "demonstrate that they have not moved from an area of low unemployment to one of high unemployment, such as my constituency"; he also opposed "a massive housebuilding programme" July '01; he voted for Iain Duncan Smith in all the ballots for Conservative Leader July '01; he asked why small farmers had to be inspected twice as often as large farmers before their animals were slaughtered July '01; rejecting regional assemblies, he told Minister Nick Raynsford that "the people of the Isle of Wight find it hard enough to cope with a Police Authority run from Winchester and a Health Authority run from Portsmouth and that they certainly do not see why their taxes sould be spent on a referendum that might result in more of their services being run from places like Woking" July '01; he complained about non-competitive ferry fares to the Isle of Wight July '01; he complained about too few Tory councillors on the local police authority July '01; he was named to the Select Committee on Education and Skills July '01; he was one of 14 new Tory MPs who together wrote to the DAILY TELEGRAPH endorsing Iain Duncan Smith as a Leader who "can unite the party on Europe" Aug '01; he objected to a proposed £60m rail tunnel promising to reverse the island's economic decline, saying "there's no evidence that the majority of people on the island want a fixed link; I'm not convinced the economic arguments in favour outweigh the economic and environmental arguments against" Sep '01; in the second recall of Parliament, he said: "let us be unlimited in our ambitions but limited in our objectives to that which is achievable and legitimate" Oct '01; he worried about demanding too many qualifications of child-minders and over-bureaucratising early-years education Oct '01; tried to amend Homelessness Bill to limit the burden on the Isle of Wight of ex-prisoners from its three jails trying to settle there after their release Oct '01; he asked how available LPG fuel was in rural areas Oct '01; in the debate on Cleaner Fuels, he advocated wind, which drove local yachts Oct '01; he insisted that the same standards be applied to overseas adoptions as applied in the UK Oct '01; he complained that the new Blair-elevated peers came overwhelmingly from the London area Nov '01;

Born: 24 October 1953, Coventry

Family: Son, of Eustace Albert Turner, schoolmaster, and Joyce Mary (Lowe); at 47, at election time '01, he said he was engaged to Carole;

Education: Rugby School; Keble College, Oxford University (BA '76, MA '81); Birmingham University (PGCE '77); Henley Management College; FRSA;

Occupation: Head of Policy and Resources, London Borough of Southwark, where he worked with Education Secretary David Blunkett "to deliver his policies" in "a failing local education authority, which was required to privatise the management of the education service" '00-01; Education Management Consultant (advising companies competing to run Education Action Zones, failing schools and LEAs, providing headteachers or school funding '97-; Manager, GDST Minerva Project '99-00; Deputy Director (Education & Training), Institute of Economic Affairs '97-99; Director, Grant Maintained Schools Foundation (which he set up) '88-97; Special Adviser, to Norman Fowler and John Moore, Secretary of State for Social Services, on health service reforms and child support policy '87-88; Conservative Research Department '84-87; Teacher, of Economics and Geography '78-84;

Traits: Long face; balding; specs; narrowed eyes; reasonable approach; likes walking and the countryside, old films, theatre, music and "avoiding gardening";

New MPs of '01 *Andrew (John) TURNER*

Address: House of Commons, Westminster, London SW1A 0AA; 2 Northwood Place, Cowes, Isle of Wight ,PO31 7TN; 58 The Mall, Carlsbrooke Road, Newport PO30 1BW (constituency);
Telephone: 0207 219 3000 (H of C); 01983 200474/522404;

Mrs Angela (Eileen) WATKINSON   **Conservative**   **UPMINSTER '01-**

Majority: 1,241 (3.7%) over Labour 4-way;
Description: The long, thin constitueny on London's eastern fringe, on the Essex border at the end of the District Line; in its northern part is the giant Harold Hill council estate, in its southern part are middle-class suburbs of Cranham and Emerson Park; in '95 it lost Conservative-leaning Ardleigh Green ward; "most of the residents of this seat have come from the inner part of east London or are members of families born there", "part of the well-known eastward drift that has taken place since the 1920s" (its previous, Labour MP Keith Darvill)
Position: On Home Affairs Select Committee '01-; Essex County Councillor '97-; Chairman, Emerson Park branch of Upminster Conservatives '01-; ex: Havering Borough Councillor '94-98;
Outlook: A beneficiary of the 'Essex effect' along with her young Romford neighbour, Andrew Rosindell, which left the Havering area with only John Cryer as its sole Labour survivor; an Essex-based pragmatic Rightwing Eurosceptic grandmother, who retook - one of only eight retaken - a longheld Tory seat, although it only ranked as the Tories' 52nd target seat; the only new Tory woman MP, she is in the Conservative Christian Fellowship and was in the Monday Club until ordered out by her Leader Iain Duncan Smith in October 2001;
History: She joined the Conservative Party '65; she was elected to Havering Borough Council for Emerson Park ward May '94; she joined the Monday Club '96; she was elected to Essex County Council for Billericay North May '97; she subscribed to Bill Cash's European Foundation from '98; she was selected to retake Upminster Sep '99; her seat was ranked the Tories' 52nd target seat Oct '00; she regained Upminster, ousting Labour's Keith Darvill by a majority of 1,241 on a 5.2% pro-Tory swing, after a 13% drop in turnout June '01; she voted for Iain Duncan-Smith as new Leader of the Conservatives July '01; she was named to the Home Affairs Select Committee July '01; she was one of 14 new Tory MPs who together wrote to the DAILY TELEGRAPH endorsing Iain Duncan Smith as a Leader who "can unite the party on Europe" Aug '01;she was briefly removed from Iain Duncan Smith's supporters' website because of her membership of the Monday Club Aug '01; she worried about cannabis plants being grown too close to the M25 Aug '01; with Andrew Hunter and Andrew Rosindell, she was ordered by her new Leader, Iain Duncan Smith, to quit the Monday Club Oct '01; she backed early diagnosis of children with special needs and opposed their total inclusion in mainstream education Oct '01; she favoured good relations with the EU and its enlargement but felt CAP had to be dismantled and the Nice Agreement "would take us in the wrong direction" by increasing qualified majority voting and weakening NATO Oct '01; she urged the expansion of police training schools to satisfy a constituency like hers which "suffers very badly from the leaching of resources into inner London" Oct '01; in the debate on Jo Moore's attempted 'spin', she concentrated on Labour's attempt to reform local government, attempting

Copyright (C)Parliamentary Profile Services Ltd   *145*

Mrs Angela (Eileen) WATKINSON

to impose unwanted mayors and causing Havering to increase its council tax by two successive major hikes Oct '01; she insisted that in adoptions too little account was taken of birth parents, even when their deficiencies had been overcome Oct '01; she backed Eric Pickles' Food Labelling Bill because it would enable UK consumers to buy higher-quality UK farm products even if slightly more costly Nov '01;
Born: 18 November 1941, Leytonstone
Family: "My paternal grandmother was Welsh"; daughter, of Edward Elliot, BRS executive, and Maisie (Thomson); m '61 Roy Watkinson, Metropolitan Police officer; 1s Roland '65, 2d Christina '68, Samantha '69; she has four grandchildren;
Education: Wanstead County High School '53-58; in what later became Anglia University (HNC in Public Administration) '88-89;
Occupation: Local Government Officer '88-95; Secretary of a Special School '76-88; Clerk, Bank of New South Wales '58-64;
Traits: Parted dark blonde short hair; young-looking although the oldest of the Tories' '01 intake; is more pragmatic than dogmatic, despite past affiliations; speaks briefly; an attempt was made to mug her on her way home Aug '01; enjoys gardening, music, Manx TT and classic car races; admits to recently resorting to readymade freezer meals;
Address: House of Commons, Westminster, London SW1A 0AA; Brick House Farm, London Road, Wickford Essex SS12 0LG; 23 Butts Green Road, Hornchurch, Essex RM11 2JS (constituency);
Telephone: 0207 219 3000 (H of C); 01288 560812 (home); 01708 443321/447592 Fax;

Tom WATSON   **Labour**   **WEST BROMWICH EAST '01-**

Majority: 9,763 (29.9%) over Conservative 5-way;
Description: Until '97 the most marginal of Sandwell's four seats in the heart of the industrial Black Country, but always Labour since its creation in '74; the area makes components for cars, aircraft and engineering; its voters are 15% non-white; Labour's strength is in the West Bromwich Central ward;
Position: On the Select Committee on Home Affairs '01-; on Labour Party's West Midlands Executive '97-; Regional representative on Labour Party National Policy Forum (on its Industry Commission '98-) '97-; National Co-ordinator, First-Past-the-Post Campaign '98-; ex: Chairman, Wyre Forest CLP '98-01; Chairman, NOLS (National Organisation of Labour Students) '92-93;
Outlook: Cheery former AEEU and Labour Party apparatchik and pamphleteer with a mission to dish the LibDems and PR and help stir up Labour; a union fixer who organised for Tony Blair '93-97 but turned against the Blairites because they treated him shabbily as an 'Old Labour' type; "'Old-fashioned Rightwing union fixer' personally well-liked on the Tribunite Left" (RED PEPPER); he believes the strength of Labour lies in the activities of its local activists and union links; he admires MPs Fraser Kemp, Peter Kilfoyle and his predecessor Peter Snape as people "who don't take themselves too seriously and are prepared to burst a few pompous bubbles", and hopes he can "follow in their footsteps"; he claims that despite the political rehabilitation of some leading SDP figures "no amount of revisionist history can get

away from their monumental betrayal"; opposes closer co-operation with the LibDems, and seeks to make Sandwell "a Liberal-free zone" (TW), the more so since the LibDems backed the successful Independent Dr Richard Taylor against Labour in the Wyre Forest seat where he used to live; is strongly opposed to elected mayors; a campaigner for West Midlands jobs as member of the Rover Task Force to save Longbridge '00-02;
History: He was "always Labour at school" and joined the party at 16, '82; he became Chairman of NOLS '92; he initially supported Tony Blair and 'New Labour' May '97; he became Sir Ken Jackson's chief lieutenant in the campaign against breaking Labour's union links '97; he became a founder-member and editor of the quarterly LIBERAL DEMOLITION to attack the Blair-favoured Liberal Democrats; the publication had been a newsletter run out of the office of Dan Norris, but he gave it union backing and persuaded others to come on board '00; he was selected for West Bromwich East after the last-minute retirement of its veteran MP Peter Snape, narrowly defeating local councillor John Edwards Mar '01; he appealed for good ideas for campaigning against the LibDems whilst urging Labour to emulate their pavement politics Apr '01; attacked former SDPers Roger Liddle and Andrew Adonis for now being in the Downing Street Policy Unit Apr '01; attacked Blairite actor Tony Robinson's criticism of the union block vote Apr '01; retained the seat with a majority reduced by nearly 4,000 votes to 9,763 on a 12% drop in turnout, yielding a 1.4% pro-Tory swing June '01; he was named to the Select Committee on Home Affairs July '01; he proposed that jailed Lord (Jeffrey) Archer be stripped of his peerage July '01; in TV duel with TRIBUNE editor Mark Seddon on fringe of annual Labour conference, Watson urged considering the possible benefits of identity cards Sep '01; he complained about the way in which the travel and insurance companies operated after the death of a 26-year-old friend, Dominic McElroy, on the island of Rhodes Oct '01; he led a motion endorsing his home town, Sheffield, as the site of a national football stadium Oct '01; although his constituency is landlocked, he backed the Marine Wildlife Conservation Bill to boast about the natural wonders of Sandwell Valley Oct '01; on the Home Affairs Select Committee he urged a study of LSD and Ecstasy Nov '01;
Born: 8 January 1967, Sheffield
Family: His grandfather, Tom Swift, was a miner and an early member of the Labour Party; son, of Tony Watson, UNISON convenor and former Wyre Forest Labour councillor, and Linda (Pearce), social worker; m '01 Siobhan (Corby); Fraser Kemp MP was best man at their wedding;
Education: St George's Primary, Kidderminster; Kidderminster Secondary School; King Charles I High School, Kidderminster; University of Hull (a contemporary of Sarah Gurling, partner of Charles Kennedy);
Occupation: Co-Founder-Editor, LIBERAL DEMOLITION (quarterly publication attacking the LibDems) '00-; Co-Author (with Mark Tami): Votes For All (Fabians 2000); Board Member: UNIONS TODAY til '01, TRIBUNE '00-; ex: National Political Organiser, AEEU '97-01; Development Officer, then Deputy General Election Co-ordinator, Labour Party '93-97; Chairman, National Organisation of Labour Students (NOLS) '92-93; Account Manager, in P Barker and Associates (advertising agency) '89-90; Fund Raiser, Save The Children '88-89; Research Assistant, Labour Party;
Traits: Dark, front-combed hair; chubby face; heavy build; specs; affable; a supporter of Kidderminster Harriers FC;
Address: House of Commons, Westminster, London SW1A 0AA; Terry Duffy House, Thomas Street, West Bromwich, West Midlands B70 3NT; 67 Birmingham Road, West Bromwich B70 6PY; 14 Yellowhammer Court, Kidderminster, DY10 4RR;
Telephone: 0207 219 3000 (H of C); 0121 553 2042; 077798 693624; 01562 824916 (home); watson@parliament.uk

Michael (Fraser) WEIR SNP ANGUS '01-

Majority: 3,611 (10.3%) over Conservative 5-way;
Description: A seat stretching from the Highlands and Grampians to the Dundee suburbs, embracing small towns and villages in the eastern part of Angus and eastern Perthshire and small parts of Dundee; its main centres are the fishing ports of Montrose and Arbroath, scene of the first Scottish Declaration of Independence in 1320; an SNP-Tory marginal since the '70s, it became the SNP's second safest seat in the anti-Tory tactical voting high tide of '97;
Position: SNP Spokesman on Rural Affairs, the Environment, Trade and Industry, Health '01-; on the Select Committee on Scottish Affairs '01-; ex: Angus District Councillor '84-88;
Outlook: Locally-born, bred and based, small-town Scots lawyer who replaced veteran SNP MP, Andrew Welsh, who switched his whole attention to the Scottish Parliament; one of the SNP's little-known 'B-team' now asked to cover four departments of state;
History: He joined the SNP as a student in its mid-'70s heyday '76; he contested Aberdeen South coming 4th, polling 2,776 votes (6.6%) June '87; he was selected to replace Andrew Welsh, who, after 19 years at Westminster, preferred to concentrate on the Scottish Parliament; he successfully defended the Angus seat despite a 13% crop in turnout and a 6.7% swing to the Conservatives, with his majority cut from 10,189 to 3,611 June '01; in his Maiden speech he complained of hospital closure threats in Angus and of "rock-bottom" morale in the Tayside NHS; he opposed renegotiation of the Barnett Formula, insisting on "full fiscal autonomy" for the Scottish Parliament, and for fuel duty cuts; he opposed threats to jobs at the GlaxoSmithKline factory in Montrose June '01; he congratulated the Co-operative Supermarkets on their reduction of chemicals in food products July '01; he expressed concern about safety enforcement in the wake of the July incident at the Chapelcross nuclear power station July '01; he was named to the Select Committee on Scottish Affairs July '01; in the Westminster Hall debate on carers, he told how difficult it was for carers in his constituency to cope with the complexities of the benefits system aimed at supporting them Oct '01; he backed a motion demanding more Treasury mony for Scottish care for the elderly Oct '01; he asked that the families of 45 Commando, based in his constituency, be forewarned of their commitment to Afghanistan Oct '01; with three other nationalists, voted against the Afghan war Nov '01; he warned that, without their income from gaming machines, many Scottish sports clubs would be in jeopardy Nov '01;
Born: 24 March 1957, Arbroath
Family: He does not disclose his parents' names or jobs; m '85, Mary Elizabeth (Jack); 2d;
Education: Arbroath High School; Aberdeen University (LLB in Law '79);
Occupation: Solicitor '81-; Partner, in J and DG Shiell '84-, Myers and Wills '83-84, Charles Wood and Son '81-83; in Law Society of Scotland; Dean of the Society of Procurators and Solicitors in Angus '01-;
Traits: Parted, dark-but-greying, front-dangling hair; specs; jowly; he enjoys reading history and doing organic gardening;
Address: House of Commons, Westminster, London SW1A 0AA; Marketgate, Arbroath, Angus; 8 Latch Road, Brechin, Angus DD9 6JE (home);
Telephone: 0207 219 3000 (H of C); 01241 874522 inc Fax; 01356 622633/625050 Fax

New MPs of '01 Michael (Fraser) WEIR

(home); mfw@dial.pipex.com;

'Bill' (William David) WIGGIN   Conservative   **LEOMINSTER '01-**

Majority: 10,367 (22.2%) over LibDem 6-way;
Description: Formerly the town of Leominster and the rest of north Herefordshire, on the Welsh border, extended in '83 to take in bits of the Malvern Hills which, in '95, were mostly shed to the new West Worcestershire seat; 2500 square miles of England's most agricultural seat, including "the most beautiful parts of the Welsh Marches" (Julian Critchley); it has a permanent SAS garrison at Credenhill; its former Conservative MP, Peter Temple-Morris, became an Independent One Nation Conservative and then defected to Labour in '98, becoming a Labour peer '01;
Position: On Select Committee on Transport, Local Government and the Regions '01-; ex: Vice Chairman, Hammersmith & Fulham Conservative Association '96-97;
Outlook: A new Duncan-Smith-backing Rightwing Eurosceptic and fundamentalist partisan; the Old Etonian banker scion of a Herefordshire gentleman-farming family, who followed his father into the Commons four years after Sir Jerry Wiggin's retirement from Weston-super-Mare; one of the Conservatives' dwindled rump of 14 Old Etonian MPs;
History: He was born into a political family, only three when his father was elected MP for Weston-super-Mare '69; he joined the Conservative Party at 18, '84; he contested a Fulham council seat May '94; he was elected Vice Chairman of Hammersmith and Fulham Conservatives '96; he contested hopeless Burnley, suffering a 7.7% anti-Tory swing, lower than the 10% national average May '97; he again contested a Fulham council seat May '98; he contested the North West regional seat in the European Parliament election May '99; he was selected to replace Leominster's floor-crossing MP, Peter Temple-Morris, in preference to George Osborne, Richard Bacon, Hugo Swire and Patrick Mercer - all later selected and elected elsewhere May '99; he retained the seat for the Conservatives with a 10,367 majority, up 1,500 on the '97 Conservative majority, with a 2.4% swing from the LibDems June '01; in his Maiden speech he mixed wit with a savage attack on Government's mishandling of the constituency's foot-and-mouth crisis, demanding an independent inquiry; he also twice demanded urgent reform of the Common Agricultural Policy July '01; he asked what value the Government placed on country sports July '01; he voted for Iain Duncan Smith in the ballots for the Tory Leadership July '01; he was one of 14 new Tory MPs who together wrote to the DAILY TELEGRAPH endorsing Iain Duncan Smith as a Leader who "can unite the party on Europe" Aug '01; he attacked the Labour Government's "lack of apology, and the televison performance that Jo Moore gave, [which] showed enormous disrespect to our soldiers, our councillors and Railtrack's shareholders and to the families of those who died" in New York and Washington Oct '01; he urged more Government help for tourist-driven small businesses hit by foot-and-mouth Nov '01; he backed Eric Pickles' Food Labelling Bill because it helped UK consumers prefer UK farm produce Nov '01;
Born: 4 June 1966, London
Family: Son, Sir Jerry Wiggin, farmer and MP for Weston-super-Mare '69-97, and Rosemary

Copyright (C)Parliamentary Profile Services Ltd   *149*

'Bill' (William David) WIGGIN   *New MPs of '01*

Janet (Orr); his parents were divorced in '82; m '99 Camilla (Chilvers), PR firm director; 1 child '01;
Education: Hill House Prep; Eton College '80-84; University College of North Wales, Bangor (Hons BA in Economics '88);
Occupation: Banker '91-: Options Sales Manager, Commerzbank, '98-; Assistant Director, for currency option sales, Dresdner Kleinwort Benson '94-98; Gold Bullion Trader: Union Bank of Switzerland '92-94; Mitsubishi Corporation '91-92; Coffee Buyer, Rayner Coffee International '89-91;
Traits: Fresh-faced boyish good looks; witty; he enjoys fishing, diving, field sports, computers;
Address: House of Commons, Westminster, London SW1A 0AA; 381 New Kings Road, London SW6 4RL (London home); 8 Corn Square, Leominster, Herefordshire HR6 8LR; The Lawns, Nunnington, Withington, Hereford HR1 3NJ (Herefordshire home0;
Telephone: 0207 219 3000 (H of C); 0207 384 2372 (London home); 0207 418 4116 (work); 01568 612565/610320 Fax; bill.wiggin@parliament.uk;

Hywel Williams   **Plaid Cymru**   **CAERNARFON '01-**

Majority: 3,511 (12.1%) over Labour 5-way;
Description: Set in a lovely mountainous setting, including the Snowdon range, it is the most Welsh-speaking constituency: 79%; its urban parts formed David Lloyd George's Carnarvon Boroughs constituency 1890-1945; it was at Pwllheli that Plaid Cymru was launched in 1925; latterly, as the base for former Plaid Leader Dafydd Wigley, it became the party's safest seat; it suffers high unemployment and depopulation; former Dwyfor was the last local government area to remain dry on Sundays, now a fading memory;
Position: In Plaid Cymru Policy Cabinet '99-; ex: Adviser to Welsh Affairs Select Committee '00-01;
Outlook: A new PFI-bashing radical Welsh voice; the locally-born-bred-and-based social work specialist who inherited ailing former Plaid Leader Dafydd Wigley's once-safe seat on Wigley's switch to the Welsh Assembly; in MIND, Child Poverty Action Group; formerly in the Welsh Language Society;
History: Born and raised in Pwllheli, birthplace of Welsh nationalism, he joined Plaid Cymru as a student during its mid-seventies upswing '73; he contested Clwyd South in the Welsh Assembly election May '99; he was selected to replace Dafydd Wigley as candidate for Caernarfon Oct '00; he campaigned on Wigley's coattails as part of a team with Wigley remaining as the Welsh Assemblyman for the seat May-June '01; he retained the seat for the Plaid but with a majority halved from 7,449 to 3,511 on a 4.8% swing to Labour June '01; in his Maiden speech he hailed his seat as "one of the heartlands of the Welsh language" and Welsh nationalism but deplored its economic decline and poor housing July '01; he attacked PFI in the NHS as "a licence to print money, money that the NHS can ill afford"; "my constituens have campaigned long and hard for a hospital at Porthmadog; one may now be on offer, but on the basis of PFI, if a private investor can be tempted;"; "people see through the 'buy now, pay through the nose for 30 years' scam"; but "they have no choice but take a bad

deal, as no other deal is on offer"; "we in Plaid Cymru call for proper investment in a reconstructed public sector that has faith in its capacities, is publicly accountable and whose activities are not shrouded because of alleged commercial sensitivity" July '01; he called attention to sackings after a strike at Friction Dynamex in his constituency Oct '01; he said there was masked homelessness even in rural Wales caused by high prices hiked by owners of second homes and concealed by emigration Oct '01; he backed Wales' extra £40m for maintenance grants for FE and HE students Oct '01; with three other nationalists, voted against the Afghan war Nov '01; he backed early eye-testing for children Nov '01; he complained about Wales' over-centralisation of postal sorting Nov '01;
Born: 14 May 1953, Pwllheli
Family: Son, of Robert Williams, shopkeeper, and Jenny Page (nee Williams), shop worker and nurse; one of six siblings; m '77 Sian (Davies), 3 d: Swenno '79, Elin '81, Angharad '91; divorced '98
Education: Ysgol Glan y Mor, Pwllheli; University College of Wales, Cardiff (BSc in Psychology '74); University College of North Wales, Bangor (CQSW in Social Work '79);
Occupation: Author: Social Work in Action in the 1980s (contributor), General Editor, Child Care Terms (in Welsh; 1993), A Social Work Vocabulary (in Welsh 1986); ex: Freelance Lecturer, Author and Consultant '95-01; Head of its Social Work Practice Centre, University College of Wales, Bangor '92-94; Lecturer, in Social Work, University College of Wales, Bangor '84-92; Social Worker, Gwynedd County Council '76-84, Mid Glamorgan County Council '74-76; (ex: NALGO/NUPE steward '74-84, UCAC [Welsh Teachers Union] '84-94); "not now a member of any unions" (HW);
Traits: Full-faced; pleasant-looking; Welsh-speaking;
Address: House of Commons, Westminster, London SW1A 0AA; 8 Castle Street, Carnarfon, Gwynedd;
Telephone: 0207 219 3000 (H of C); 01286 672510/672003 Fax;

Roger (Hugh) WILLIAMS   Liberal Democrat   BRECON & RADNORSHIRE '01-

Majority: 751 (2%) over Conservative 7-way;
Description: The largest seat in Wales, with 750,000 sprawling acres, it is the UK's sixth most agricultural constituency; it includes the spectacular landscape of the Brecon Beacons, the small towns of Brecon, Llandrindod Wells and bookselling Hay-on-Wye, and a strip of the old South Wales coalfield at Ystradgynlais; 10,000 Labour voters in other fringe mining areas were transferred out in '83; since the '80s it has been a very tight LibDem-Conservative marginal, won by only two or three-figure majorities in four of the five most recent Westminster contests;
Position: Powys County Councillor '81-; ex: Chairman: Brecon Beacons National Park '91-95, Brecon & Radnor NFU, Brecon & Radnor SDP '81-82, Mid Wales Agri-Food Partnership; Vice Chairman, Powys TEC; on Development Board for Rural Wales;
Outlook: A locally-rooted farmer "very well-known in and around Brecon" (Rhodri Hornung, WESTERN MAIL) and a "seasoned campaigner" (LIBERAL DEMOCRAT

Roger (Hugh) WILLIAMS   *New MPs of '01*

NEWS) who replaced the retiring MP Richard Livsey - but not winning as comfortably as Livsey did in '97; one of only two LibDem farmer-MPs; in the NFU, Farmers Union of Wales, Country Landowners Association;

History: He joined the SDP, becoming their constituency chairman '81; he was elected to Powys County Council May '81; he joined the Liberal Democrats '89; he was selected to succeed Richard Livsey as LibDem candidate for Brecon & Radnorshire largely because he was a wellknown local man June '00; he retained the seat with a majority slashed from 5,097 to 751, on a 4.9% pro-Tory swing June '01; in his Maiden speech he emphasised his constituency's dire economic prospects because of decline in manufacturing and the impact of foot-and-mouth both on farming and tourism July '01; he urged a single rail franchise for Wales to improve services to rural areas such as his Oct '01;

Born: 22 January 1948;

Family: His father was a farmer; m Penny/Penelope (James); 1s Brychan, 1d Rhian;

Education: Llanfilo County Primary, Christ's College, Brecon; Selwyn College, Cambridge University (BA in Agriculture '79);

Occupation: Farmer '69-, on an inherited farm near Talgarth;

Traits: Dark, forward-falling hair; chubby, full face; Roman nose; Welsh features; "a large, good-natured man" (Rhodri Hornung, WESTERN MAIL), "with his feet in the soil of Brecon and Radnor" (Jamie Gibson-Watt, local supporter); the same public-school-and-Cambridge pedigree as fellow LibDem MP Simon Hughes;

Address: House of Commons, Westminster, London SW1A 0AA; 99 The Street, Brecon, Powys;

Telephone: 0207 219 3000 (H of C); 01874 625739/625635 Fax; brecrad@cix.co.uk;

Pete(r) WISHART   **SNP**   **NORTH TAYSIDE '01-**

Majority: 3,283 (8.5%) over Conservative 6-way;

Description: A lovely, huge, mainly rural seat of over 2,000 square miles, put together in '83 from northern parts of former Perthshire and Angus; Forfar and Blairgowne are the only sizeable towns; Brechin, a small cathedral city was added in '95; the Highland clearances began here; it embraces what was probably the largest berry-growing industry, several distilleries, and the ancestral seat of the Queen Mother's Bowes-Lyon family at Glamis;

Position: SNP Chief Whip '01-; SNP Vice Convenor for Fundraising '99-; Deputy Spokesman on Justice '98-; Director, Scotland Against Drugs and Fast Forward Positive Lifestyles '92-; ex: SNP Spokesman on Drug Issues '97-99; Assistant Spokesman on Education '97-99; Honorary President West Fife Cultural Initiative; on Campaign Committee of Scotland Against Drugs '97-99;

Outlook: An expert on fighting the drug culture; the Commons' first former rock musician, formerly with the band Runrig: "the first Member who has ever appeared on 'Top of the Pops' in his own right" (PW); one of the SNP's second team, he replaced SNP Leader John Swinney on the latter's withdrawal to the Scottish Parliament; a self-described former socialist with Fife coalfield roots; "most rock bands on tour are about sex, drugs and rock 'n roll, but with Runrig we were in the back of the van talking about Scotland's constitutional future" (PW);

New MPs of '01   *Pete(r) WISHART*

History: Reared in Dunfermline in a political family, he was a socialist at school, and joined the Labour Party; he was politically active as a student at Moray House College, but Labour's prevarication over home rule turned him towards the SNP; in the early '90s Skye-based Runrig campaigned against Skye Bridge tolls and nuclear dumping; he joined the SNP '97; he became SNP Spokesman on Drug Issues '97; he was selected to replace departing-for-Holyrood SNP Leader John Swinney in North Tayside May '00; "It's going to be close," he warned potential supporters, "the Tories will be getting the toffs out of the glens"; he retained the seat with a majority reduced by nearly 1,000 to 3,283, on a 12% drop in turn-out, producing a .3% swing to the Conservatives June '01; in his Maiden speech he claimed that "music has so often been the soundtrack of political change", pointing out that "in the counter-culture of the 1960s, there were those who rallied against unwarranted international aggression and those who championed and pioneered the rights of minorities and women"; apart from also extolling the beauties of his constituency he insisted that the NHS in Tayside was "in chaos" July '01; he urged an early debate on "the effect that the Barnett squeeze will have on Scottish public services" July '01; he asked about the access to broadband of smaller businesses July '01; he asked about subsidies to different types of music, from opera to popular July '01; he asked about Government assistance to football July '01; accepting that "the demise of Railtrack was as predictable as it was overdue", backed a not-for-profits investment policy but urged ScotRail be turned over to the Scottish Parliament Oct '01; he urged a full debate on humanitarian aid to Afghanistan, to which Clare Short could report Oct '01; he led a motion opposing a restriction on the cash jackpot payout from gaming machines Oct '01; he said Jo Moore should have resigned or been sacked but it was a waste of Parliamentary day on her when there were more important subjects like Railtrack's failure; Scottish railways should be removed from "the Strategic Rail Authority in London" Oct '01; since UK legislation seemed likely to be delayed, he urged allowing Scotland to be allowed to ban tobacco advertising Oct '01; he insisted the Scottish Parliament be allowed to keep its numbers, regardless of the Scotland Act agreed by the non-SNP parties Nov '01; he spoke expertly about problems in fighting drugs Nov '01;
Born: 9 March 1962, Dunfermline
Family: His great grandfather was a miner, as were both of his grandfathers; son of Alex Wishart, engraver, and Nan (Irvine), teacher; m '90 Carrie (Lindsay), Education Advisor; 1s Brodie '91;
Education: Townhill Primary, Dunfermline; Queen Anne High School, Dunfermline; Moray House College of Education, Edinburgh (Diploma in Community Education '84);
Occupation: Keyboard Playing Musician, initially with Big Country '81-; "he left, following a row, just before its massive international success began"; "his subsequent career was less stellar but more sustained after he joined Runrig" in '85, at the age of [23]; fifteen years on, Wishart says he has probably 'hit his last keyboard in anger' with the Rolling Stones of Gaeldom, having contributed to the album which the rest of the band is launching on Skye" (Glasgow HERALD) (MU) '85-01; Community Education Worker '84-85;
Traits: Long, oblong head; front-combed hair; dour-looking; because he is from Fife, unlike most of the rest of Runrig, which is from Skye, he is not Gaelic-speaking; says of his former rock band: "we were never seen as dangerous, which for a Parliamentary candidate is probably just as well";
Address: House of Commons, Westminster, London SW1A 0AA; 22 Main Street, Low Valleyfield, Fife KY12 8TF (constituency);
Telephone: 0207 219 3000 (H of C); 01250 876576; 07974 437109 (mobile); wishartp@parliament.uk;

Shaun (Anthony) WOODWARD   **Labour**   **637]]ST HELENS SOUTH '01-**

Majority: 8,985 (26.6%) over LibDem 8-way;
Description: A seat created in '83 comprising the town of St Helens with its glass-making industry (Pilkingtons) and engineering; "a mess of mini roundabouts, pedestrianised shops and depression" (A A Gill, SUNDAY TIMES); the town is a Labour fortress, never out of the party's hands since '35; from '45 to '58 it was held by Sir Hartley Shawcross, who eventually left the Labour Party, and was mockingly dubbed 'Sir Shortly Floorcross'; in '01 it attracted attention as the seat into which Labour's Millbank machine parachuted the floor-crossing former Tory MP Shaun Woodward;
Former Seat: Witney (as Conservative '97-99, Labour '99-01)
Position: Conservative: Spokesman, on London June-Dec '99; on Select Committees: on Foreign Affairs Jan-June '99, Broadcasting '97-99, European Legislation '97-99; Communications Director, Conservative Central Office '90-92;
Outlook: The second floor-crosser since Labour defector Reg Prentice in '79 to move seamlessly from a safe seat of one party to a safe seat of another without interrupting his Commons membership; this feat was first emulated in '97 by Alan Howarth, who took three years to shed his Tory loyalties; the speed of Woodward's turn of coat produced a hostile consensus: "the only election issue on which the MAIL, TELEGRAPH and GUARDIAN agreed [in '01] is that Woodward is the ballot box equivalent of syphilitic rape" (A A Gill, SUNDAY TIMES); in their detestation, commentators ignored the political reality of his being given a safe seat: PM Tony Blair was sending out a signal to other possible Tory defectors: "We will take care of you!"; Woodward carried the banner as an audacious, quick-flipping Tory-to-Labour renegade after only two-and-a-half years in the Commons; as a sharp Labour-baiter before his defection, he left the suspicion he remained a 'wet' Tory but with special sensitivities about the Tories' homophobia and Europhobia; "to go from the Tory frontbench to Labour's backbenches in just three weeks is a hell of a journey" (his friend, Tory MP Stephen Dorrell); a socially-mobile one-time Tory 'Golden Boy', who had a safe seat, beautiful and costly homes and a Sainsbury millionairess wife; he quit the Tories as a campaigner on homosexual rights, claiming "someone has to stick up for homosexuals, and the new extreme Tory Party obviously won't"; he said, "I'm not a natural Tory; I come from an extremely modest background", "the Tory Party is obsessed by class", and it "has been hijacked by the rabid Right"; "I am not leaving my party, my party has left me" (SW); claimed he had thought of joining Labour when Blair became Leader but couldn't desert John Major on Europe and a classless society; "bright, ambitious and very well connected" (NEW STATESMAN); "very talented and able" (Tony Blair); "one of life's strivers" ('Peterborough', DAILY TELEGRAPH); was close to Chris Patten, Kenneth Clarke, Douglas Hurd; from his initial Commons outings, although he showed himself a supporter of Ken Clarke and Chris Patten on Europe, prior to his shock conversion he displayed a Rightwing attitude on economics and a sneering and bitterly partisan attitude to Labour, which new Labour MPs found provocative; he was "good at attacking Labour" (Robert Shrimsley, DAILY TELEGRAPH); bitter Tory references to him include: "no principles and not a shred of credibility" (John Bercow MP), "I have never felt able to take him at face value" (Party

154   *Copyright (C)Parliamentary Profile Services Ltd*

Chairman Michael Ancram), "the man is not a Conservative, and he appears to be more attracted to Europhilia and homosexuality than to Conservatism" (Lord Tebbit), "a ruthless careerist who has used both his marriage and his wife's money to advance his career" (a senior Tory); he has been further excoriated by journalists: "Woodward isn't just a former Tory MP and official, but one marked by the most shallow opportunism" (Hugo Young, GUARDIAN); "a transparent opportunist of the most unprincipled type, [who] by marrying into a respected, very private, abstemious family, has used his wife's wealth to elevate his own vaunting self-esteem and ambition" (A A Gill, SUNDAY TIMES); but more sympathetically - "a strong record on civil liberties and social tolerance (Steve Richards, NEW STATESMAN); close to Labour peer Lord (Tom) Chandos;

History: He was Leftwing at Cambridge and claimed to have joined the Conservative Party only in '88, after having married a very rich Tory Minister's daughter; he was on the short-list for Woodspring, where he was pipped by Dr Liam Fox '88; was head-hunted by party Chairman Chris Patten to be the party's new Director of Communications Jan '91; brought Saatchi & Saatchi back from the wilderness after their '87 falling out with the Tory leadership; together they planned the 'Labour Tax Bombshell' campaign Oct-Nov '91; unsuccessfully contested Avondale ward, Kensington May '94; on the short-list for Witney, from which Douglas Hurd was retiring, clashed with local authorities over his unauthorised alterations to his Wren-style home, Sarsden House: "we don't want another Teresa Gorman here" a local was quoted as saying Sep '95; at his selection conference, according to Stephen Hayward, the Conservative Mayor of Witney, "we were led to believe certain facts: Shaun approved of fox-hunting, would support the reintroduction of capital punishment, would support the existing ban on homosexuals in the armed forces; he was a mild Eurosceptic and supported the 'wait and see' policy of John Major"; he was duly selected for Witney, defeating ex-Minister Francis Maude Oct '95; co-signed a loyalist letter to DAILY TELEGRAPH with five other candidates, backing John Major's negotiations as putting Britain's interests first but warning that "if Economic and Monetary Union is based on unsound economic foundations, it will fail, with potentially disastrous consequences both for those inside and outside a single currency" Dec '96; he retained Witney, despite a notional swing to Labour of 13.6%, by a majority of 7,028, down by two-thirds from Douglas Hurd's '92 result May '97; in the Tory Leadership contest, was initially one of the few who backed Stephen Dorrell, then joined Kenneth Clarke's campaign team; at the Vincent Square home of his father-in-law, Sir Tim Sainsbury, he played host to two Clarke-Redwood meetings to do a deal to stop Hague May-June '97; backed an attempt to kill the Government's Bill to further ban handguns June '97; in his Maiden speech, in addition to tributes to his predecessors in Witney, he paid homage to the Hongkong reign of his friend, Chris Patten; he emphasised the rural basis of his constituency, attacking as "ill-considered" the "recent moves in the name of progress and reform to prohibit the legitimate pursuit of country sports", "I do not hunt, but I have become aware of the role that hunting plays in the life of the people of West Oxfordshire", he wound up by suggesting that Budget leaks had come from the Treasury but, unlike Hugh Dalton, no apologies would be forthcoming July '97; asked Chancellor Gordon Brown why, since he "justified his breathtaking 17 tax rises on the need to curb the consumer boom" how he explained "£5b of his £6b tax rises were taken from the corporate sector?" July '97; attacked the Budget as "totally incoherent", as part of an attempt to mislead observers; "it proves, first and foremost that Labour's first instinct is always to tax, and to raise taxes, again and again" July '97; he again attacked Labour's damage to pension funds July '97; co-protested punishment by beating of defeated Iraqi football team July '97; visited Japan as guest of British-Japanese Parliamentary Group Oct '97; baited Health Minister in Select Committee on banning tobacco advertising in snooker but not Formula One racing Nov '97; attacked Welsh devolution for inadequate powers and lack of support in referendum; was rebuked by Deputy Speaker for "shouting from a sedentary position" Dec '97; believed National Minimum Wage would cost jobs and not remove poverty Dec '97; doubted Labour's 'Welfare to Work' would do much longterm for unemployed Dec '97; initiated debate on threatened Burford Community Hospital Mar '98; visited China and Hongkong with all-party Britain-China Group Mar '98; claimed Budget "piles tax on tax, savages incentives, and distorts the workings of the marketplace" Apr '98; opposed fuel tax rise for impact on rural areas Apr '98; sought adequate compensation and apology for POWs of the Japanese Apr '98; defended loss of BBC and ITV rights to televise sport with advent of cable and digital TV June '98; explained why he would vote to lower age of consent for homosexuals in DAILY TELEGRAPH article June '98; was one of 18 Tories voting to lower homosexual age of consent to 16, June '98; urged Government to veto EU withholding tax on savings income Nov '98; backed sustainable development but opposed higher Vehicle Excise Duty's impact on rural areas Nov '98; expressed concern about 150 former sex offenders in the Oxford area Nov '98; criticising the Water Industry Bill, claimed water disconnections had increased only minimally since privatisation Dec '98; wanted revenue from higher Vehicle Excise Duty hypothecated for the environment Dec '98; initiated debate on a sustainable fisheries policy Jan '99; visited Israel with Conservative Friends of Israel as guest of Israeli Government Jan '99; was named to the Foreign Affairs Select Committee Jan '99; voted and spoke powerfully for lowering the homosexual age of consent to 16, comparing it with abolition of slavery Jan '99; told John Prescott his policies were regarded with "absolute contempt" in Oxfordshire Jan '99; opposed threatened closure of RAF Brize Norton Feb '99; accused Foreign Secretary Cook of failing to act on 15-month-old Spanish threat to disrupt Gibralter's economy unless granted joint sovereignty Feb '99; called on Robin Cook to have an ethical foreign policy of his own and resign in wake of Select Committee leaks on Sierra Leone Mar '99; visited Paris for 'Club of Three' conference Mar '99; visited Auschwitz with Conservative Friends of Israel Mar '99; visited Cadenabbia, Italy, for British-German Round Table for CDU and Conservative MPs as guest of Konrad Adenauer Foundation Mar '99; visited Paris for Franco-British Council seminar Mar '99; warned of Kosovo conflict spreading, asking if Government was prepared to commit ground troops Mar '99; claimed Labour's New Deal had failed 60% of those participating Apr '99; opposed sex education in primary schools: "the innocence of the child needs to be preserved" May '99; visited Jordan and the West Bank as guest of the Council for Advancement of Arab-British Understanding June '99; was named to the frontbench Environment team with responsibility for London June '99; doubted Labour's target of 60% new housing on brownfield sites, given transport problems and lack of consumer demand July '99; attacked damage done to greenfield sites by park-and-ride schemes, "bringing cities like Oxford to a standstill" July '99; attacked Labour's roads policy and dubbed proposed congestion charges "anti-motorist" July '99; sought to make proposed London Mayor dismissable by the Greater London Assembly Nov '99; dubbed Labour's Dobson-friendly mayoral selection process as "autocracy" Nov '99; go-between Labour MP Ann Keen reported to Downing Street that he might be about to defect to Labour, because of the Tory Shadow Cabinet decision to back the retention of Section 28 Nov '99; said he would refer Ken Livingstone's undeclared lucrative speaking fees to the Standards Commissioner Dec '99; in the INDEPENDENT ON SUNDAY he claimed Section 28 "hangs like a sword of Damocles" over teachers dealing with "homophobic bullying" Dec '98; he was sacked by pager as Spokesman on London for backing Labour's decision to scrap Section 28, Dec '99; in Social Market Foundation lecture he attacked Conservative mantra of giving people greater freedom over their own lives as "a kind of possessive individualism" and attacked Section 28, Dec '99; he resigned from the Tory Party and crossed the floor to Labour citing: "the increasingly

Rightwing policies of the Conservative Party over the last two-and-a-half years" under William Hague, claiming the party had "thrown away the sensible policies of John Major on Europe", had made a "reckless promise to reduce taxation year-in, year-out", and backed Section 28, Dec '99; he rejected calls from his local Conservative Association to resign, claiming "I have not changed; I am still the Tory the people of Witney elected; it is the Tory Party that has changed" Dec '99; accused Tory Party of planning the privatisation of the NHS Jan '00; made first speech as a Labour MP on RUC reform, hissed from the Tory benches Jan '00; visited US to "advise" the Gore campaign Feb '00; was barracked by the Tories in a further speech on lowering the homosexual age of consent Feb '00; in the race relations debate attacked the Tories for their "repugnant" racist prejudices and Hague's "populist" immigration policy Mar '00; his claim about "unanimity" for repealing Section 28 among local headteachers was dismissed by his successor as Tory candidate, David Cameron Apr '00; his speech at a Labour Party fringe meeting was billed: "Never Forget the Threat of the Tories"; flanked by Stephen Lawrence's father, Neville, he claimed most Tories were "instinctive racists" Sep '00; the hard-Left CAMPAIGN BRIEFING opposed scrapping the two-year membership rule to enable his selection for a winnable seat before the next election Sep '00; he applied for a grant to convert derelict farm buildings for use by a charity Oct '00; he denied the BIRMINGHAM POST allegation he was to be parachuted into safe Perry Barr after Jeff Rooker's retirement Oct '00; he was not invited by Witney Town Council to lay a wreath on Remembrance Sunday Nov '00; following rumours of Millbank attempts to drop him into various safe Labour seats - Huddersfield, Telford, Erdington, he was selected for St Helens South on the eve of the campaign, in place of the swiftly-retired Gerry Bermingham, aided by an imposed shortlist excluding strong local contenders such as St Helens Council Leader Marie Rimmer; he won by a majority of four votes, with the backing of AEEU delegates ordered by Sir Ken Jackson to back him; he had joined the union two days before the ballot; "they are straining our loyalty," said a local party official, "they know we accept him or vote against the party Leader during an election campaign"; former Liverpool City Council Leader Harry Rimmer denounced his selection as "cynical manipulation by the Labour Party heirarchy" May '01; he told the DAILY TELEGRAPH that he felt like Winston Churchill after he left the Tory Party for the Liberals, "I don't want to go on saying stupid things" May '01; after campaigning with the help of his wife and butler -and the hindrance of six phoney butlers provided by the DAILY MAIL and Conservative Central Office - he retained the seat for Labour with a majority cut by 14,000 to 8,985 over the Liberal Democrat, on a 14% drop in turnout, yielding an anti-Labour swing of 14.3%, June '01; a press-speculated Ministerial post did not materialise after the election June '01; at short notice, he pulled out of appearances on both BBC 1's 'Question Time' and Radio 4's 'Any Questions' June '01; he urged the recruiting of more respiratory specialists to speed the compensation claims of former miners July '01; after four months, Peter Mandelson, his boyfriend, Reinaldo Avila da Silva, and two pet dogs finally moved out of the Woodwards' £4m home in Queen Anne's Gate, Westminster, back to Mandelson's West London flat, where security work had been completed Aug '01; he posed to Clare Short five written questions on aid for Afghan refugees Oct '01;

Born: 26 Oct 1958, Bristol
Family: Son, Dennis George Woodward, porter who became a director of Maggs furniture store, Bristol, and Joan Lillian (Nunn), former barmaid and cleaner; "my parents were very loving but they were quite old" (SW); m '87, Camilla Sainsbury, heiress daughter of ex-Tory Minister, Sir Tim Sainsbury; 1s: Tom '89; 3d: Ella '91, Olivia '93, Kate '96; his brother Leslie Patrick had a sex change, becoming Lesley Patricia;
Education: Bristol Grammar School '65-77 ("I was fat, slow and hopeless at sport; I was bullied until a teacher realised there might be something in this roly-poly child" (SW)); Jesus

Shaun (Anthony) WOODWARD

College, Cambridge University (MA; Double First in English Literature; "bolshie but outstanding" - tutor Lisa Jardine);
Occupation: Shareholder, J Sainsbury Plc; Author: Tranquilisers (with Ron Lacey; 1983), Ben: The Story of Ben Hardwick (with Esther Rantzen; 1984), Drugwatch (with Sarah Caplin; 1985); Director, English National Opera '94-; Professorial Fellow, in Communication Studies, at Queen Mary and Westfield College '92-; Director (unpaid): ENO, Childline, Oxygen FM Radio; Trustee: Woodward Charitable Trust, Royal Shakespeare Company Development Board, Victoria History of Oxford Trust, Institute of Continuing Professional Development, The Mulberry Bush, Bath International Music Festival, Macmillan Cancer Relief, Cancer Research Campaign; ex: Fellow, Institute of Politics, Kennedy School, Harvard University '94-95; Communications Director, Conservative Central Office '90-92; Producer, of BBC's 'That's Life' '89-90; Director, Jerusalem Productions (promoting Christian broadcasting) '89-96; Senior Producer, 'Panorama' '87-89; Reporter/Producer, 'Newsnight' '85-87; Researcher, 'That's Life' '82-85; Parliamentary Affairs Director, National Consumer Council '81-82;
Traits: Long face; high, retreating forehead; limpid eyes; an eager networker; "bright, ambitious and very well connected" (NEW STATESMAN); "one of life's strivers" ('Peterborough', DAILY TELEGRAPH); "an eclectic but fashionable circle of friends, ranging from Peter Mandelson to Michael Portillo" (Robert Shrimsley, DAILY TELEGRAPH); "hot-tempered and given to pique" (BBC driver); "Shaun was too arrogant when he joined the family; he's an adventurer; they thought he was on the make" (a Sainsbury family friend, quoted by Rachel Sylvester, DAILY TELEGRAPH); "Woodward is a man whose mouth says one thing and everything else about him says another" (A A Gill, SUNDAY TIMES); "to his enemies he is a social climber from a modest background who was dazzled by money, power and glamour"; "a skillful tennis player who works out at the Bath and Racquets Club" and who "danced with the Princess of Wales at a wedding reception" (Robert Shrimsley, DAILY TELEGRAPH); "Shaun has butlers, Labradors, two stunning homes and lives like a lord; I know New Labour likes grand types, but even they are going to find Shaun a bit much" (a Tory frontbencher); asked if he had had homosexual experiences he said, "If I had any homosexual affairs I would tell my wife, Camilla, but I'm not going to discuss it with the public" (SW); allegedly spent £20,000 on his 40th birthday party; is a ravenous book-buyer;
Address: House of Commons, Westminster, London SW1A 0AA; Queen Anne's Gate (£6.75m mansion), Westminster, London SW1; Sarsden House, nr Chipping Norton, Oxfordshire OX7 6PW (17th century Wren-style building to which he allegedly made unauthorised alterations; "bigger than Brideshead" [a guest]); a new home in St Helen's centre; a holiday home in Mustique;
Telephone: 020 7219 2680 (H of C); 01608 659223; 020 7792 8181 (home); 01608 659617/659708 Fax (Oxfordshire); 020 7629 7298/7297 Fax (London office);

PROFILERS AS BARBERS

When we started illustrating our volumes, we never anticipated outdated MPs' photographs would force us to double as barbers. In every volume ever published we have incurred cries of "I no longer have a moustache!" or "I have shaved my beard" or "I haven't worn my hair that long for five years". There is nothing more dismaying than telling your artist how good his sketch was and then seeing the woman MP portrayed with hair five inches shorter two hours later.

David WRIGHT   Labour   TELFORD '01-

Majority: 8,383 (27.2%) over Conservative 5-way;
Description: An altered mid-Shropshire former marginal seat based on Telford New Town, but encompassing old towns such as Coalbrookdale, Ironbridge and Coalport; the Telford New Town was designed to revitalise its historic but declining mining, foundry and engineering areas; having over 30 years become the fifth most populous seat it was split in '95 into Telford, a safe Labour seat, and The Wrekin, which Labour retained more marginally in '97 and '01; it has attracted inward investment, especially by Japanese and Taiwanese companies; it also has Aga and Brinton's carpets;
Position: Ex: Wrekin District Councillor '89-97; Oakengates Town Councillor '90-00; Chairman, Secretary, Wrekin CLP;
Outlook: A son-of-OMOV local worthy who represents his home town in which he has lived all his life; a former councillor, chairman and secretary of the constituency party and local government officer, self-dubbed a "specialist in the development of housing strategies and public-private partnerships"; he replaced late-retiring Bruce (recently Lord) Grocott, former PPS to three successive Labour Leaders, including PM Blair;
History: He joined the Labour Party '87, becoming Housing Strategy Manager for Sandwell the next year; he was elected to Wrekin District Council May '89, elected to Oakengates Town Council May '90; he was selected to replace Tony Blair's PPS Bruce Grocott as Labour's Telford candidate; as the local man he defeated Nula O'Kane, the former West Midlands European candidate, Simon Stevens, Alan Milburn's Adviser, and Sue Woodward, Assistant to Tony Wright MP Mar '01; he found that the quality of some local housing estates was a key issue in the campaign April-May '01; he retained the seat with a majority reduced by 3,000 to 8,383 on a 14% cut in turnout, yielding a 1.6% pro-Tory swing June '01; in his Maiden speech he showed concern about the "proliferating of agency work and temporary employment contracts" which were sometimes "acceptable and give flexibility"; "but too often they are used to circumvent giving people the employment rights they deserve" June '01; he urged an early debate to devise a strategy to co-ordinate services on local housing estates and establish funding regimes that could regenerate them July '01;
Born: 22 December 1966, Telford
Family: He does not disclose his parents names or jobs or his wife's Maiden name; he married Lindsay in '96;
Education: Wrockwardine Wood Comprehensive, Telford; New College, Telford; Wolverhampton Polytechnic (BA in Humanities '88);
Occupation: Ex: Housing Strategy Manager, Sandwell Metropolitan Council (TGWU [ACTS]) '88-01;
Traits: Thin face; retreating hairline; strong chin; a former instructor with the Boys Brigade; a supporter of Telford United and Shrewbury Town FCs;
Address: House of Commons, Westminster, London SW1A 0AA; Suite 1, Matthew Webb House, High Street, Dorley, Telford; (constituency);
Telephone: 0207 219 3000 (H of C); 01952 507747;

Richard YOUNGER-ROSS   **Liberal Democrat**   **TEIGNBRIDGE '01-**

Majority: 3,001 (5.1%) over Conservative 4-way;
Description: A seat created in '83 between Exeter and Torquay from the old Totnes and Tiverton constituencies, stretching from the rugged granite grandeur of Dartmoor to the seaside resorts of Dawlish, Shaldon and Teignmouth, including the light industrial town of Newton Abbot; it was where William, Prince of Orange, landed, the home of 'Hornblower' (Lord Exmouth) and where Sir Arthur Conan Doyle created 'The Hound of the Baskervilles'; in '97 it became a knife-edge Con-LibDem marginal; in '01 the LibDem candidate Richard Younger-Ross finished the job of polishing off the abrasive Tory, Patrick Nicholls;
Position: Ex: On Liberal Party Council '79-84; Vice Chairman, National League of Young Liberals '79-81;
Outlook: A third-time-lucky seasoned campaigner who ousted the abrasive maverick Europhobe Tory MP, Patrick Nicholls, giving the Liberal Democrats their fourth seat in Devon, compensating for the only LibDem loss in the southwest, at Taunton; the former Rickie Ross, who has been hyphenated by marriage to Miss Younger, not by snobbery or high birth; in the Anti-Slavery International, British-Kurdish Friendship Society, Howard League for Penal Reform;
History: He was born into a Conservative family in suburban Surrey, where his father, Arthur Ross, was a Conservative councillor in the early '50s; he joined the Liberals at 17, '70; he became the organisational Vice Chairman of the National League of Young Liberals '79; he was elected to the Liberal Party Council '78; he contested Chislehurst for the Liberals, retaining second place with 9,658 (23%) votes June '87; he fought Teignbridge for the first time, coming 9,548 votes behind Tory MP Patrick Nicholls Apr '92; at the annual LibDem conference, he moved to commit the party to the "disestablishment of the Church of England" which caused a furore Sep '93; at his second attempt at Teignbridge he dramatically slashed the Conservative majority to 281, the Tories' third smallest majority in the country May '97; targeting Nicholls' record as a constituency MP, he shaved 2,000 off the Labour vote and, helped by Viscount Exmouth's 2,269 UKIP votes, he finally ousted Nicholls by a 3,001-vote majority on a 2.8% anti-Tory swing June '01; in his Maiden speech he emphasised the recent blows to local agriculture and tourism and the obstacles to local young people wanting to enjoy sports June '01; he led a motion urging a Royal Commission into the workings of the Crown Estate to "ensure that its operations are to the benefit of Her Majesty's subjects" July '01; he staged a debate on the low employment and low wages in South Devon Nov '01;
Born: 29 June 1953, Walton-on-Thames, Surrey
Family: Son, of Arthur Ross, insurance broker, and Patricia (Flint); m '82 Susan (Younger);
Education: Walton-on-Thames Secondary School; Ewell Technical College (HNC in Building Construction); Oxford Polytechnic;
Occupation: Architectural Design Consultant '90-; formerly in various architectural practices; helped run his father's insurance brokerage '79, and family shop at Shepperton Film Studios '79-83; he worked in Iraq '82; Commons Researcher '81;
Traits: Heavily built; full face; parted, forward-combed brown hair; pleasant smile; specs; 'Rickie Ross' (LIBERAL DEMOCRAT NEWS); enjoys cooking, riding, gardening, football

New MPs of '01 Richard YOUNGER-ROSS

(Arsenal); "I am passionate about sport";
Address: House of Commons, Westminster, London SW1A 0AA; 41 Higher Brimley Road, Teignmouth, Devon TQ14 8JU;
Telephone: 0207 219 3000 (H of C); 01626 777169/777162 Fax;

INDIVIDUAL SEARCHES:
The compressed political insights in our books are boiled down from the most comprehensive political files available. Access to our computer and cuttings files is available on Peers as well as MPs, from £35 per Parliamentarian.

TO EACH ACCORDING TO HIS NEED
MPs, journalists and others use these books for differing purposes. In committees, MPs on either side tend to bait each other with embarrassing information culled from our pages - like former MP Ron Brown's "snip" as his wife called it. When one Tory MP goes to another's constituency, he likes to be able to ask about his colleague's children by name. Journalists like to have additional telephone numbers. The biggest all-round use is to mug up on an MP before taking him for a meal, to prove that you know just how fascinating he or she is.

TRACKING SCANDALS
By noting the warts in our portraits of MPs, we have long tracked their scandals. Sometimes we have been the first to notice a wart. In the Profumo scandal, we were the first to publish, in 1963, his letter to Christine Keeler in our newsletter, WESTMINSTER CONFIDENTIAL. We pushed another hole in the dam holding back disclosure about the corrupt lobbying activities of the Ian Greer organisation when, in 1989, our PARLIAMENTARY PROFILES volume published, in its profile of Michael Grylls, the fact that he was accepting from Ian Greer an unregistered percentage of all the business referred to Greer's firm. Press Gallery colleagues declined to report this disclosure after Grylls pretended that he was going to sue us for libel. The story seemed to die for a long time until Greer and Neil Hamilton, with the full support of the Major Government, threatened to sue the GUARDIAN. In the preparation for that trial-which-never-happened, it was discovered that Ian Greer changed his whole accounting system when faced with our publication of his secret relationship with Grylls, giving the game away to the GUARDIAN lawyers.